D0853206

OPEN SECRETS/
INWARD PROSPECTS

OPEN INWARD

REFLECTIONS ON

PAUL DRY BOOKS   *Philadelphia 2004*

SECRETS/
PROSPECTS

WORLD AND SOUL

EVA BRANN

First Paul Dry Books Edition, 2004

Paul Dry Books, Inc.
Philadelphia, Pennsylvania
www.pauldrybooks.com

Text type: Adobe Garamond
Display type: Schneidler Initials
Composed by P. M. Gordon Associates
Designed by Adrianne Onderdonk Dudden

1 3 5 7 9 8 6 4 2
Printed in the United States of America

Library of Congress Cataloging-in-Publication Data

Brann, Eva T. H.
Open secrets/inward prospects : reflections on world and soul /
Eva Brann. — 1st Paul Dry Books ed.
p. cm.
ISBN 1-58988-019-6 (alk. paper)
1. Life—Miscellanea. I. Title.

BD431.B746 2004
110—dc22
2004017933

ISBN 1-58988-019-6

To Robin and George,
my friends in Kypriotianika,
for that annual idyll, my Voyage to Cythera.

CONTENTS

Preface ix

2 INWARD PROSPECTS

PREFACE

I wrote these thoughts down on about two thousand sheets, two to three thoughts per paper, and I kept them in some used manila envelopes, the earliest of which bore a postmark of 1972. The sheets themselves had no dates or venues and no proper names on the now somewhat comical assumption that these jottings were timeless and universal. And indeed, decades later they are still tightly attached to times, places, and attendant persons, whose images snap back with great vividness. Yet if the same should happen to a possible reader of these abstractions from life, they would be proved to have a certain scope.

Whether about 5000 articulated notions per person per lifetime is about average or over or below I cannot tell; they certainly stacked up high.

Because they made a heap rather than a composition, they naturally have a number of alternative titles. Among them are:

Skariphemata: an obscure Greek word, meaning *Scribblings,*

Maxims and Minims: "Maxims" was suggested by La Rochefoucauld; a minim is, serendipitously, a fluid measure equal to one twentieth of a scruple, or a half note,

Reflections and Refractions,

Diary of Delight and Depression—the title on all the
 envelopes,

Drop by Drop: Distillations

 Open Secrets/Inward Prospects won out because all these
scribbles divided in a rough but ready way into two sorts:
1. observations about our external world well known to
all but not always openly told, and 2. sightings of internal
vistas and omens, looking at myself as a sample soul.
 "Reflections" is meant in the double sense as when
thinking bends pensively back on itself and when the
mind casts a coolly critical glance at what is before it.

INSTRUCTIONS FOR USE:
Open anywhere and if it irks you try another page. This
book can be long or short—As You Like It.

1

OPEN SECRETS

1 NATURE: SIGHTINGS

Once we live in an environment that is altogether an artifact, artificial, we live in a world that has no being in the ancient sense: "Being" is cognate with *physis,* that which grows on its own, that is, nature.

Living entirely out of nature, even if that artificial or even virtual world has become second nature to us, means being entirely encompassed by human rationality and human irrationality: Then only we and the dust mites will be as nature made us—well now, only the dust mites.

Nature is to science a mystery beckoning to be profaned, an X asking to be solved for. The wonder is that it works, that she is amenable to construal, to answering to a lucid, beautiful rationalization that leaves appearances and perceptual affect behind to reveal mathematical structures, patterns, processes, and creations of superlative interest. And then, a second miracle: This second nature, the nature of the intellect, which "saves the appearances" for reason by superseding their sensory affects with abstractions of number and shape, turns out to be eminently useful. We can bind nature to our convenience and comfort by applications of hypernatural construals: The theory of nature is practical! This is the wonder of wonders. The great question is how far this grand transformation of nature into second nature, of natural growth into sheer materiel can go before aboriginal nature simply gives out, and its transformed residue grows vicious towards us and mounts the ultimate slave rebellion against its masterpiece, the human animal.

Landscapes and the slow-growing cityscapes sealed within them are the most heartliftingly beautiful sights there are. That's because cultivated nature environing human sociality is the soul laid out in space.

Nature always achieves her comeuppance, when every solution develops an unforeseen problem and every cure an unexpected side effect and every plan an unintended consequence. Then that's not benevolent nature at work anymore; it's nature gone rebelliously rampageous. What if she were to shut down on us, like any abused system?

A double engagement, of mind and imagination: reading severely intellectual texts within sight of magical beauty. A porch hanging out into a spacious landscape. The *Critique* on my lap and out there in the blue middle distance the conical cinder hills against the very far off long light blue mountains. What a strange experience: to look now and then into so enchanting a spaciousness while reading of the transcendental sources of that sensibility within myself: St. John's College, Santa Fe, in the seventies.

Sign of the times: A student, asked what is meant by second nature, offers this example: "Take a can opener."

(He meant the kind they call a church key hereabouts.) "That's nature. Now take an electric can opener. That's second nature."

My own state still has in stretches that beauty the early colonial "Relations" note: a soft, mellow, pastoral, muted beauty, especially in fall, quite different from New England's brilliant displays. The hills are low, the little brick towns moderately elegant. A friend calls Maryland the shallow South. It really is the betwixt and between state; I'm fond of it.

The sights of nature come home to us in different modes: the robust romance of natural picturesques, the fragrant romance of old cultivated scenes, the surprised delight at nooks and crannies overlooked by development, the planned astonishment at natural wonders, etc.

Weeping willows close up, clumps of majestic trees behind and beyond ranks upon fading ranks of mountain ranges, and a church spire in the middle distance: the Blue Ridge. I love its rocks and rills, its woods and templed hills—except the temples tend to be communications installations.

The world used to offer a free bonus, the bonus of beauty nearby, the free and easy sight of natural beauty. Now that, like everything else, needs arranging. But though it's receded, it's not gone. This is a big land.

Pleasant breezes, glorious vistas: The heart expands and the intellect is activated.

There are natural settings so intensely atmospheric that the *genius loci* seems to step out from among the trees and regard the willing watcher, like that "Piper at the Gates of Dawn," Pan to the ancients.

A beautiful natural scene enters the memory much more permanently than the events that came and went in it.

Unforgettable: lovely talk in the sight of beauty.

Ducks in Walla Walla, at it in spring: A thingy like those rolled-up trumpets you blow out on New Year, a brief commotion, an unconcerned fluffing of feathers, he struts off with a waddle, she looks deeply uninterested; all this in view of a far from uninterested public, me.

Landfall on a Greek island, in phases: a thin dark swath of blue haze lies on the edge of the wine-dark sea; a blue outline like a shield upon the waters develops; it grows detailed; a beach is discernible; we land and find a sunken path between banks of glowingly blown red poppies, wildflowers, and fragrant warmth; the nausea of the sea recedes; soon we come to the habitations of men. Though the meat is not a cut from the chine of a boar broiled on a spit (it's *kephtedes,* savory meatballs), it's an archetypal memory image.

Landscape is a setting for love and friendship but it is older; it comes before and survives human affairs, and that is how it enters the imagination.

Golden stubble where the wheat's been harvested, chocolate brown earth where the fields have been plowed, mauve where they've dried under the sun—for mile upon spacious mile like an endless standing wave broken by canyons, gold on one side, dark on the other with clumps of cotton trees and silvery shacks. Beyond the sharp-faceted foothills and way beyond, far off, the blue saw-toothed mountain range, and above it all a pastel blue sky with clouds enough for live shadows to play over the scene. And bouncing before the car mat-gold balls of tumbleweed and little whorling dust devils, like sprites showing the way. I saw this a quarter-century ago: Walla Walla, Washington, where I was playing hooky from my college.

2 DOMESTICITY:
AT HOME AND AT WORK

Work starts when the mind's mainsail is tautly filled, the decks are clear and to shift figures, the world—that attractive nuisance—is with us but not impending.

What a miracle that any good work ever does get done when the world is one big blockade.

There's business and there's work. Business is as the Romans say, *neg-otium,* "non-leisure," and is to be disposed of. That gets you to base level, leisure, and thence to real life.

A perfect life would be one in which pleasure was the steady descant to work—halcyon days of lordly and liberal leisure, easy intimacy, smooth passage from the pregnant study into the blue day. Well, it happens.

The blithe spatial integrity of a life in which the workplace and home are close: easy transiting from public to private, from giving out to stocking up.

It's when labor is done that people need company, when first away at school that students need *in loco parentis* attention, when there's a first taste of success that colleagues need admiration, and, of course, when any of these are sad that they need conversation. There is world enough, if only there were time!

Self-forgetfulness in activity is being truly collected. That's what Aristotle calls *energeia*.

When there's a work impending (as does a benign incubus) everything is under its imperium. Even recreation—wonderful word—is only work by other means.

Fanaticism, the practice of orgiastic rites about the god's shrine (*fanum*), which is murderous in the public sphere, is in its mitigated version the condition of accomplishment. Work is faintly orgiastic (in fact *orgia*, Greek for secret sacrifices, is derived from *ergon*, work). It is surrender to compulsion and ritual-subjected excitement.

Publishable production is light relief from the inner labor of mastering experience and thinking things out.

We are kept from work happily by outer pleasures or inner dreaming, unhappily by moody distraction and intellectual confusion. For passing from bleak vacancy back to blessed occupation there is that secular analogue to prayer, thinking things out, driven by the antithetical forces of the longing for serenity and the need for getting it right.

Return: There's the effort of re-entry, the respinning of the cocoon of daily life, disposing of accumulations, reversing the downhill slide of unattended objects, repairing the alienation of absence, facing the evidence of bygone life. The enigma of return is in the "back again," in the reparable rupture of time.

The sense of possibility is a goad: not yet. And an enticement: might be. And between these the work gets done.

The more atmosphere an office has, the less gets done by that book, the one that turns human eventualities into exceptions when they ought to be expectancies.

Some help others, some do "their own work"; if there's got to be comparisons, the edge is with the helpers.

What's the difference between obsession and purpose? Love.

You can't tell about your self when you were fully at work—your self wasn't independently there.

When seized by a revelation, take a hot bath.

Chiseled definitions come from slow futzing around with that rough, shapeless bulk which is the mind's proto-material. Carve too soon with precision and you get a finely worked klutz of a thought.

Making things is a way of bypassing intractable confusion and unfaceable fear.

Vacation by gradations: anticipatory surge, arriving fuss, exploratory pleasure, full-blown bliss, gratified reflections, inchoate tedium, precipitous escape. I have limited talent for vacancy.

Why older people have more working energy than the lusty young: because interest that has a thousand old roots is convertible into physical vitality.

Three aspects of this working life: teaching, studying, writing, which requires the flexible alertness of going from responsible and helpful public conversation smoothly into tentative and self-directed inner speech; taking care of life's business, which demands compressed efficiency; dreaming, which wants only the readiness.

"Work and pray," say the monks; add: "and contemplate."

Who doesn't know about the great cycle of eros into work and work into eros? Did we need a degrading psychological theory for this sublime experience?

Be an easy-going monomaniac: don't always do *the* thing but never quite let it out of your mind, where it stews while you attend to necessary affairs.

An integral life: when everything, your serendipitous loves, your adventitious friends, your chosen living, turn out to work as one.

How differently shaped are the lives described by being (fully) at work (Aristotle's *energeia*) and doing one's work and having work and going to work and working.

It sounds like a mere conceit, but it's a haunting thought: My house, my home, is full of inanimate things that derive their use, their value, their significance from me. What are they when I'm gone? When I come back they are as I left them, the static witnesses of a bygone time. What was their mode of existence without their owner? When does my investment in them wear off (as the study of my house has long since ceased depreciating on my tax return) and how do they manage to grow more valuable by the decade (as my house's estimated value increases with every reassessment by the tax people)? The relation of people to their things is treated with imaginative thoughtfulness most often in young children's books. But it's an adult topic, the objectification of the spirit in things, or (without Hegel) the human ambience.

The inexorable routine of work which is also a job is at once a weariness and a saving grace.

That fanatic perfectionism which means that every look at the work suggests starting all over is the antithesis of the expansive ardor which goes for scope and leaves perfection to the very end.

Elements of sudden glory: a friend rediscovered, an absorbing project, a love reconfirmed, a business resolved, a successful occasion, a class come alive, a novel discovered, the intellect alight.

The weekday office is filled with loquacious confidences, animated communication, sociable chatter, relaxed mentation; what you have to realize is that this is a highly efficient, competent life form.

Two life-gestalten live side by side: that in which the bulky foreground figures of work interrupt the background of free time (the life of play which we knew from childhood, return to on scheduled vacations for rest and recreation, and hope to regain in retirement); and that which is configured quite differently: foreground and background, work and play, have melded, but there are little bright blanks of restorative vacancy. This latter gestalt is certainly the happiest, but so is there contentment in the first.

After a prolonged period of withdrawal from the active life, of leisurely study or writing, there is an inertial resistance to re-entry. It takes a while to be re-encapsulated in business.

All the firsts of return, sitting on one's chair, sleeping in one's bed, taking a bath, filling the refrigerator—there should be a *bracha,* a blessing, to mark, even sanctify, the arrival in one's place, the restarting of an old life. There probably is.

We immigrants naturally value roots more highly than do the native-born, albeit we pull them up for inspection now and then. So they are not so deep as those of untouched nature—but very well tended.

Do you get the impression that you've caught your house at it when you come home? What was the *genius loci* up to in my absence, agitating my atmosphere?

Kids crash in their pads; German bachelors have *Budenangst,* "den-anxiety"; Englishmen are at home in their castles. Pad, den, castle, the house is a kind of bastion against and for the world, a place where I preside: I may shut myself up to do what requires privacy or isolation; I may mount a decorous conviviality; I may fuss the place into my notion of comeliness.

"Home is the place where, when you have to go there, / They have to take you in . . ." or ". . . Something you somehow haven't to deserve." I think Frost's people are talking of a homeless shelter. Because for my money, home is exactly what you have to deserve, in fact to make. And the first part seems to be true mostly for the houses of parents of wayward kids.

Why were the ancients capable of grander style and deeper thought? Because what they did have was servants and what they didn't have was information.

The duties and delights of the little life: feeding, cleaning, fixing, paying—expending time in small coin; but there are also the reasonable routines and spontaneous rewards of teaching, the pleasure of conversation now witty, now deep, the enjoyment of playing with children, the relish of good reading. And then there is the imaginative life, and so it's not a little life after all.

The *incipit* of any enterprise, by reason of sitting on the time line with one of its sides exposed, stands out and seems to determine the whole. But human time consists of specious presents, discrete moments, and if moment one went wrong, moment two can repair the damage. In any case, in the long run a false beginning makes a great comic anecdote. Now if there is no long run . . .

Some homes are conceived as unkempt, hospitable in-and-out places with flailing children and shedding dogs, others as secure houses, stably tidy and ordered to one specific taste. The one is lovely to visit, and the other conforms to my life.

The house: that shelter of companionable spirits, of sunlit domesticity and conviviality, but also the space of desolation, *acedia,* and flight from obligations. Could it be that our dwelling is the spatial analogue of our interiority? We, our conscious selves, live within our souls which are furnished with the accumulation of our life, our memories. We, our somatic selves, live within our homes which are furnished with the accumulation of our life, our possessions. Both venues house investments turned into obligations.

What is familiarity? It is living without looking, and its confirmation comes when our glance is once again engaged and delightedly surprised.—*Viven a nuestro lado, / los ignoramos, nos ignoran. / Alguna vez conversan con nosotros:* "They live by our side; we neither know nor heed them, they neither know nor heed us. But sometimes they do talk to us" (Octavio Paz, "Objects").

Here's my taste in a home: My things should be homely, imperfect, of middling quality, jibing with each other, not intrusively precious, but invested with the significance of their provenance.

"Renovation" has the, sometimes intended, consequence of laying ghosts. Generations have lived in my house, and until this moment I haven't given them a thought.

Return by moonlight? I come on my own ghost of a month ago—eerie. Well, an animate body trumps a ghost on this earth.

I glance over my thousands of books, well knowing that most of them will not be opened again by me, except insofar as they happen to be my letter filing system. Of course, when, one day, they go to the college library, they'll sanitize them. But oh, what company a reader with my tastes might find! What a blessing, incidentally, that books have soundless voices; I'd go crazy.

Clean the house first, and a duty will fill in the time you thought you cleared. When I was a child I'd eat first everything on the plate I liked least. So a friend of the family, a bearded lady, leaned over and took my hoarded last bite, because, she said, I must not want it. Why didn't I learn my lesson? It's constitutional.

If you must flout convention do it away from home or do it candidly. Candor is good concealment, since people don't hear what they're candidly told in these matters.

The difference between keeping house and playing house is the difference between doing the weekly family shopping and picking up some nice-looking salmon and fresh asparagus. The point: Those who have more fun don't necessarily have more joy.

3 DRAMA: FLAWED TRAGEDIES

A wounded soul has a certain fragile poignancy: Weak nerves look like sensibility, an empty spirit like pathos, the defensive expense of spirit like determination. But this psychic fragrance is fugitive—a prolonged look behind the scenes, and the odor is pitiably frowzy.

There's this to be said for grief: It's easier to come by than happiness and much less laborious to maintain.

Just see the comical nonchalance with which the soul wipes its hands of the muck of midnight stews, once it's got what it wanted.

The medieval monks had it right about *tristitia,* "world-weariness": *laborare et orare,* "work and pray." But at what and to whom? Figure that out.

In the murk, the drab hell, of the psychically crippled it is confoundingly hard to tell weak character from pathology. Is it inattention or amnesia, selfishness or self-protection, coldness or apathy, fickleness or lability, shallowness or deadness—in short, badness or illness?

Whence comes the power of a blemish to transform adoration into poignant love? Does it highlight perfection as, they say, beauty spots do, or does a touch of pity perfect love?

A real sorrow, as from a loss: that the human being you love had an antecedent life—as if you heard a fugue without its first statement.

After a blow to the soul, the sensibility is numbed and all the world seems to be under glass: clearly detailed and quite intangible.

Wherein is genuine human equality to be found? I mean not assumed rights but an actual condition. Surely it is in suffering that we are all each other's equal: A toothache is a toothache and heartbreak is heartbreak the world over, be we smart or dumb, rich or poor.

Misfortune and failure can have their poignant dignity. The piteous apathy born of early deprivation, the unapproachableness that comes from a rebuffed childhood—all these induce a kind of tenderness, though that's just the trouble—it's love's labor lost.

This is human catastrophe: to learn what it means not to know how to live, to feel time as a malicious slouching beast, to taste the nothingness of despair and the taut vibrancy of utter forsakenness. And then to add insult to injury, to be drummed out of the elite corps of companions and to be returned, disgraced, to the indifferent mass of the "Other Ranks." Schiller: *Wem der grosse Wurf gelungen, / Eines Freundes Freund zu sein, / . . . Ja—Wer auch nur eine*

Seele / Sein nennt auf dem Erdenrund! / Und wer's nie gekonnt der stehle / Weinend sich aus diesem Bund! A somewhat merciless but truthful consigning to Arctic exile of the unlucky, that glorious Ninth: If you haven't managed to be at least one friend's friend, creep weeping out of our company.

Life next to a cripple not of limb but of life has its pain and its sweetness; the first comes from the absolute curtailment of psychic capacity, the second from the laborious gallantry with which the incapacity is borne.

A friend's depression feels like hopeless rejection; you simply aren't effectively there.

The gusto for the monstrous is particularly powerful in those in whom nature is strong: Archaic Greece.

We can show no greater trust in the vitality of our nature than to try to master our passions: The more firmly you prune back your foundation planting, the more vigorous and shapely it grows.

It's a fearful comfort to realize how great is the difference between good and bad fortune and how different is the acquired wisdom of those who live in a good country where family, friends, and possessions are safe and sound, from that of a people whose world is in ruins and whose life is grim. What those victims of fortune have learned—and here's the double hit—is a lesson expensively acquired and worth nothing or less than nothing. For the wisdom distilled from dark misfortune is poison to a decent land. I would rather be governed by the comparatively unscathed, the innocently, even ignorantly naive, than by those whose souls have been seared and whose experience is with hell. Why? Because well-fed, prosperous, protected people have a more definitive recoil from badness—a more instinctive reaction and a more reliable resistance.

The rejected soul is a squirming worm; it writhes and coils up and rears and again lies low; it schemes and plots, turns in circles and gives in, gives up. In its lowness it takes comfort in sob stories, trite tales, vulgar lyrics, sappy songs; it finds a comfort in the community of the abandoned. And it is a large community—witness country music.

Despair has a taste and feel and a sound—the nauseous taste of nothingness, the throbbing feel of forsakenness, the jaunty sound of damnation. The last can be heard in the aria that the High Priest sings in Judas's behalf after his suicide (*Matthew Passion,* No. 5).

Some people seem to live lapped in a soft pall of sadness, a mat melancholy, within which their life has a sort of gray contentment.

When people cry on strange shoulders, the relief evidently outweighs the shame. But it's probably like taking pain pills: When it wears off it's worse than ever.

The bitter aftertaste of dissipation: no residue of profit and "th' expense of spirit in a waste of shame," the soul stuck in its taste for morose diversion, soggy, inelastic, unable to snap back, the imagination blacked-out, and even the minimal efforts of self-maintenance overwhelming. Whyever?

The nauseating vertigo of loss: present shock and the distant trumpets ushering in desolation to come. And then the strange oscillations of time, of being for one, two, three moments yet in the moment before the news came and the world was well.

Insult added to injury: the ignominious exile from the blessed land of the lucky.

Leave-taking is a little death—a very little one, since we are yet together in the land of the living. What will it feel like the last time?

Sadness and sorrow steal away the lithe élan that is part of our self-possession and leave us pulpy and shapeless. Pretending helps.

A human being who has no story of suffering can hardly be a subject, meaning an inwardness that has been touched.

Judging by myself, there is an appalling specificity in human fellow feeling: Misfortune induces a detached, sometimes repelled pity; acute sympathy is reserved for those who are, as the Germans say, *sympathisch,* appealing.

Is it possible to love someone who has never been touched by suffering? Even a god, it seems, turns mere adoration into love through pity. Aren't Christians brought to salvation through their sensibility?

This turns out to bring real comfort to people: unaffected interest in the details of their misfortune. They become storytellers, and the listener's sympathy becomes incidental to the engaging tale. They tell and find relief; you listen and learn something. No shame on one side, less helplessness on the other.

Every grievance has behind it some grief which it is humane to discover and address, though the complaint itself may have no merit. In the young, once you're past their gawky intransparency, the real matter turns out to be some ideal rebuffed. Then you have to persuade them 1. that their expectations were unrealistic and 2. that they're not to relinquish them.

Nietzsche glories in tearing away transparent veils. "The sense of the tragic," he says, "waxes and wanes with sensuality." "What constitutes the excruciating voluptuousness of tragedy is," he announces, "its cruelty (*Grausamkeit*)." Any child who demands a gruesome story, as I used to (gruesome equals *grausam*), has an inkling of this human lust for being excruciated. But we grow up to have scruples.

Life offers this rough compensation: Grief has lessons, or, as Aeschylus says: *pathei mathos,* learning by suffering (*Agam.* 177). But you're double taxed on this profit: First you pay in grief and then in labor. For it takes work, digestive work, to get, so to speak, the good of the bad: You have to decoct your affect into a concentrate of thought.

Some griefs ask for chocolate, others ruin the appetite. What's the metaphysics of that?

How long can a grief last, once it's crystallized into a clear psychic possession? Forever.

Watching a tragic figure and being a tragic figure are disjunct experiences: grandly heroic vs. abjectly miserable. Antigone, that teenage monster, has for us a forbidding dignity as she commands the public stage, but to herself, in the minutes and hours and days of her private life, she must feel in turn bleak with loneliness and rigid with resistance. But then the thought: There is no interior, no off-stage Antigone. The protagonists of Attic Old Tragedy are not human beings but incarnate principles.—That's what's monstrous: a monolithic girl.

It is part of the tragedy of tragedy that you eventually have to present yourself in public with it. And there the young are touching because they haven't yet learned that we don't look like our images of ourselves. So they look like lost children while they feel like tragic heroes. But it is nonetheless the image you have to speak to.

Persistent unhappiness whose cause is too deep and too old for discernment begins to look like willful entrenchment. It's perfectly intractable because it's tragedy as a *modus vivendi*.

There is a small sadism of love: the urge to see the loved one under a tragic aspect, to see the loved soul raked up and writhing, partly for the frisson and partly to offer consolation. It is very shameful.

Some people carry about them an air of neurotic anxiety which does not have the musk of tragedy but the fetor of misery.

Why do some sufferings have pathos while others are pathetic? Why, for example, are some cripples distinguished and others demeaned by their condition? It must be that the former bear it with psychic panache and residual physical deftness, while the latter are—but that's not right to put in words.

The worst fear after a great disaster is that the survivors' souls may have been stretched past restoration and wrenched past straightening.

In great crises the delicate anxieties of normalcy are overborne by the urgencies of survival. But that's no way to live, this trivializing of those of the soul's by-paths that flourish in prosperity.

In the continuities of ordinary life its limits are out of sight. But in the trauma of dispersal, when some segment of life is closed forever, we get a glimpse of the ultimate end and, oddly enough, sudden images of our beginnings, early childhood.

In unbalancing transitions, true things are (temporarily) tarnished by the terrors of fleeting time.

There is a curious nostalgia *for* the present *in* the present, when all we love appears as a wan ghost of itself, and we feel an anticipatory mourning for what is right next to us.

Clarification, inner articulation, is our ultimate relief from a tragic embroilment. The rest is mere follow-up.

Silent suffering is always moving, provided the silence isn't noisy.

Women love to nurse the war-wounded. That's because pity can be an aphrodisiac, provided its object is heroic: "She loved me for the dangers I had passed / And I loved her that she did pity them" (*Othello* I, iii).

The dilemma of pity is its asymmetry: expansive for the giver, humiliating for the receiver.

People who have been assaulted and maimed lead a life behind the barricades; they are trained on the past in horror, recoil from the future in fear, and want to kill the present.

Three lovely sorts of humanity: when the same person who preserves severe grace in adversity also has tender grace in normalcy; when someone very efficient in practical life turns out to have a vital imaginative life; when someone faces the troubles and tragedies of the world not without a sense of their poignant dignity but is determined to transform them into soluble problems and livable comedies.

It must be hard to be excluded from the free-flowing community of the inconspicuous and unstigmatized by reason of celebrity or defect. What a blessing congenital obscurity is—my own lovable way of life.

Pity is compounded of unwitting condescension, appalled distance, dutiful kindness. Sympathy weaves together poignant fellow feeling, desire for closeness, and warm care. At least, there are two feelings, worlds apart, which these words might distinguish.

Well-being is a flotational, buoyant state of life. Expect a letdown, plop.

Living tragedy, say a fatal disease in the midst of life: It makes no sense and has none, and that realization seems to be a sort of comfort to the victim—no more agonized searching for fault or cause. But for the bystander the relief from fear comes from the dry fact that fatal disease is not the norm. As Aristotle says, "Nature is what happens always or for the most part." It is a real though impersonal solace that the norm is normal.

Heraclitus says, "The dry soul is wisest and best." What *he* means I wouldn't know, but what *it* means to me is: A little pathos goes a long way; brisk brusque cheer is the deflating antidote to the melodrama of life.

Living tragedy is to be efficiently dismantled, fictional tragedy is to be receptively savored. Strange!

It is a goblin pleasure to flatten the peaks of young melodrama with adult kindness.

People say we overlook flaws in those we love. I don't think so since in love we overlook nothing. Instead we love the pathos of imperfection; it is the beauty mark of the soul.

In elegant souls somber graciousness turns to playful grace when a burden is lifted.

Undecidable: Do character or nature or fate shape the tempestuousness of the wounded, the sourness of the stinted, the indecision of the insecure? And is irritation permissible or are we bound to endless patience? Take all you can and blow up when you must.

It is next to impossible to be deeply attached to anyone, man, woman, child, who doesn't have a touch of pathos, for passionate pity is one ingredient—just a pinch—in all love.

Luck probably makes you better quicker than does suffering, if you're careful to control triumphalism. You're not the darling of the gods. Just call Luck by her true name, Happy Accident, and you'll see she's no goddess.

The double jeopardy of physical deformity: spectacle and disability.

Pain isolates although suffering is what most equalizes us: We are all the same in pain yet we feel it only for ourselves. Our taxonomic togetherness is disrupted by our individual separateness, but it is just in the resultant vulnerability that we find a new universal.

The abnormal want to be treated as normal but not quite. They want the world to forget while attending. I wonder if this mantra comes from them or their professionals and if the demand is too logically strained. They might really wish for friendship that comes about not in spite, but in view, of their defects.

Pathei mathos, learning by suffering is tragedian's wisdom. Learn for the love of it, say the philosophers. Those who experience tragedy are naturally going to agree with the dramatists—they want some profit from it all. But I hold with the effort of wiggling out of, defeating, subverting the setting of such wisdom wherever possible and returning as soon as we can to the happier wisdom of philosophy.

Is the life of the religious liberal, say a secular Jew like myself, a life of levity compared to the disciplined self-confined life of the orthodox? Without doubt. But then levity is Latin for lightness, and what is light rises by nature, so there's hope.

Genuine bad luck (that is, not lack of prudence) has no antecedent but no end of consequences—a sad asymmetry.

The neophilistines: They want their souls seared of an evening, and they pay to be excruciated.

As with stage tragedy, so in life: See the protagonist from a distance and you glimpse a timelessly heroic, poignant shape; get closer and it is a daily battle for normalcy; enter within (at least in imagination) and it is a minute by minute fight against amorphous misery.

Sensible people would much rather feel for others' tragedy—and, if encouraged, even savor it—than conduct their own. *That* they try to circumvent by cunning and, that failing, turn to some account as an "experience." But mainly they acknowledge to themselves a truism whose truth should be more fervently proclaimed: that to live well is by far the nicest thing, and also to be well and to be well off. From *The Way of All Flesh:* Ernest—"Don't you like poor people very much yourself?" Townley—"No, no, no." So much for the "culture of poverty" they used to talk about.

Those who plan to found their dignity, their pathos to themselves, on their suffering, have come to the wrong country—a kindly but persistently optimistic land, that expects its people to temper their sense of election, of being chosen to embody tragedy, to the busy mainstream. Americans attend very nicely to figures of fate for a while, but then they go about their business—whose large, unconscious aim is to subvert tragedy. Here the proper reply to the non-question "How are you?" is "Fine."

For the young, at least, the pathos of physical imperfection is centered on the possibility of attracting love, of being loved not for, nor despite of, but *with* one's defect. For they want to be loved neither with perverse pity nor with averted face but just as they are. With a little luck, it's possible.

If there's consolation in beauty, that's a sign the grief is melting, since beauty requires an unconstricted chest to enter.

When you wake up tense and startled after midnight to find that your own life has got away from you, that you're seeing it through the wrong end of the telescope—then all the decades are compacted into a partless and pointless whole, all these people are unmoved impassive ghosts, all the present is a grind of doing and redoing. Well, get up, make some hot chocolate, and get down to some work.

Who is wiser, those who are once-born or twice-born, those whose life has continued in homeostatic calm or those who've gone through a season of hell and have come out? I would go for the innocent over the catastrophic wisdom, because while the fears of the former may be less informed, its hopes have a more concrete content.

Misfortune nonchalantly borne in the light of day may turn to despair at night, while a tragic mask worn abroad may reveal a sunny visage at home. You never can tell.

Those who go in for putting up with it stoically are less likely to scramble themselves into a better situation, while those to whom outrage and rebellion are second nature are more likely to bull their way past it.

If you're miserable, take a bath or a walk, or pig-out on TV or Swiss almond ice cream, but don't pick that time to pontificate about life.

Some people carry about a decoction of their griev-ances bottled as an essence to be, skunk-like, periodically squirted into the common air.

When fissures appear in the ground of faith, music is mere sound, people mere wraiths, the relish of work a mere memory—read a Gothic novel.

Exercise your imagination occasionally on correcting the negative deprivation of a prosperous life: Imagine hell with exactitude.

Life's little ironies: that weeping eyes bring on a runny nose.

It is one of life's satisfactions to hear your friends acknowledge sincerely that your griefs are fairly felt and gallantly borne.

A crisis sweeps comet-like across life, first the flashing head and then a whole swath of suspended consequences.

The saddest, most hopeless case: when someone's very person is an irritant to another sensibility. It trumps the greatest respect and is irreversible by time.

The German folktale of "little Hans who sallied forth to learn dread" is abysmally wrongheaded in its melding of culpable innocence and guilty curiosity. Our business is to convert all fascination with the uncanny into sober repulsion and to consider that every soul or place that presents itself under the aspect of demonic pathos is apt to be grayly miserable within.

The awareness of living with some marking fact, be it stigmatizing or distinguishing, must be like being accompanied by an ever-present doppelganger, continually asking "Why me?"

Those who are hurt, unless it is abjectly, are already the winners: They're having an experience. That's one of those open secrets.

People grow unsleek with grief and rough with loneliness—and repellent with pride, because they know it.

The really lost souls are those who can't find their way to the bread-and-butter beauties of daily life. That's what Satan couldn't bear: the everlasting ordinary bliss of Heaven's eternal day.

People who rely on their troubles to attract friendship had better recall that sympathy has a shadow called aversion.

Causing pain for enjoyment is twice repulsive, once and first for the harm to the victim, but again for the soul-corrupting perverse estheticism of sadism—a supposedly human being moved sexually and unmoved humanly. Yech!

Tragedies are spectator sports, that is, the spectators have the sport, whilst the heroes and heroines are busy trying to discern whether the fault is with fate, themselves, or just luck. But here is what the tragic figures themselves don't experience: what Aristotle calls the tragic pleasure. There is, I think, no such thing as subjective Tragedy that's all for the onlooker. The same holds for comedy: Whoever was a buffoon before his inmost self?

Is it to laugh or to cry that heroes, tragic or epic, become *cases* for us moderns, duly catalogued in the Diagnostic and Statistical Manual?

Gallantry under conditions of unwanted conspicuousness attracts moved admiration.

Diversion, *pace* Pascal, has its uses: a holding pattern while the turmoil on the ground is dying down.

Can there be a thoroughly candid, cleanly perspicuous relation to the world: someone who has no hidden guilt or pain, whose *jocunditas* goes through and through, who is truly simple? Perhaps a person of faith? Here is what such a one would *not* be: boring.

Under certain circumstances people go prophylactically crazy, as any sane person would.

Two kinds of chronic pain: living with personal disfigurement or disability and living in a disgraceful and corrupt community.

The tragic life is a burden, the comic life a shame; the serio-comic life is my life of choice: work and hilarity.

Who knows more? Those who have faced ultimate things or those who have stayed well within the borders of life, those who have attracted disaster or those who have evaded catastrophe, those who have experienced final impotence or those who have managed affairs within the limits of their ability? Well, I know this: Disillusionment isn't wisdom.

The comfort of a traumatic catastrophe is to tell the tale. "It is an ancient Mariner, / And he stoppeth one of three." Humanity requires listening if you are that third, and more than once; besides, it's apt to be interesting. Now tales of contentment have less gripping content: "How did you fare in the last half-century?" "Well." "Where were you?" "All over." "What happened?" "Nothing much." Except I lived, I saw, I learned.

An exact imagination can configure us internally in every posture of suffering from being rheumatic to being bereaved. But it can't bridge the rift, of hairline breadth and infinite depth, to existence.

Life is not a fiction, where the tensions of mutual misunderstanding are prolonged for the reader's enjoyment. Too much real suspense makes the soul inelastic. Resolve discords quickly and generously, never mind pride. This particular spice of life, the lovers' or friends' quarrel, is too hot for prolonged use.

A sound constitution has a modicum of determinate needs and a definable cause for its griefs. Fulfill the former and resolve the latter and all's well. The sick soul has infinite, vagrant desires and vague, elusive miseries.

The proud pretenses of the heart: People make a show of being content with a stingy gift when the heart says "more, more." They mask crying need with nonchalant humor. Should we pretend not to penetrate the pretense? No, unless there's been too much of it, we should be generous—and when it's children, unconditionally so.

You're telling me your troubles, like, you've got too much to do. That's exactly my trouble, too. Now does that make me have more or less sympathy for you? Both.

4 MUSIC: "SOUL OF THE WORLD"

No one leaves before royalty, and it's the same with music; you don't switch it off. When it's finished you can go.

An exalted heart and a steady beat—Bach.

Music—and all heaven breaks loose.

Music, for the amateur, can be focal (in attentive listening, perhaps score in hand), applied (to dance or march, perhaps even to calm nerves), or environmental. This last, the delight of amateurs and the scorn of purists, is also the most magical. It is not overheard; on the contrary, it is listened for behind the foreground activity. It becomes the expression of the *genius loci,* its aura made audible, and within it people appear more beautiful and move more gracefully, as the Toltec gods were said to walk swiftly above the ground shod in blue sandals.

The love of music is the secular person's devoutness.

As the descant is to plainsong, so is music to work.

Whatever sophisticated theories supported the modern and postmodern styles, this seems to be a fact, surely an open secret: Concrete is cheaper than marble, steel than wood, plastic than ivory, prefab than handmade. Similarly, making few or large strokes or drippings is less time-consuming than realizing a design in detail and by tool. Are two economies getting mixed up here?

If you cut out a piece of background from a baroque canvas and stretched it on a frame, wouldn't it pass for a work of non-objective art?

If the purifiers ever drove stereotypes (= types) from the scene, could literature survive? It is impossible to imagine and cast into words an absolutely unique and typeless being. But neither, except in comedy, is a fictional being merely a token, an instantiation, of a type. The peculiar charm and the human interest of fictional characters (as of people) surely lie in their embodying their kind with enchanting variations: deficits and intensifications and aberrations. So Natasha Rostov is a young Muscovite princess, who shows herself on that unforgettable night at "Uncle's" to be all Russian, knowing out of nowhere the peasant grace of a Russian folk dance, and she is also all girl. She belongs to a whole hierarchy of types; she is an incarnate intersection of three classes— princess, Russian, girl—at least. And also she is totally inimitable; several men want her and no one else, which is proof of uniqueness. But her one-and-only personality is seated in her types: It is her warmheartedly spirited way of realizing them that makes her Natasha. So in literature as in the visual arts, and above all, in music, if the types and the canons fail, individuality becomes vagrant, antic.

Trendy art: the collusion of the poor in spirit with the rich in pocket.

I hate formal concerts: The music comes through as if I had cotton in my ears. Why should I want to consume that piece at that time amongst strangers? And what do I care if he can play better than anyone else? The music I care about would be moving if it were played with the deformations a figure undergoes in a fun house mirror.

It's a miracle that musical form not only expresses musical substance but human meaning as well, for example, Bach's theologically learned devoutness.

What I think of as characteristically Greek, *pace* Winckelmann's famous "noble naiveté, silent grandeur": sophisticated grandeur, subtle substance, perverse soundness, and naiveté nowhere in sight.

Visual art requires focused inspection, while music enters the ears circumambiently. The visual arts (excepting architecture, rightly called "frozen music" because it too environs) are occasional pleasures while music belongs to the day. Of course, there's the consequence of living with it; surfeit: "Enough! No more / 'Tis not so sweet now as it was before"—getting enough of a music is a positive irritation, while a picture is simply no longer visible.

For two intense years I studied Greek pots and pot-painting and found every detail engrossing. But that was work. I trained myself to see, and I learned to describe. It was a professional's relation to a visual art. But with music I'm an amateur, which means an unobligated lover—from childhood on, when I used to take my scratchy gramophone under my blankets and shiver with the delight of "feeling my feelings" (as a young friend of mine said when I swung him high on the park swing).

Music both patterns the motions of the soul and expresses them. It makes us inwardly shape up and it expresses those shapes in sound—or the other way around.

Architecture is the house of all the arts, but least of all in the form of a museum.

Greatness, on slightly better acquaintance, is not in the least repelling. These works were made for us, and they are hospitable, almost homey. They speak to us, even if we are only minimally prepared, with expectant familiarity and trustful originality. They want to be understood.

Sudden music is an impromptu festivity of the soul, it opens all the inward prospects.

Conrad, a passionate sailor and a great novelist, who thought that sailing and writing were two endeavors of a kind, says: ". . . nature . . . is an indispensable condition to the building up of an art" (*The Mirror of the Sea*). He is contrasting steamships with sailing vessels; the men in the one are mastering nature, in the other conducting an intimacy with her. I think that just as you need recognizable human types to write fiction, so you need nature. We do have a literature of second nature, denatured nature—

science fiction. But it's hard to see how the writing of novels could survive the final transmogrification of nature into artifacts, for how can you be intimate with, say, an electronic device (to wit: the cyberspace genre)? A novelist needs human nature as a foil for individuality and nature's nature for humans to define themselves against.

The word, by its nature of being one-over-many, is meant to convey sum and substance briefly—to abbreviate experience. Novelists who attempt to render interiority exhaustively (e.g., Virginia Woolf) can also be exhaustingly boring. Concerning consciousness, intimations are better than court reporting.

There are realms, realms of grandeur, admission to which is not by effort but by gift. Yet who but a mucky egalitarian wouldn't agree that it's better to be an outsider looking in than that there should be no such exclusive Edens?

Music has the power to make a gnawing want into a flowering wish.

Sheer glory: a place and its music. I once wandered into St. Paul's when the organist was practicing a Bach toccata-and-fugue—fifty years ago.

A carping connoisseur is harder to bear than a gross boor.

Combinatorial pleasures of the young: in love, in a beautiful place, in the company of a friend likewise employed—and music.

No one has sufficiently said what a feeling is. It is *pathos,* something passively suffered, affect. Yet it is also motion, being moved out of oneself, emotion. No more do we know what pleasure is, especially psychic pleasure: It seems to be the aboriginal accompaniment, not so much reaction as concurrent comment—but every analytic description covertly involves the word "pleasant." All the definitions I've read of feeling or pleasure are either diversionary or circular: Even my trusty *Heritage Dictionary* can do no better than to lead me from feeling to affect and from affect to feeling. And the definitions given in books circumvent saying what passions are by telling how they arise and what they're good for—as if origin and effect were what is wanted.

Could there be another person with less ear and more love for these strange structures composed from pitched sounds (tones) ordered in systems (the Greek word for "scales") according to rules and their felicitous breaches?

What synesthetic serendipity makes my silver flute give out purling runnels of liquid silver?

They say that hypocrisy is the respect vice pays to virtue. Well, kitsch is the tribute vulgarity pays to beauty, which is why bowdlerizations, popularized settings of great music, sentimental visions of sublime scenery, are so touching: They show that we all long for the same archetypes.

Music elicits the particular pathos that each human being possesses by reason of sharing in the general human condition.

Living without the natural aptitude for what we love best could be a small local tragedy, were it not that most of us are good (and busy) at something we love less but esteem perhaps even more.

That literature invites thought most which is quite bare of deliberate symbolism and interposes no separable literary devices between its world and *the* world: Jane Austen, Fontane, Tolstoy, Paul Scott.

Why is music that is a mere cranking of the style-machine or poetry that is rhymed emoting so irritating, while a romantic novel, written to formula and unfetteredly sentimental, can be enjoyable, like a mild debauch? Why is narrative prose more forgiving of bad taste than music or poetry? It must be because in prose fiction the mere matter trumps the execution, and that matter is recognizable enough to the day-dreaming imagination in its aberrantly lurid mode to make the thing absorbable.

I imagine that it takes thousands of elegant females scribbling away in their boudoirs to produce one consummately fine woman novelist (though come to think of it, the English didn't have boudoirs; Jane Austen wrote in a parlor with that famous creaking door to warn her of approaching visitors). We're in that state now (how many alumnae manuscript novels have I read?), and so the novel flourishes—though the females aren't elegant anymore, they're quirky instead.

There is a kind of English novel that is great for that rare truly vacant afternoon: emotionalism under a veneer of reserve, demure melodrama. Usually a mousy, steelily moral governess (capable of blooming in love) withstands her tempestuous, rich employer who is rendered helpless by an act of heroism. *Jane Eyre* is the masterpiece of the type, whose attraction is that it shows women to be principled (eyre = court) and men emotional, contrary to modern theory (Carol Gilligan).

The melodramatic gesturing of crooners and the wild antics of rock stars seem to me inversely proportional to the passion-content of the music; the less it means the more stylized body-emoting. To be sure, when the gyrating was fresh and young and the voice was inimitable and the songs stolen from a good tradition, the whole effect was rousingly charming: Elvis, of course.

Painting seems to me more dispensable than music because every face is its own portrait, every landscape its own painting. Nature even produces non-objective compositions: a piece of sycamore bark broken off, a view of the Painted Desert from a Cessna. All these can be framed in the observer's mind *ad libitum*. But there is no cantata-trouvé.

Are the concisions and obscurities of the poets delphic or antic? I can tell—and love to discover—what makes a difficult great poem great (Hopkins, for example), but I have no idea how you tell better from worse in the average run. That inability is the mark of an amateur.

James speaks of the author's "muffled majesty" (*Golden Bowl,* preface). Isn't it interesting that those authors who really do muffle their majesty by letting their people reveal themselves are more like the Author—who endowed his creatures with free will—than those who attempt to create their characters' interiority for them by speaking from within them?

Who among us can't turn a poetic phrase, compose a short chorus in the shower, doodle a villa? But since we have neither inventive momentum nor learned skill, we are the readers, listeners, dwellers—and it's all for us.

Amateurs are good at appreciation but their critique tends to be articulated aversion.

"Soul of the world" (from Purcell's *Ode for St. Cecilia's Day*): Music as the bond that binds the material atoms into one harmonious ensouled body—that is, *mutatis mutandis,* the definition of a *world,* a cosmos, as distinct from a sprawling universe. We, being similarly ensouled bodies, want to live in a world, that is, a musically resonant environment. If astronomy, which first disclosed the cosmos, has outstripped itself, and the Whole cannot be comprehended as a world now, then we must make subworlds, make them or maintain them, as required.

Connoisseurs, buffs, amateurs are often in love wholesale with the whole genre, though they can also turn picky and love only what they love—a self-willed tribe.

There is a whole current tribe of civilized women writers who are perhaps not "significant" (to the critics, those preening parasites) but plain good: in rebellion against rebellion, sophisticatedly human, cultivatedly experienced, lovers of language and of men, women, children, land-scapes, cities, houses. Any being that came within their imaginative purview could count on fair treatment. They write novels but make no attempt to be novel about it.

Some decades ago the novel was pronounced dead. Well, it wasn't the novel but the novelists. Genres don't die, they go into a catatonic state until awakened by the kiss of a young prince (or just as likely, a princess). Then they spring back to ruddy life not having aged much. All these death announcements by the undertakers of art, the theoreticians!

You can see in young students how calling and craft are complementary: Something beckons; they train themselves to follow.

Tolstoy: apotheosis of the human mean.

Hearing a Bach harpsichord concerto: This is bor-rowed joy without debt to pay. Is the elation elicited or infused?

There is the *sapor sapientiae,* the savor of wisdom (I made this up out of my very deficient Latin) that science-fiction exudes, far from the insufferable intellectualizing it undergoes in literary criticism. —A year later: No, I got it from *Paradise Lost.*

The moral import of fiction: Almost every calamitous tale invites the reader to imagine an alternative event, to ask: What could have been done to prevent it? What should I have done?—just as we do in life, where also it's usually too late. To draw the moral wisdom from a serious fiction, you have to relive it as if the possibilities were still open and the tragedy still preventable. For example, could I have stopped Bartleby from inanition? But it doesn't have to be a moral labor, this alternative fiction— it could just be a satisfying daydream in which you made good some fatal omission or refrained from a destructive act. Whether you retell the story to yourself in earnest or in levity, variations on the subject, riffs off the theme, are the sign that the fiction has entered your life.

There are these participatory cybertexts where you make the story advance according to a decision tree. I think authors are paid to make determinate decisions, and these enable readers to imagine alternatives. The imagination takes off best from firm ground.

Some music rectifies, some music ruins souls; some saves them, some sends them to perdition. That's why Aristotle ends his *Politics* with the consideration of children's musical education and Luther somewhere speaks of music as next to theology.

Paradise must be the place where what music signifies becomes manifest in sights and expressible in words. Or, perhaps, music is heaven's native tongue, signifying no less immediately than on earth but far more tellingly.

What makes the meaning music intimates so elusive in articulation? The reason is not, as people say, that it is too general. On the contrary, music means too specifically for words, its intimations are far too subtle, its meanings far too particular—way beyond the articulating threshold of specifying language. Music expresses motions of the soul so fine that the intersection of a thousand mortal words couldn't render them.

Bread-and-butter glory: Bach.

Lusty, roiled, shiftless spontaneity makes good copy but not great literature. The heroes and heroines of the monumental novels tend to be oppressed, conscience-ridden, love-sick stay-at-homes.

The events of life are usually buffered from each other by expanses of ordinary time, while the events of literature follow each other—perforce—in concise succession. For there is no way to get the effect of expansive passage except by letting real time really pass: "Ten years have now gone by . . ." is an imposition on the reader's temporal imagination who cannot really fast forward like that and has the events of the previous page in mind undimmed by that imaginary decade. That's why fiction is more experience-inspissated than life, in which the ten years really passed. Life of course has this advantage (not to be overestimated): The events are moderately real.

All the actions of a Greek drama take place within one day, because they are meant to be *moments* of truth, culminations.

Let an event of life end dramatically, definitively, and life will immediately get to work on it: subjugate, digest, bury it. Let it peter out and there's no eradicating it—it's sunk into the fabric of life. I think that's why epics and epic novels never end on the high point but fade away: They want to creep into our experience ineradicably.

Distrust revelatory visions under stress and turn-on-a-dime recantations of life. Dostoevsky's people do that sort of thing and their novel ends (among other reasons because they're dead), while Tolstoy's people have the grace to outlive their great moments and go back to a (faintly illuminated) normalcy. Backsliding is a healthy human recoil from the heat of an inflamed spirituality.

When children worry about the practical detail of an imaginary tale you know their imaginations have been activated. Book: "Then the dinosaur put Matthew on his back, and they ran across the desert." Child: "But there's nothing to hold onto!"

Where do children spend their time? On the last page of the dinosaur book: "Then the big fiery meteor came, and all the dinosaurs died." "No, they didn't." "How do you know?" "I was there."

I sit and look at my library shelves and am amazed. There *they* sit, always to hand, like good children never heard from until addressed, each taking up a diminutive share of my house. And scarcely one of them that doesn't know far more than I do.

I wonder whether "stylized" art that is not primitive but primary, that is, not made with style in mind, such as archaic Greek or pre-European African art, doesn't look highly natural to those who see it in its representational habitat. It simply emphasizes the most notable features of familiar figures. It is selective naturalism.

Aristophanes: titillating and deep, pornographic and pure, rambunctious and conservative, vulgar and lyrical, fetid and noble.

Ugliness seems to come in two kinds: formless insipidity (empty parking lots on a gray Sunday) and aggressive deformity (cartoon monsters). Evil does too: nullified Being and perverted Good. Is that because Ugliness is the emblem of evil?

"Wondrous machine," the organ, from Greek *organon, the* instrument just as the Bible, *ho biblos,* is *the* book. In the chapel of St. Mary's College, Moraga, the organist and his students were practicing: little runnels of sound down the columns and then cascades booming off the walls. ("Wondrous machine" is from Purcell's *Ode for St. Cecilia,* the patron saint of music; poem by the Queen's Chaplain, Nicholas Brady.)

Science is what makes the West legitimately history-bound, for its advancement recoverably encapsulates its beginnings: To study science from a contemporary text is to swallow formulas that are the abstracted result of millennia spent in finding the terms, the elements, the relations that make nature mathematically expressible. The bare results are in themselves beautiful and coherent, but in their history they reveal the revolutions of thought that made humanity's most successful enterprise possible, as well as the cost in distance from naturally experienced nature that had to be paid. The arts, on the other hand, have no history at all, in the sense that from first to last they are all equally present, now. The *Aeneid* may presuppose the *Iliad* but it doesn't supersede it, nor is it, properly speaking, its effect. But then, is there historical causation in History proper, the sum total of time-expired human events? Well, was Napoleon's march on Moscow inherent in Xerxes' crossing of the Hellespont?

Several times, on talking to taxi drivers about the classical music they were tuned into: "It's relaxing." I don't think they meant "tensionless"; they meant "not raucous."

Paintings elide appearances. The sensory world is an aspectual continuum: Wherever we stand and look we can dig deep into surfaces, split wholes, inspect infinitesimals and then face round to scan and tunnel into infinities. But paintings choose a band-width out of this interminable great-and-small, and a viewpoint. There is no going beneath their painted veneer, no cutting them up, no getting very close or receding very far. They break appearances out of their spectrum and raise them into a space of privilege.

5 COMPANIONS:
USAGES OF FRIENDSHIP

A friend is surely not a second self. Why would I want one more of myself? A friend is the first and closest *other*.

Some friends were once lovers *in potentia*. But once the form of friendship has set, that possibility is unthinkable to the point of taboo. Not so the reverse.

The admiration of friends gives unaffected pleasure because it has both facets: It comes from a cordial desire to give pleasure, and it is knowledgeable. Whereas public praise rouses only a hollow sort of exhilaration; it adds nothing to the achievement but, on the contrary, somewhat deforms it. And it has this unedifying side effect: Although it gives only a muted pleasure, you begin to find it a little galling if it's omitted.

Trying to be friends with certain airless souls is like beating your wings in a vacuum—a precipitous plunge into nothingness, like Milton's Chaos and the dark Night.

What discontinuities of mood could make someone eagerly claim our friendship one day, and on the next know us not?

Some people are black holes: No service or care leaves a deposit of affection; their need is bottomless.

Counting on friends is not relying on them. We count them among our blessings but that doesn't mean that we plan to depend on them—even less so if we know we might, in a pinch.

It's a gratifying confirmation of our good judgment when lovers turn into old friends.

Friendship is the school of eloquence, since we talk to our friends equally in presence and in absence and as well as possible.

We save up the events of our days to tell our friends, feeling that until our affairs have been told they haven't quite happened: Thus do our friends confirm our lives.

We confide in our friends and reveal ourselves to them. But the self-revelation isn't telling our secrets, and our confidences aren't, for the most part, complaints and griefs. There are hundreds of things short of embarrassing indiscretions left to tell no one but a friend; in the same spirit we digest our complaints and shape our griefs so as to make them somewhat more interesting than burdensome. Friends get the idea in any case.

When lovers are friends, the world becomes supremely snug. The converse seems odd—rare—impossible?

To make a friend of a vigilant, armed, and brave soul is a victory, but not one to be sung.

There are friendships (of a sort) which are totally *de facto*—nothing takes root and nothing develops and you're always back where you were: vagrant souls.

In certain friendships, a systematic flat-eyed evasion of furtive demands for sympathy serves long-term loyal amity better than effortful production of responsive sympathy. When the others have gotten tired you're around, callous but unwearied.

Dictionary of Random Preferences: friendship over hobnobbing, growth over construction, development over accretion, nature over second nature, preservation over obsolescence, maintenance over innovation, freehand over jig, talk over communication, love over relationship, contemplation over conceptualization, and on and on.

"Significant other," forsooth! Are all the other others then insignificant?

It is lovely to have a friend who is an incarnate type.

It makes you smile inside to watch someone trying to bring you out—on the friendly but false hypothesis that it needs effort.

There is a certain prejudice against self-consciousness in human matters as dimming the spontaneity of sympathy. Not so, I think: By superintending our responsiveness we contain and concentrate feeling.

If a friend asks me about myself I'm straightway suspended between warm pleasure and utter non-interest. The pleasure comes from being asked in such a friendly way and from the chance to be expansive *ad libitum*. The indifference comes from not expecting to hear anything new.

Inarticulate people say clumsy sentences with delicate meanings.

Inarticulately good people are simply lovable.

Friendship is a mutual aid society only in a pinch. Ordinarily it's a company for producing delight.

Friends rephrasing each other's meanings: an acknowledgment, a compliment, a service.

Social occasions can work a certain magic. You see your friends in costumes and onstage as it were, and suddenly they turn from ordinarily familiar to strangely familiar: They achieve sudden glory.

A friend in trouble, especially an ordinarily salubrious soul laboring under some hurt, arouses a new kind of affection, like all love, not totally innocent. For it encompasses a certain pleasure in seeing a familiar human being in a tragic light and a certain satisfaction in being called on to help. Well, that's how we are when we aren't worse, that is, cold and careless.

Why the casual touch of chance affection is so comforting—because it carries an assurance of well-disposed indifference.

You can't abandon friends because they've stultified themselves and become boring, but you don't have to listen so carefully either.

There's a certain apprehensiveness about being really looked at. Even the best of friends look at each other diffusely. Certain animals get aggressive when eyed fixedly. Certain civilizations don't permit looking into people's faces. Only lovers and babies look directly and prolongedly into our eyes. Lovers' care may be for the soul, but their desire seeks the surface. Babies seem to be searching for our very being, though that's—probably—an illusion. But when a friend looks attentively, there's a danger.

"Cordial" is an underappreciated word; we don't signify enough when we sign a letter "Cordially yours." It means "of the heart," heartfelt, and betokens gracious warmth. There's this nice bonus, that it also refers to a restorative liqueur: "a taste as sweet / as any cordial comfort."

One of the most companionable of modes is parallel looking, and the car is its venue of choice: Our lovely land comes flying toward us, we each look into it, delight in it, and talk to the friend beside us.

Except in times of very low vitality, we want our friends more as recipients of our plenitude than as ministers to our need.

There is a charm, that of expectant delight, in incipient, inchoate friendships: present pleasure and great things to come.

Our friends are doubly our benefactors: They take us out of ourselves and they help us return, to face together with them our common human condition.

The reticent sympathy of friends feels like snowflakes on the face, quick, cool, refreshing.

There's a tacit sympathy that is offered as a form of gallantry and can be received with panache.

It is a wonderful and shaking experience to be *seen,* as the Germans say *ins Auge gefasst,* "clasped into the eye"—wonderful and also embarrassing, because the same life time that prepares you for internal scrutiny makes you feel less fit to pass external muster.

"Being understood" is, hopefully, taken to mean "being validated," even loved. Well, that's taking a lot for granted. "To know each other is to love each other" has—this is an open secret—a realistic complement: "To know each other is to dislike each other." Viz. a wittily snobbish English author: "To dislike her was the mark of a liberal education" (Angela Thirkell).

Aristotle says that friends have to live within sight of each other, one of those obvious truths it's nice to have a citation for. There's something appalling in the speed with which the skin of reality grows together about the hole left by the departure of a colleague. Though, to do the heart justice, we forget only to remember, unexpectedly and vividly. But since being friends depends more on talking than on seeing, there's a post-Aristotelian cure for distance. What would old *Ipse dixit* have made of the telephone?

By friendship—as by fiction—the world is multiplied.

A man's sensibility seems to me very fine, partly because it is a little mysterious, partly because it is so close to his intellect; men make the most inexhaustible conversation partners and the rarest of friends. But now come matters of the heart, confessions and confidences, and then I'd tell a woman what I've never say to a man, except on occasions of trans-friendly intimacy—and then in three words.

There's an impregnable enigma to an other's being; the most mutual efforts to breach it come to naught—and a good thing too.

How wonderfully the wells of conversation fill up after apparent total exhaustion!

You want to enter the permafrost of discontent? Get fixated on possibilities, denigrate actualities. Example: Get to thinking of the billions of people out there among whom there is bound to be one made to your dreamiest specifications.

People who hang around are accepted as buddies but with a little contempt. Busy people are respected for their scheduled availability, but there's a little annoyance in it. People known to be at leisure but seldom seen are admired for evidently liking their own company best, but they're also counted out.

The fascinating specificity, the preoccupying uniqueness, of our friends does, eventually, turn into a typical pattern, in unequal parts lovably and irritatingly predictable. Me too.

A really good party: Come late, leave early, in between talk about the ordinary old stuff to the usual old friends—and perhaps meet a couple of potential old friends to whom to talk about the ordinary old stuff in a novel variation. And if they have those little quiche tarts, it's perfect.

"They are devoted to each other"—a nice sisterly phrase that gives me the creeps.

Even nowadays, boys are sensitive, girls get offended. Boys are made brittle through their sense of honor, girls are made resilient through their sense of grievance. A half-truth, which isn't a bad score for a generalization.

There's a certain blackness lurking that refuses all lightening: Intimacy is irritating, distance chilling, familiarity insipid—then the cool warmth of friends is best.

Why is he my friend? Not only because he's good or because he's interesting, but because he's interestingly good.

Can you trust people who have flatly no relation to divinity, no faith or doubt, love or hate? I don't mean trust in their personal fidelity, I mean dependence on their soul's depth, their groundedness.

Friendship, that love without desire, sensibility without sensuousness, steadiness without urgency—what a recreation of the spirit!

A friend is that human being we might fall in love with but haven't in fact.

The tragicomedy of very old friendships is that nothing is forgotten and nothing is said. There's very wisely, and perhaps also foolishly, a taboo against breaking open the crust of years to expose old resentments and deep-rooted sentiments. There is a *gêne* about recalling our youth, adverting to that awkward and passionately loyal adolescent we still detect in each other and examining too closely the self-willed and unsentimental elderly woman we each occasionally see in the other. Are we going to be sorry we took, or rather let creep upon us, these vows of silence? We must be right: We'd both sink through the floor with embarrassment, like the two adolescents we've remained for each other over threescore years.

We love people for what their soul keeps company with.

Three friends are a mutually enhancing threesome; three lovers make for mutually assured destruction.

The wall of silence we live behind over the years, why don't we just breach it? The deflating truth is that it's in part because we know that on our side at least there's not much news, and what there is you won't want to hear.

Rule No. 1 of friendship: Never feel guilty but often sorry.

The reward you get from a friend for reading small signals correctly is being told the rest.

Making a new friend is something like entering one of those walled towns of old. If you come in through a postern you get a back-to-front first view and it takes a while to learn that all the central structures face the other way. ("Making a friend" is, incidentally, a pretty truth-telling idiom, much better than "acquiring.")

Getting to know somebody chiefly means learning to distinguish the patterns from the spontaneities.

At first a friend's virtues seem his natural possessions, but then the life's work behind them appears and enjoyment deepens into admiration.

"To him (or her) who has shall be given" holds eminently of friendship.

Here's one in the endless parade of reasons why men and women don't understand each other: Men adore very young girls, a relatively mystifying taste to an older woman. Now if a woman worships a boy, that's another matter. A serious youth is poignantly godlike, and a moving god is irresistible.

When two friends are companionably together the spirit of pleasure attends as a third.

It grows pointillistically: a flash of wit instantly gotten, one thought striking both at once, sudden simultaneous laughter, a quick mutual gesture of fondness—each leaves its residue until the canvas fills up with the perfect shapes of friendship.

Two ways: Fine-honed reticence and homely friendliness, both are lovely. The interesting fact is that the more candidly cordial person sometimes has the deeper reserves.

Just as there is a satisfaction when a shy animal approaches you, so there is a kind of proud pleasure in watching a reserved person opening up.

It is a delight to be the recipient of gratuitous care. It is ungenerous not to take some pleasure as well in being on the receiving end of necessary assistance.

Some people are mysteries that don't beckon: You don't know and don't want to know what is beyond the limits you seem to have reached; in fact you wonder if a human being might be opaque all through: self-opaque.

There is a bemused pleasure in being well and truly fussed over, but getting one's just deserts is less embarrassing.

There are friends not of choice but of circumstance. I don't mean the intense quick bonding of special occasions, wilderness trips and emergencies, which immediately fall apart, but the comradeship of common hardship and suffering, that of soldiers and prisoners. These friendships prove something wonderful, masked by our daily comfort: that real love can arise from necessity.

Can women be friends? Well of course, the best of friends, and they can conduct the friendship as women or as human beings. What's the difference? Well, I think the ancients were perfectly right, that the intellect is what we have in common as human beings, so such a friendship will be mainly about matters intellectual. And as women? Who doubts that men and women are equally beings of feeling? But there may be a difference in the way feeling floods the body, in the diffuse poignancy of our passion: ". . . immediately a delicate fire has run under my skin" (Sappho), and that makes for intimate mutuality. Oh, what do I know.

Yet another boon of friendship: not only to be understood here and now but to be remembered later.

The angels must listen to friends in colloquy with delight: We forget our natural opaqueness in our eagerness to open ourselves, and for the moment we are all candid, all manifest, as must they be to each other.

Friends look at the world together as if through one of those old stereoscopes: The slight parallax resulting from their different positions gives the scene its depth.

We never forget a friend's remembering what we said or did.

How we impose on our friends: We come bearing gifts that it is more blissful to give than to receive, such as inscribed books of our own inditing. We come bearing a pent-up flood of travel stories which our friends can't wait to hear; to make it perfect we bring slides . . . Well, you can complete this list; these are open secrets.

Best friend, closest friend, oldest friend—we are lucky to have one of each: to open our self to, to live with, to be silent with.

Nothing can touch those moments of perfect understanding, not the quotidian quarrels nor the distancing years.

I have a friend who babbles like a brook and requires only that I nod, a duty I discharge in two senses.

Men have this great advantage over women: They say (and who am I to doubt it) that they need sex in general. Women tend to want it in particular. So the male field is far larger.

Aristotle says there are three kinds of friendships: of pleasure, of utility, of virtue. He forgot the comradeship of work and war and, above all, the companionship of the imaginative life.

I think most people would prefer to be seen as invulnerable, untouching, and unpoignant as possible, in other words as doing pretty well. So try to look at your friends not from the outside with sympathy, but from the inside with empathy.

What people tell you is obviously only the tip of the iceberg (a bad metaphor for our tangled internal jungle). Kindness requires a calculation: How much more are you being asked to figure out?

It is a cordial courtesy to return a confidence for a confidence received.

I have a friend who wants only one thing: to tell me factoids. They're unforgettable, and I can't recall a single one.

Benefactors induce furtive rebellion against their very being. It takes a large soul to feel simple friendship for someone you need.

6 CUSTOMS: "TRADITION, FORM AND CEREMONIOUS DUTY"

Children who are not acquainted with reverence tend toward panic.

Even when the firsts of life—acquaintances, places, projects—are quite unceremonious, if something of importance develops from them, it turns out that they remained in memory, small sharp pictures retrospectively fraught with the ceremony of beginning, like the *introit* of a sacred celebration.

A tradition that is ours less by birth than by adoption can go suddenly very alien, namely with respect to the human intimacies. Would I wish to meet in the flesh these great men who are the objects of my study and the guides of my thinking? Would I want to live close to them in a place of luminous Pentelic marbles and dinky private spaces, where men were able to talk at leisure but women stayed home, where beautiful boys worked out in gymnasia but no one had an aspirin? Not much. But then, it is time to remember, the tradition is not historical, bound to epoch, place, people, all destined for destruction and disappearance. The tradition is just that component of an inhospitable time which is not mortal and not alien, and what I made mine has next to nothing to do with once live Athenians in all their otherness. So this temporal culture shock is misplaced, and I can return from my uncanny fantasy to this familiar land of ours, where that tradition is so perfectly at home as to be mostly unregarded. Well, I'm glad to be back. And yet, if I could have just three days . . . ?

Tradition has at least two senses: a sediment of styles, rituals, "ceremonious duty"—cherished continuities—and just the opposite, a winnowing of texts, a series of works of intellect and sensibility, whose meaning is vibrantly unsettled and unceremoniously dialectical.

Innovation means busyness; tradition is kept alive in leisure.

Progress, insofar as one may still believe in it, is not linear, nor cyclical, but helical: It spirals upward in a widening gyre, leaving us with similar orientations but on a higher and wider level of technique and quantity. But there's also a different kind of temporal event: the periodic recovery of the tradition, its reunification—renaissance, the recapitulation of old wisdoms in new settings.

Communities that cherish a tradition, be it intellectual, military, or political, are each a little *polis,* a town (cognate with *Zaun,* fence), enclosed in some sort of wall: our Naval Academy's brick wall, our campus's privet hedge, our town's old town lines (of which Southgate and Westgate Streets are reminiscences). Not that these communities are particularly exclusive: They are in fact more or less self-selective, but they need to be compact, demarcated places for their essence to flourish.

To have the gift of a good tradition is a blessing, like having a good physical constitution, a well-working family, or a well-governed country. To try to destroy or deconstruct it is as reckless as the dissipation of an inheritance. It looks daring and noble at the time, but it is monumentally silly in retrospect. For what then is next? Why would you call an era *post*-modern unless you had no clue?

It's a truism by now, or, at least, an open secret, that avant-garde is self-cancelling. For how can there be novelty except within a tradition that serves as baseline? Innovation outside a traditional frame is just forcible idiosyncrasy.

A life without solemnities is prone to binging, that secular ecstasy.

Ceremonies are deftly performed because they are perennial practices, and that practiced elegance (as, say, of a priest serving Mass) gives rituals their connoisseurial aspect.

Tradition is the background against which we manifest ourselves. Can a traditionless human being show as either individual or natural?

We appropriate our tradition by self-initiation in the company of older friends. Current culture is acquired by peer-pressure and hanging out. Well, our students manage both at once; which is why we're half in, half out of their lives—a good thing.

The forms and terms of the past seem passé to us, but I wonder from time to time who it really is that's been superseded.

The past seems sealed, in the double sense of being locked up and not amenable to amendment and of having been perfected, perfect, and subject to nostalgic reminiscence. This hermetic past doesn't do us much good in either mood.

My, perhaps idiosyncratic, distinction: History is the past-perfect of human lives and deeds, tradition the past-present of human thought and sense.

Simple forgetfulness is the cause of much revivalist rethinking. Conversely, a good memory can be the cause of intellectual stuckness.

What have we lost in having missed the lives of great men? Mostly their smallness.

How I imagine the God of my Fathers: ugly to the point of beauty, wrathfully temperamental, ready to translate personal slight into moral iniquity, dead serious and cumbrously antic, stiff-necked, stubborn, jagged, mystifyingly abrupt in his communications, sorrowful from way back, unrelentingly judgmental, magnificently self-unaware—impossible to live with and not easy to forget. The Greek gods sometimes take on human shape; my fellow Jews sometimes adopt their God's personality.

Why are tradition and beauty allied? Because crafted beauty is significance made apparent to the senses, and the tradition is the storehouse of all meaning made unforgettably accessible to the soul.

People who, be it from conservatism or reflection, speak the traditional language of morals and metaphysics sometimes sound curiously fresh and future-bound, as if the spirit was just waiting to re-enter the words.

The question concerning the Western tradition, understood as the record of epochal intellectual discoveries—Being, the diatonic scale, axiomatic geometry, mathematical physics, methods, techniques, etc.—*the* question is whether these discoveries are the orderly self-revelation of nature or the contingent constructions of the human mind. And that question is itself an element of the tradition.

Scholars, students rather than lovers of the tradition, face a double bind: Either they suppose that they've learned something of value and start living off their intellectual capital or putting it out at good interest, or they learned only to know that they know nothing, in which case you might well ask: *cui bono,* what's the good?

Even—or especially—the most intimate social relations, love and friendship, require ritual to punctuate time and ceremony to express attentive regard. There are, to be sure, young boors who capture companions by their lusty insouciance alone. But they get left, as far as I know.

The principle permitting the reading of great books: "A cat may look at a king." Is that from *Alice?* Well, anything not otherwise attributed is.

A Roman says: *nil admirari,* wonder at nothing. But more than one Greek has already said: *thauma,* wonder, is the beginning of philosophy, the love of wisdom. So from way back experiential wisdom is pitted against inquiring wisdom.

No one doubts that our Western tradition strives for universality, but whether it thereby evinces a proclivity for dominion or for egalitarianism is hotly disputed.

Old works are not dead for live souls.

Are we fixed in place like sea anemones or free in the stream like leaping trout? Are we so seated in our time and place that we would die of alienation if removed, or are all human times and all inhabited places potential home to us? Given a friendly reception and plenty of time we could eventually disport ourselves like fish in water anywhere. Yet there'd be nights when we would wake up feeling utterly unaccommodated. For the heart may be trout-free and flexible, but the memory is anemone-stuck and fixed.

Those originals who, in the absence of all learning, reinvent the wheel of reason, are the real thing, but at the price of subtlety: Homemade philosophy is usually as crude as it is vigorous.

The various assaults on the tradition of the intellect have so far either merged with it because it is dialectical and thrives on opposition, or they have faded away because it is selective and resistant to fads. Could there be something so truly new that it was neither rational nor irrational, neither dialectical nor dogmatic, neither transcendent nor secular, ontic or time-bound—nor an amalgam of any or all pairs? So far, those who've tried to be radically novel have all ended up as books side-by-side on the shelf marked "Philosophy" with those they intended to supersede or deconstruct.

7 COUNTRY: "AMERICA, TIME'S NOBLEST OFFSPRING"

The American Eden: where lions don't lie down with lambs but all stand around arguing—in the courts, often.

The brat syndrome: A lot of Americans act toward their country like brats toward a parent; it doesn't mean they don't love her or won't come through when needed.

Only immigrants, mid-Westerners, and military are permitted to be patriots these days. Americans think they're beyond all that "chauvinism"; immigrants (this one, at least) think they're brats. And yet—the natives are being comically American and the latecomers are a little out of line. For self-criticism is the American mode of self-importance. Funny, how it's always in the plural: "We" are guilty of this or that. I hardly ever hear anyone say "I am prejudiced" or "I exploit the environment" or "I watch a lot of really awful TV." Well, it's companionable culpability; I can think of worse national ways, and it has its limits: A colleague, an Indian immigrant, tells me that the old Immigration and Naturalization Service, not otherwise known for its wit, put out a pamphlet of advice for newcomers. One item: "Americans are very self-critical. Be careful not to agree."

America at her best: simple grace, homey comfort, rational convenience, and casual civility.

The latter-day Europeans disdain American flag-waving as retrograde and prefer mutually assured dislike. Probably our artless rambunctiousness is humanly safer.

If Whitman lived now what would his feeling for America be, when her expansive beauty is partly overlaid by the ever-expanding structures of convenience? I think he'd have found something to rhapsodize over, he, whose "immigrant Muse" was "By thud of machinery and shrill steam-whistle undismay'd, / Bluff'd not a bit by drain-pipe, gasometers, artificial fertilizers." The unsightly appurtenances of commodious living engender a certain affection, even exhilaration: It works.

"Time's noblest offspring is the last" says Bishop Berkeley ("On the Prospect of Planting Arts and Learning in America"). Could this continental country really be the final act of history, as he thought over a quarter millennium ago? And its noblest? *Civis Romanus sum,* said the proud citizen of the greatest ancient empire. But to be a citizen of this modern empireless imperium seems to me calls for a feeling different from mere pride— maybe awe?

If we all live in each other's cultural pockets, who's going to mind the cultural store? In anthropology, the professionals have now been dealing with the revolt of the studied for quite a while. There ought to be a rebellion of the understood as well.

Melting pot: Play ball on Saturday. Pluralism: Play ball on Sunday. Multiculturalism: Watch black stars anytime.

Hyping of everything: What would make my evening would be if one of those sedulous tasters that stand by at cooking shows on TV were given a sample and said "Yech!" Or if there was a really frowzy old woman-anchor.

Neighborhood—what's nigh: the place of daily serendipitous coincidences. Also of blowups.

Inertia protects those mediocre arrangements that are viable without being great and make America so livable.

Cherish the local anomaly, the natural hierarchy, the distinctions of wealth, all under the tent of American civility; beware of engineered universality.

To rebel against Britain (America, India) and to lose a war with America (Germany, Italy) is the way to prosperity. That's history's morality.

Americans go in for rituals not only because, like everyone else, they like pomp and circumstance, but because it gives them an exhilarating sense of being founders and of having come from way back and on high, both at once. *Novus ordo seclorum,* "A New Order of the Ages," says our dollar, but around the unfinished pyramid with its eye it adds: *Annuit Coeptis,* "God favors our ventures."

Our federal republic is in conception what the scholastics call second-intentional: not the thought of a thing immediately but the concept of a concept: a nation of states, devised not discovered. But it is a potent abstraction which has extruded its own body. It all began when Washington devoted serious thought to the proper honorific for an American president. Now the most powerful man in the world is called "*Mr.* President," a glorious title.

What is wrong with Jefferson's natural aristocracy (which that sensible curmudgeon Adams knew would lead to no good) is that "the best and brightest" are almost guaranteed to have no sense. We don't need an aristocracy, meaning the "rule of the best"—"moderately good" will do fine, where "good" means both sufficiently smart and fundamentally decent. And that's about what we've got. And the intellectuals should stop making outsiders of themselves; the public is just turned off and the kids are co-opted into snobbish squawking.

Our American middle class—mannerly without much breeding, civil without necessarily "caring," home-loving without deep rooting—is also extraordinarily receptive to quality, authenticity, and intimations of transcendence.

"Thinking for yourself," that American mantra, ought to be a redundancy. But maybe not, since we have that strange capability for absorbing thought from on high as a kind of intellectual tan, a surface coloration.

The trick of humanity, particularly democratic American humanity, is to be fully aware of all the public idiocy while thinking of nobody (well, hardly anybody) as an idiot, to believe only forty-nine percent of what's said in public while calling nobody (well, hardly anybody) a liar, and to know full well (from introspection) that most deeds have hidden agendas, without falling into self-indulgent cynicism.

In times of crisis the people of this country treat each other with a delicacy and discretion accorded to the honorably wounded. The American "masses" show a good deal of mandarinism, exquisite courtesy democratized by camaraderie (9/11). Of course, then the hype starts while we go back to our natural state of shoulder-rubbing indifference or irritation.

American philistines show their invincible good sense by preferring—in their private dwellings—fake half-timbering to pre-fab habitats and classical kitsch to post-modern constructs. Those last they appreciate in public buildings visited on Sunday outings.

America's democratic ethos is largely based on the adroit use of the vernacular, the folksy wit, easy banter, swift throw-away idioms that lend people's encounters a quick glow of fellowship. Nations whose public tone is stiffly formal, guardedly hostile, inhibitedly domineering are dangerous.

A New Englander once told me that they hang strips of dripping bacon over the troughs in which they are boiling off the maple syrup to dampen the bubbling. (Truth to tell, we were eating maple syrup over fresh fallen snow at the time, and knowing I was Jewish, he wanted to see if I would choke—I nearly did, laughing.) Anyhow, I wish those Whitmanesque waves of rapture over America's largeness and variety had a drop of bacon fat to tone down the billows so I wouldn't feel silly joining in.

England is—to me—mostly a literary venue, a place where, if you know what to look for, your book-illustrating imagination is confirmed, where you find what seem like the primeval scenes behind the literature. But there is also something confusing, almost repellent in the museum atmosphere of all the places of pilgrimage. Not to speak of the fact that you soon long for America's beautiful largeness—more spoiled, but better at tempering, so to speak naturalizing, the spoilage, which is, after all, the fallout of her livableness.

Travels over—and through—America: the car racing (always a well-gauged number of mph ahead of the law) over thousands of smooth miles, through beauty of varying variations (i.e., sometimes the same for two hundred miles, sometimes changing by the half-hour), over state lines that seem, although artificially straight on the road map, to bound physically distinct territories. Then time out, at truck stops with the fraternity of drivers on their phones or thumping their huge tires with mallets or expanding their already massive bottoms with 4-egg omelets. Or in one-street towns with homey greasy spoons, old-timers shooting the breeze before we come and presumably long after we go. Putting up the tent in a Midwestern town park where a baseball game is in progress with all its casually inexorable ritual, bratty children bearing the marks of freedom; keeping ourselves to ourselves but slipping on demand into easy chat—at home in the whole continent.

Maryland once again: a soft but not yet deep Southern charm. Soft light, soft fall colors (nothing as brilliant as a New England hardwood turning). Modest hills, little stands of trees, an occasional pond, moderately gentrified towns. But there's a dark side: In Annapolis Lincoln got nine votes in the 1860 election.

Innocence at home: Some of our students read their Nietzsche assignments as if that author was as indefeasibly nice as they are. Oh, the wicked pleasure of hearing all that nervously nasty transatlantic subtlety neutralized by the all-American balm!

The net of uncomely uniformity that covers this aboriginally paradisical land and its wonderfully varied Edens with its homogenizing mesh not only provides for the handily familiar comforts we're accustomed to but induces a kind of connoisseurship of small differences: People develop observations about the texture and taste of hamburgers over the fifty contiguous and non-contiguous states. In this country there's happily someone to sing anything: Read J. B. Jackson on strip malls.

Lolita is a pretty hairy book, but it is the immigrant's finest tribute to the dreamy vestigial loveliness of the American landscape as discovered under the driving lash of a degenerate lust, a prolonged, perversely romantic rape by a sophisticated European child molester whose obsession is finally transformed into simple, heartfelt loving pity when his nymphet Lolita turns into plain housewife Dolly.

A chief reason for American happiness (for as history goes we are, our general grousing and our particular misfortunes notwithstanding, unusually happy with our lives) is the do-it-yourself mode, which gives both independence to our enterprises and activity to our weekends. The democratic jacks-of-all-trades and near-masters of many make their own world with standard parts and jury-rigged solutions. And being at ease with their things, Americans can afford to be friendly with each other.

At those feared extremes of American religion I found something astounding: do-it-yourself faith, Protestantism protested, independence taken to a second power—little sects that believe the Bible is 1. literally true, and 2. to be interpreted in radical independence with no more tools than the English we come with and the Greek we care to learn.

If cleanliness is next to godliness Americans are mostly going to heaven. I've often wondered that there is such fastidiousness about the flesh being able to withstand close inspection in a country so spacious. In the Japanese it's not so surprising.

Immigrant: In five years you've become an American, in ten years you always were. But an Old Annapolitan—never.

You can have a real feeling for something you don't have a real feel for: American popular culture and me.

Our most vaporous American sage says: "A foolish consistency is the hobgoblin of little minds." Well, OK, I get the point, but is it really what people most need to hear? Here's one they do need to hear: "An elusive complexity is the false mantra of modern minds."

It's hard to trust someone, or at least to regard him as all there in all dimensions, "who never to himself hath said, / This is my own, my native land" (though of course not everyone can say the "native" part). Such people have no gravity. But those who do it noisily, self-righteously, bigotedly, ignorantly have no grace.

To love your country loyally is to love it open-eyedly, sometimes for its flaws, sometimes with its flaws, and most often in spite of its flaws. It's not so different from personal love.

Summer in Santa Fe: a kind of Knossos without the Minotaur; white columns, projecting balconies, sun flooding the campus and the hills changing contours with its course, the moon-range of cinder cones in the middle distance against the light blue silhouette of mountains far off (a magical landscape), and close up children at play, colleagues and students stopping for talk—the summer palace of the intellect.

Southwest: the pure, unfraught, unobligating pleasure of panoramas whose ghostly inhabitants are too ancient and too distant to arouse my current anxiety.

All over the world people love their country, if necessary, against reason, but the most American Americans love theirs *for* reasons. It's not the unconditional love commanded by ancestry, tradition, and above all, land; for them this country has to live up to its rational *raison d'être* (which is succinctly formulated in the Declaration)—or else. What is wonderful is the way our continent cooperates in the concrete realization of these abstractions—offers its largeness and its localism, its soft and its wild beauty, its coziness and its grandeur—to the working out of all their consequences, even to supporting that utilitarian overlay which material prosperity spawns. Let's hope we don't push her, our matrix, too far.

Some nice brickwork, a fan ornament, a gilded cupola, a reflection in a skyscraper—how much more moving these are to me—acquired but naturalized tastes—than the surfeit-inducing superabundant monuments of the museum-countries.

There's something America seems to me particularly good at: the golden prose of ordinary daily life—commodious living with a hint of glory. Though to read the journals you'd think everybody here was miserable.

It takes a lot to live in this country because you have to have a citizen's judgment, a parent's prudence, a consumer's canniness; the pursuit of happiness is pretty laborious.

Take a stranger around your town, and you'll see 1. what love does for a view, and 2. how infectious it is.

To be sure, incontrovertible beauty trumps every attachment, but short of that, there's nothing for making a place glow like being the seat of a thousand memories.

The little elaborations of prosperity, the sober beauties of good joinery, the pleasant parodies of Old World grandeur, the antique reminiscences of republican elegance—all this muted local music gets to me more than the gorgeousness of transatlantic palaces.

American bad taste has this saving grace: The plumbing is good.

Scratch a cowboy, find a poet.

I don't know how it is elsewhere, but in this country, almost every time you lose your temper because of some annoying inefficiency, it turns out either you're yelling at the wrong person or there really was no other way.

Americans dressed up: the most amazing extremes; short short skirts and black stockings, ankle-long skirts and sandals, flare-bottom slacks and tight black pants and always blue jeans, painted, tinted, speckled, be-pearled and bespangled—the bizarrerie of fashionable individualism; and out of these multiform uniforms they're perfectly sensible people. And then there's American casual: the legend- or logo-bearing T-shirt, the washed-out torn jeans, the un-run-in running shoes and the rangy-kid body bearing—the conformism of comfort-seeking; and these people often turn out to be sophisticated makers of rational order. There are even Americans who by nature and design are truly formal in bearing and dress—the signal of aristocratic reserve; and they, as often as not, come from the plainest of mid-Western families.

Americans are for normalcy; "normal" is a term of approval. What a miracle this seems to immigrants who are from countries where a rabid contingency rules—that there should be a land where "normal" means "desirable."

American liberals: a. Everything is our fault, and so b. we should fix it; a. is plain false, but b. may be true.

Ubi bene ibi patria, "Where I'm well off there's my country," isn't a very noble sort of patriotism, but alter it a little, and it tells the truth: "Where I thrive, there I love."

The young aren't required, they aren't even able, to make this unabashed pronouncement: I'm a member of the middle class, a wage earner, a houseowner, taxpayer, registered voter, TV watcher—and mighty glad of it. To be able to say so is to me a mark of maturity.

American English is this country's chief gift to receptive immigrants—this plenitude of linguistic possibilities: Anglo-Saxon, Latinate, low, high, local, technical, pungently idiomatic and slyly euphemistic. Where else can you insult a guy and keep a civil tongue by calling him the north end of a horse going south? (I think I got this from that corrupted populist Huey Long.)

Ethnicity: It gives people a sort of specimen look within which their individuality appears. But when people turn American, in a generation they lose that and seem to be stamped by a lack of stamp, as if they were a bland matter formed by individual choice, attaining to a specific sort of cross-Continental unspecificity. Some try to specify themselves by idiosyncrasies which have a way of all looking alike. Some adopt an ebullient, splay-legged noisy assertiveness. But it all looks unracily American—until you see this non-ethnic type (of any color) on its travels in Europe. Then it suddenly appears that Americans are very "ethnic" indeed, that they are a strong breed with considerable character. It is a European illusion that they themselves are reserved, subtle, and high-bred and Americans are loud, obtuse, crude, and breedless.

9/11 revealed to us that we think of this country, the New Jerusalem, as sacred and an attack on it as blasphemy. There's a solid reason: More people have been modestly happy here, I'd guess, than in any other land, and to taint that is an offense against the spirit of well-being.

Country music is often saccharine and mawkish and sentimental, and since we are all that way in those situations that it's mostly about—miscarried love—it's common in the better sense, that is universal and so, touching. Who hasn't sat in a diner, mourning?

I don't like the blood mysteries of the "folk" and I'm against the forces of "society." What I'm for is the feel of the country with its folks and their raucous but fundamentally principled politics. I like America's continental scope from sea to shining sea and the changes in its landscape that take place as if those straight lines on the road atlas were drawn according to nature (from, say, Tennessee to Arkansas, to Oklahoma and Texas and on to New Mexico, all different as if to rise to their statehood). I love the heart-rending beauty of the aboriginal land,

and I'm not immune to the heart-rendingly familiar ugliness our commodious living has spread over it. All these muted or garish glories I'm for, and I'm for these people you can talk to.

A run-in with fanatical outrage makes one appreciate the schizophrenia, that is to say, split-mindedness of American life, where people can hate one another but be fair, despise each other and be civil, consider another soul damned to perdition but leave it be. At their best Americans can have deep convictions for themselves and act with tolerant forbearance toward others. Whether they do it from indifference, doubt, or practical considerations, who would want to investigate?

It does not detract from our immigrants' feeling for this country that we found the good life here. To my mind love for cause beautifies its object more than that famous unconditional love.

An immigrant's attachments are elective affinities which have turned into natural bonds. What could be more like marriage? For those of us who were fleeing for our lives it was perhaps more like a marriage of convenience where the partner wakes up one morning to find that expediency has turned into unpremeditated, pure love.

Since most young Americans want to be "different," and since they don't usually articulate what they want to be different *from,* just as they want to be "relevant" without saying what they want to be relevant *to,* they're pretty much alike in having these unfocused urges. And then one day the urge is gone and they've somehow become interesting people and appreciable citizens.

Americans are shallow by their very creed: optimism (plus a lot of fussing), faith in solutions, end runs around tragedy, trivialization of grief (by "grief-management," forsooth!). We expect to be absolved from sin by our facile self-criticism and to ward off bad luck by grousing. It's the wisdom of non-sages and works better than the grander sort.

Some Frenchman, I read somewhere, said that when he sees a German trying to be graceful he wants to jump out the window. I wish he would. Meanwhile I'll say, when I see a Frenchmen succeeding in being intellectual, I say God bless America—except that's immigrated here. Why am I talking like this? The EU will eradicate it all quite peacefully.

God bless stereotypes, the amateur anthropologist's guides to American life.

Being a beneficiary, I can't forget that America got Europe out of its messes in two world wars, set it up economically, protected it from Eastern invasion. So why shouldn't they despise us? We arm ourselves against evil-doers, invent new gadgets, devise techniques, are pretty nice people, have a smaller percentage of crazies then you might expect. Very irritating.

The intellectuals who, believing nothing much themselves, think that leaders who feel the same should encourage religion as a kind of spiritual stabilizer, haven't looked at America: Our leaders have the naiveté to be themselves some sort of believers and that's what makes them leaders to begin with. Americans take care of their own faith, from hokey to solid.

Working it out: All these ignoble American therapies, talkative navel inspections, turning passions into problems while trying to rouse the languid tigers ("getting in touch with your feelings"), bureaucratizing the human condition and managing the hell out of it—the private application of the American mantra, that you can organize your way out of the most profound difficulty. Well, if it works. . . .

I've read that our young, when queried, aver that only ethnics have a culture but that there is no American culture. (They should see how pungently American is an American abroad.) Why is that? Well, partly it's the diversity vocabulary which leaves out—and quite rightly—being American, since America is the unifying ground of all the differences. Partly it's that we don't sense the air in which we live and breathe; the atmosphere of ordinariness is not an aura. But it's also something beyond that: Americanism itself is ordinariness, normalcy raised to another dimension; you might call it the apotheosis of the mundane, where it flips into sheer though subliminal poetry.

Why does a concrete arabesque, a nicely molded brick, a painted wooden acroterion in an American neighborhood give more pleasure than the inspissated splendor of Europe (I got "inspissated" out of T.E. Lawrence: "tightly filled")? Because these little aesthetic moments have more free air around them, which brings out the poignant memory behind them, and because they're home—not particularly my home but home in general, homey. The non-touristic eye is not so much more forgiving as more completely attentive.

All the American virtues: tolerance, religiosity, know-how, pragmatism, energy—the whole litany—can easily go over into babbittry and philistinism. And they can also rise to a humane grandeur.

The jury-rigged comfort of the whizzing capsule, snoozing in turn on top of a pile of book boxes and sleeping bags, bowling through Idaho, a landscape that's taken how-to-look lessons from Grant Wood, now and then driving with both hands otherwise occupied, taking pleasure in hokey lyrics—"Loving's a lot of pain and trouble"—camping under the tent's green, moon-translucent canopy. And seeing the eidetic imagery of the day's sights streaming vividly and incessantly by: travelling in this cozy continent. Well, of course, I know it can be brutally dangerous.

Is there another country that has a town called Normal (IL)?

We are full of hubris, ignorant of others, tactless of their feeling, have no staying power, make ourselves hated, are needlessly aggressive, shoot from the hip, are ever over-confident, *ad infinitum:* heard within twenty minutes at a dinner party during our war with the most terrible tyrant since Hitler. And above all, the majority of our fellow citizens are gullible, brainwashed captives of the media (the same on which I hear the tyrant address his nation and opportunistic gloom being spread). That's our chauvinism: inverse boasting; and our elitist egalitarianism: Everyone in general but nobody within listening distance is a little stupid.

8 TRAVEL:
RECREATIONAL ADVENTURE

When adventures in the world have to be expensively organized, inward journeys are what we go on without getting reservations and shots.

Eventfulness is what kids want, and it underlies their reformist impulses: adventurous togetherness and demonstrative high-mindedness. It's politically nugatory and humanly grand. (Yesterday in class: "Is Aristotle right when he says that the young don't understand politics?" A decided chorus: "Yes"—and a loud supplementary voice: "Nor the old.")

External adventures, when adventitious, seem often to end in misery and ignominious rescue, even in catastrophe and the end of everything. If organized, they are, for all their warmth of quick bonding and their frisson of well-regulated peril, episodic charades. The most genuine adventures take place internally: The body stays put and the soul ranges.

To hope to be taken out of oneself by war is sheer madness. Every sane person should engage in apotropaic trembling for the peace that lets us lead the life we have. The telling popular advice is: "Get a life!" And no one who needs to be told that should ever have a say in making war.

Scheduled adventuring is more for having been done than for doing. External adventures are hardly real before they've been told. Internal experiences are rather de-realized by being uttered, except in a very skillful account. Sartre: "Adventure does not let itself be drawn out; it only makes sense when dead" (*Nausea*)—a quarter-truth.

Photograph of a sightseer in front of the sight: the record of a case of not looking.

A tourist is a pitiable person, cut loose from respect, reference, and responsibility, subject to fawning and xenophobia, victim of foul-ups about tickets and rooms, the continually unaccommodated man, the voluntarily displaced person.

The Germans have wonderful words for experiential stultification: *Neugier:* "news-greed" (curiosity), *Sehenswürdigkeit:* "sight-worthiness" (point of interest). Well, tourists pay dearly to be delivered to the sight catalogued as worthy to be seen. And what do you do before such a sight? Well, you have your picture taken with your back to it (that is your tourist's identity card; it shows that you are you and it is it and the two were within one viewfinder). And then you gawk and the sight goes blank with embarrassment. And then, greedy for a new experience, since the last one denied itself (as they say in English novels when the lady of the house doesn't wish to be "at home"), you traipse on until you finally come to a café, where your soul longed to be.

Why do we do it? Because we keep forgetting that seeing is not having a look, which can be scheduled and directed and accomplished. Seeing, fulfilled looking, is ocular lovemaking: It wants its prologue, its mood, its moment. Tourists' sightseeing is—I'll stop here with this metaphor. But that's what we forget when we join a sightseeing tour.

Chaperoned walking tours are pure hell. But left to your own devices a place of pilgrimage can be moving: Here, on the road to Piraeus, Socrates walked and was stopped for a conversation (though two meters below, to be sure); here, up on Little Roundtop, Joshua Chamberlain's 20th Maine turned the tide; and later, here on Cemetery Ridge, Lincoln spoke those most memorable three paragraphs. But that's not gawking—that's participating.

What we want, some of us: to be again part of a high-pitched, soul-straining, pathos-laden, beauty-suffused story—again, because we've been there in the heart-in-the-mouth times of dreaming youth. This is the sound of the Sirens' song. Plug up your ears and plug on, and it will come in some more elderly but more survivable shape, for sure.

"Life, friends, is boring. We must not say so," goes a line by John Berryman. The devil, they say, finds mischief for idle hands, and even more for disengaged minds. Travel is therapy, tourism is snake oil.

The "identity of indiscernibles" is that sage philosophic maxim that says that if two items differ in nothing they're one. Of course you can't come across such items exactly in life (because they'd be one), but in a rough way the notion applies to much travel today: We sit in a hermetic cabin, hear the same monitory sing-song, eat the same pretzels (featureless enough to be *ipso facto* indiscernible), and look at the woolly white haze. What is more indiscernible than an airplane trip? And when we get there . . . ?

9 AGES: VERY YOUNG
TO PRETTY OLD

Adolescent miseries: when, poiseless and inexpressive, we maunder about just to maintain contact, talk without the boldness to beg or the backbone to sign off, prolong embarrassed pauses in the hope of encouraging responses, get stuck in banal locutions, mystifying circumlocutions, insistent repetition! If only one could say to the kid: Learn to express yourself. But that's half the problem: The "yourself" isn't quite there either.

Of course, the sexes differ, *ab ovo* I should think, e.g., little boys have pride, girls "sensitivity." So boys get insulted and girls get offended. Since being insulted is spontaneous and being offended is self-willed, boys are more vulnerable than girls.

For the young every loss is the end of the world. They're right, since every event might well be a turning point and determine a whole long life. The (comparative) serenity of old age comes from the fact that most of the turns have already been taken, and the life left to go wrong isn't that long anyway.

Heine sings: *Aus meinen grossen Schmerzen mach ich die kleinen Lieder,* "Out of my great pains I make those little songs." Well, there's a lot to be said for expressive mastery. You have some complex burdensome grief, great or small; you search for its shape, its roots, its ramifications, which means casting it into language, and presto! it has been, if not exorcised, at least externalized, made a thing already half-remembered. Awful though the prospect be, one must wish *all* the young wrote poetry.

The young look for complete enveloping bliss; they tend to be little Wagners seeking to produce and experience a *Gesamtkunstwerk,* a total work of art, a sensation in several modes at once: studying while amorously intertwined, saturating themselves in voluminous music while doing their homework, ingesting substances and making poetry. It may be a necessary stage in the development of the sensibility: First it is stretched to the limit of its quantitative capacity and a little past, and then, the impulse to totality exhausted, comes the time for qualitative concentration and discernment—let's hope.

The young see their elders as corrupted by that all-responsible "system." Well, it's worse. That system *is* adulthood objectified: privacy, property, power established, and what's more, it is the frame that defines youthful exuberance.

Those "privileged" kids live with a whole slew of problems unknown to generations back: They have to go more miles to walk in nature. Traditions of authority being gone, their relations to adults are too personal. They live in an environment making for a fragmented and frantic sensibility. Their natural docility is frustrated by premature freedom. Their sense of rights turns desires into demands. Their relations to the opposite sex are at once too immediate and too denatured by new social constraints. They see principles of conduct turned into calculi of convenience. They have the high-tech means for miraculously broad and speedy communication, but their expressive capacities are stunted. And they live with an insidious war without foreseeable end (2003 C.E.).

Childlike and childish: the ever-young at heart and the willfully infantile. The first are quirky but lovable, the second just irritating.

The contemporary secular child is just us with an astigmatic shift, and it's sad: knowledgeable and informed way beyond its means, full of articulate pseudoscience, acutely psychological without much self-knowledge, flexible beyond the point of resiliency, needing without heeding the insipid language of adult-induced self-esteem (at my nursery school, "Good job" is obligatory to even the most cursory daub of a daily project), trained to do a lot of wasteful discarding of food (these are sanitary liability issues), and living with an ambience full of stimulants—images, music, materials—meant to be half-attended to. Is there nature enough in a child to overcome the benevolences of our child-rearing?

Those of the young who fall for modish trash (because no grown-up says them nay), for ephemeral gurus, cheap musical experiences, and tendentious ideology are preparing for a life of letdown, because having to disown your youthful enthusiasms is like cutting off the branch you're sitting on.

The essence of the youth rebellion of the sixties seems to have been that the kids weren't needed for anything else.

What the young are deprived of: nearby green groves with a hidden observant Pan, open churches with their hierarchy of pomp, stifling cities and their heavy neighborhood-auras, brooding pasts with beautiful archetypes, stern courts with dangerous power, the elegant malevolences of smart strong teachers. What they get is prosperous freedom. Does it have a savor?

Those among the young who are fanatically focused, uncomfortably intense, are the ones who will gain enough masterful distance to be really open, open with that discriminating receptivity which finds some fondness for much that it cannot honor.

The best of the young seem to be willfully immune to their times; they've heard, but barely, of the current mantras and live untouched by peer pressure, innocent of the merely now and already familiar with the ages; they're the readers.

Little children are the aboriginal conservatives. The rules can't be changed; they're traditions more than prescriptions. Every reading of a story has to be canonical or it's a transgression, like an ancient Roman ritual, which has to be word-perfect or it's blasphemy. Their questions aren't rebellious questionings but real inquiries: "Why?" doesn't mean "Why should it . . ." but "What's behind it?"

By nature, children love the *terra abscondita,* the *urbs secreta,* the *domus arcana,* the *magnitudo minima* (why on earth am I talking Latin suddenly when I can't even read it for real?): the hidden earth, the secret city, the mysterious house, the tiniest size. These imaginative modes may be displaced by jetting space rangers and dancing dinosaurs, explosive alien intrusions into the child's imaginative privacies, violent rather than haunting, cute rather than magical, hard-edged rather than atmospheric. But can the homelands of the imagination be obliterated? If so it's a greater loss—and this isn't hyperbole—than the laying-low of an earthly region.

This principle may be passé in evolution but it still works for children: Ontogeny recapitulates phylogeny, the individual being goes through the tribe's developmental stages. Thus children think as young Aristotles. They are fixed on goals rather than motions, movement rather than time, places rather than space. It's just the natural world before it was mediated by science, a clockless world of purpose and containment.

Here's the latest innovative idiocy—whatever, but take comfort in the young. They'll rebel against this rebellion, and we'll be back where we started, more or less.

Les enfants s'ennuient le dimanche: "Children are bored on Sunday" goes an old French children's song, and it spoke truth: That non-weekday was our first taste of world-without-end sheer drear (an Elizabethan noun), a child's first run-in with Nonbeing. It's also the first experience of Satan's opportunity: enforced, dressed up idleness and its imaginative sadism. But that's all gone—Sunday is now a day of compulsive recreation. The satanic sadism was possibly a better soul-deepener.

Life's ever-confirmed lesson is already well-known to children: Our daily dose of expectable pleasure and holidays coming slowly but steadily, day after torn-off day, over the horizon of hope—these are the conditions upon which we contentedly do our daily duty.

The ardent, or rather emotional, young are not much for meticulousness; they're impulsively productive and sympathetically kind, but not exact. Their slipshod emoting and formulaic self-expression doesn't yet do justice to their spirit. We have to hope that when they've collected themselves and learned to say what they think, some of the latitudinous wildness will still be there to be disciplined.

My generation: personal rectitude, social indifference. This generation: social sensitivity, personal laxity. For example, students (not all, of course) think discrimination is an intolerable evil, but taking the money out of a found wallet a very venial sin. This has got to come back into balance; then we'll be in heaven.

Thinking back: The young, for whom falling in love is a natural state, are really in no condition for it: They can't manage the radical otherness they've got entangled with, the infeasibility of making a project of an other, the inevitable hydraulics of feeling, the dangers of focusing all their light on one heap of tinder, the fact that disaster always strikes out of left field. (In Camden Yards I love to concentrate on the way-out left field to see what's lurking there: usually just a lonely Oriole.)

Why are little kids more expressive than grown-ups? Because children not only react more spontaneously at first but also because they then have every interest in drawing attention; e.g., it starts as genuine weeping and soon becomes a will-driven crying jag. Adults have learned that the world's not a stage for self-revelation but a workshop for getting on with it, though we're nonetheless meant to walk on not naked-faced but as mask-wearers, persons (from Latin: *persona,* mask).

Youth should be impracticably pure: despise money but not fame, be radical not realistic, suspect the establishment and believe in making the world better; a prudent youngster is a little repulsive. Equally so are adults who got stuck in culpable innocence and idealism and who refuse to learn which side is up.

The semi-literate young talk grandly in a cunningly careless incomplete way: They want to "make a difference" (from what?); they want to "be relevant" (to what?). To be grown-up is to supply, at least mentally, the prepositional phrase that completes these praiseworthy intentions and makes them determinate.

To grow up well is to overcome childishness without losing our childhood. For example, we might still like what children like: excitement with security. But we also know that's mere fun and games.

The many contemporary young who were brought up to hate social bigotry more than individual dishonesty will probably make very nice fellow-citizens, but will they be reliable partners in the business of life? Is even a passionate tolerance (almost a contradiction in terms) a substitute for personal integrity?

Monomaniacal children have the predicate for a happy life: all-consuming interest in a project. So don't try to distract them.

Ardent intellectuality and heroic dreams: the unselfconscious display of this lovably youthful frame of mind used to be the prerogative of young men. But now there are more young women (there always were some) who, untouched by ideologies of self-assertion or victimhood, unreluctantly display the same fine spiritedness.

Our students have the half hopeful, half fearful notion that "reality" comes after school, "out there." They'll be surprised to learn that reality isn't all that real and that, anyhow, life doesn't get much realer than it is in our program's pressure cooker. But you can't tell them.

Here's a difference between youth and old age: If, when I was twenty, I'd been given the choice of an hour face-to-face with the human being I was in love with or an eon before the throne of God I'd have chosen the one, and now I'd choose the other.

Certain young women two generations after me resemble boys in their pride and pathos, their arrogance and despair (just as some of us did in our time)—without conceding any of their womanliness. There seems to me to be some truth in the ancient categories (and PC be damned) which attribute to the male a certain high-strung brittleness and intellectual abstraction and to the female a certain opportunistic flexibility and down-to-earth earthiness. What is everlastingly fascinating is how these features turn up mixed and melded in individuals, and how preponderances change over the decades. We're at a pretty good moment.

It's pleasant to live around the harum-scarum instability of the young as long as you don't have to participate. But how they'd like you to, and how hard it is to persuade them that decibels might be disagreeable! Oh, for the return of the tea party. (In fact we've had revivals.)

The young—not all—compromise their boundaries, the shape of their being, from sheer uncertainty and embarrassment. It's part of maturity to have firmed up enough to stay oneself during these assaults on one's dignity, and in old age that escalates into not giving a damn and being more or less immune to invasions, even finding them funny. It was in that spirit that the poet entitled a comedy *As You Like It*.

Up to late youth, even early middle age, a deprived childhood (love, money) is explanatory; thereafter it's self-exculpatory.

Our neighbors, the midshipmen, certainly in some respects more naive than our students, have a stiffness that comes from carrying the uniform, a formality that sets them off from the world. Name tags and patches and piping announce who they are, not differences in get-up. But when I see them I recall that they have taken an oath to go in harm's way for us and perhaps to die, and all their callowness assumes a certain dignified pathos.

The young are given to sudden fugues of the spirit which look to a teacher like the soul playing hooky.

I could never make out what it is in a certain baby's eyes that makes him look as if he were a starry messenger come from outer space with some news. But it sure made me understand better that other religion—because on the face of it to make a Messiah of an infant is absurd.

Very young men: physical deftness and psychic panache.

Let no one say that there is no totally non-erotic physicality: Babies are totally appetizing and there's nothing remotely erotic in it. They are so physically pleasant that even changing a smelly diaper is a kind of pleasure. Mystery of mysteries: Why does this universal appeal vanish as humans grow up, so that eventually the flesh is much more rarely but much more acutely attractive?

There's nothing like the awkward grace of a boy embarrassed by his own gallantry.

Children are the most consistently engaging of humankind because they stay themselves by changing.

There's a certain nostalgia in seeing a little boy leave behind his affectionate little-boyhood and become the confident lout you want him to be. The starry messenger baby became the comical toddler and the toddler a little proto-man, and he lengthened into a kid. Are those beings simply gone or are they preserved somewhere else than in memory? Does the fact that these figures were absorbed into the making of this little person mean they're somewhere, somehow still present in him? Does development cancel or preserve its stages? How odd to come on a Hegelian question in reminiscing about a child!

There seem to be two ways to come upon one's (happy) childhood, the way of nostalgia, Housman's Land of Lost Content, and the way of homecoming, the sense of an ever-present Edenic back-up.

Giving students helpful hell is good as long as they don't turn themselves into pretzels of contrition.

Sanitary suburbia: Can a child's imagination do without the nooks and crannies, wardrobes, and wild woods of old neighborhoods? Are walk-in closets and child-proof playgrounds venues for the imagination? Well, there are always flashlights under blankets.

Here's a paradox of early youth: Glands and spirit are all set toward love in general, but the sensibility tends to be exigently particular; the list of required features is exhaustive. First love sends the whole checklist to hell, and thereafter we know that ideals are eminently amenable to *ex post facto* revision: The person we got turns out to be the person we were always looking for.

A really intense adolescence seems to me of all human ages the one farthest removed from childhood, because it is so fiercely concentrated on an emerging, complex, self-conscious inwardness and its expression, whereas children, who surely have a secret inner life, have—as I remember it—next to no interest in articulating it.

There's nothing so exhilarating, moving, and teacher-inspiring as a really serious youth.

The young after the '60s, even after the general return to real life, are different from the preceding generations: tolerant (to the point of being flabby), not only in social matters but in their sensibility, which sometimes seems as if anesthetized to blanket-music and public privacies, more given to unspecific intimacies, more keenly alive to social injustice and somewhat indifferent to the finer points of personal morality. That's in the dorms, but in class they preserve, with evident satisfaction, an unassumingly easy decorum.

My law of intellectual property: 1. Whoever thought a thought at an earlier personal age is its originator. (When some of my seventeen-year-olds come up with the notion of intelligible forms, they are the discoverers if Socrates was eighteen when it came to him; trouble is, he was probably more like fifteen; see Plato's *Parmenides*.) In any case, origination is an irrelevancy where atemporal truths are at issue; in the way of the world priority matters, in the realm of the soul appropriation. 2. Truths are held both jointly and severally by all who cherish them, at whatever age discovered. (Note: Clevernesses belong to those who invent them; hence you can steal wit but not wisdom, which is free for the taking.)

10 EDUCATION:
"GLADLY LEARN AND GLADLY TEACH"

Education is both the release from and a recovery of one's own times; it uncovers roots while it imparts traditions.

An "experimental" school is a sin against the young. For who are the subjects? Why set up to teach if you aren't convinced of your course?

I've never known a devoted teacher who didn't have stage fright before every class and who didn't welcome a snow day.

Scholars: Bacon speaks (I think in the *Advancement of Learning*) of "vermicular studies," wormy learning.

Goethe and Hesse both imagined a pedagogical province, a Castalia (spring of the Muses on Parnassus). Both reservations are run by a mandarin-formality, a reverential aura, that captures half the enterprise—loving respect for greatness. But they're missing the other half: the amateur-rudeness of free inquiry. Their life of work and festivity, discipline and beauty, is lovely to imagine, but our boisterous college is *real*.

We teachers of college students who rely on the biddable civility of our young are really parasites on the thousand "noes" and hundred "time-outs" of those who did the real upbringing.

There are two sets of readings: the trusted great texts, studied with devotion in hope of illumination, and the accident reports and fever charts of our condition, studied with revulsion for prophylactic purposes. (They are very roughly as books to articles.) The trouble in educating our young on the latter is that they become fixed on curing evils rather than achieving good.

Studying is not "making studies," and "what the studies show" is what still later ones refute.

The demand for productivity is a perversion of the sabbatical: "Thou shalt neither sow thy field, nor prune thy vineyard. That which groweth of its own accord of thy harvest thou shalt reap." Teachers should have a time for letting things come to unpressured, unexploited fruition, free time for rumination and reflection.

The possessive and mercantile locutions of scholarship reveal something of its nature: "my work," "my author," or "I am indebted to X for thought Y." Such talk is alien to the spirit of gladly learning and gladly teaching.

Jane Austen speaks of establishments where girls "scrambled themselves into a little education" (*Emma*). I can think of worse ways to conduct a school.

By liberal education we are supposed to gain wisdom, by vocational training competence, and the two together (related as amateur to professional learning or roughly as undergraduate to graduate schooling) should make a fully formed human being. But it doesn't work that way anymore. Liberal education at its most respectable has contracted itself into preparation for scholarship, so that professional training is not its complement but its arcane culmination; leisurely learning is left nowhere.

Willful willessness: to surrender human affairs to experts. That's where an educated citizenry is needed.

There is an almost voluptuous surrender in the narrow specialization of academics. Some professions are so engrossing or demanding that an exchange of breadth for depth is required. But that a teacher should live with a willfully incomplete humanity? For the mastery of what? For preeminence over whom?

In forming education policy there's a perpetual call out for another study, more information, advanced techniques—just anything to postpone facing the hard simplicities: principals able to enforce discipline and teachers alight with learning.

Sancta simplicitas: "More research is needed"—when you already can't see the trees for the pulped wood.

Anthropology used to mean philosophical analysis of embodied humanity carried on by limited eye-witness observation and lots of introspection. And then it became an amateur study carried on by lady travelers and colonial administrators. And then it became an academic science. And then it developed methodological problems: If you go native, what you gain in insider knowledge you lose in objectivity; if you remain coolly outside you forego empathetic sympathy. If you collect anecdotes from native informants you have skewed insight; if you are a number-cruncher you get accurate non-insights, etc. And then anthropologists ran out of *anthropoi.*

How they must envy their founder Herodotus who had a whole world, center and periphery, of which to be *autoptes,* a "see-for-himselfer," and interpreter, unembarrassed by academic taboos and embroilments. But probably they've never read their founding classic.

What ingrate doesn't feel an occasional twinge of guilt at the privileges of the free professions, for whom duty and pleasure, strain and excitement, are convertible? But an odd relief comes from the incomprehensible fact that it is not true of everyone, what Chaucer says of the Clerk of Oxenford, that "gladly wolde he lerne, and gladly teche."

I think of myself—as do my colleagues—neither as a professor nor a scholar, nor even as a teacher, but as one of a company of curators of a community of learning.

Reasons why we learn best together: Practical—because it makes us listen well (our access to alien wisdom) and speak clearly (our way to ourselves); psychological—because in company we get ourselves over that mental miasma called *acedia* by the theologians (the student's occupational disease); pedagogical—because most of us need to be jump-started (Socrates calls it a *periagoge,* a conversion); philosophical—because thinking, by the very fact that it is first and last the soul talking with itself, naturally longs for other partners in between (though the sociability of the contemplative soul is something of an enigma, even for Aristotle, who is generally so magisterial about the life of the intellect; see *Nichomachean Ethics* X 7).

There are checks and limits to teaching—when you long to convey incommunicable grandeur. You just have to stand by till you either conclude that this moment will have gone unseized or see the carefully laid fire catch on. After that your little lit spills are unneeded.

There's a difference between a scientific and a scholarly article: The former has two authors or more, the latter one author or less.

What can be a sounder setting for our soul, for exhilarating challenges and uncompetitive companionship, than to hold converse with books superior to ourselves and with colleagues who are our equals?

The inner life of learning is full of what the Germans used to call *Allotria* (Greek for "what doesn't belong," "isn't to the point"), signifying the darting levity, the untethered playfulness of the mind. If people knew how much futzing around goes into one determinate sentence, would they think more or less of it?

What is good teaching? Not a performance, though one certainly has a strenuous sense of "being on"; not a broadcast, though where there is a classroom of students one can't help now and then talking to the air between them. The teacher's problem then is how to talk *with* students rather than *to* them and how to address *each* student rather than *all*. But that's the least of it; listening to them is the real art.

Students have a right, it seems to me, to get candid answers to serious questions about my thoughts on anything from philosophical to theological, from literary to human matters. I say this because we are committed to professing little and eliciting as much as possible in class. If asked outside of class, I will give straight and clear accounts of my opinions on everything but current politics. It is a betrayal of the student-teacher bond, only second to getting involved in intimacies, to reveal one's politics—but perhaps not one's political philosophy (e.g., I'm a Madisonian, heart and soul, and might be gotten to say so in a properly thoughtful setting). Are students similarly entitled to me personally, to my passions, fears, loyalties? No, but they are welcome to conjecture about them (as they inevitably will about their teacher), and if they come near the truth they are laying the basis for a friendship when they cease to be students and become our alumni, our adult "nurslings." So never rebuff serious inquiry and seldom indulge mere curiosity.

There's delicately farcical fun in speaking with a straight face of intimate matters knowing that the unready will never clue out the comical candor and the attuned students will find it headily revealing.

Academics (among whom my own colleagues are not really to be counted) have a propensity for regarding the heat of their indignation as a measure of the justice of their cause, forgetting that trivial annoyances are apt to be more roiling than a deep injustice.

The "morale" of a faculty is an atmospheric and fungible mystery. It's an exudation of guesses and fond hopes about each other's mood—vague, but negotiable when packaged as pressure. It's a humor of self-righteous self-solicitousness: what pitiable (but dangerously potent) victims we are! Yech.

The apparent popularity that faction-makers get from a sudden coagulation of shared interests turns out to be brief compared to the long-lived respect given to communal leaders whose passion is not for an issue but for a place and expresses itself in meticulous objectivity—if the community is fundamentally sound. A permanently faction-ridden faculty may well achieve a Madisonian stability in a large university but in a small college it is a misery to itself and a bad model for the students, who are there not least to learn what a community might be.

Students think that reality is "out there" or "afterwards." Well, it depends on what you rate higher on the reality scale: the wide open indifferentism of the large world, or the enclosed intensities of the small community.

Academic crises are addictive and the "what we've been through" cries are partly melodrama—when, after all, we talked ourselves into it, cultivated our passion for it assiduously, and prolonged it perversely.

It's much easier to be carried along by a common opinion than to say why it's true—and that's of course exactly what Socrates means by an opinion: a notion that has you rather than one you have. Does the locution "the faculty thinks" even have a meaning? On a sharply defined issue, heads can be counted or consensus obtained; that's "the sense of the faculty." But the thinking behind it is as ungatherable as a herd of cats.

All is well, they say, if only the faculty is unified. What if we're all one and all wrong? Or is that unthinkable?

I bring certainties from home to the faculty meeting; my colleagues dissolve them, and we resolve otherwise. I go home and I wish we hadn't. Well, at least I've achieved perplexity, the Socratic state of grace.

We teachers are tainted Arcadians, who don't think much about who's keeping the beasts fed and the picnics packed. Arcadia means "Bear-country," not for nothing: The stock market could be our nemesis. The real Arcadians (the ones who exist only in pastorals) keep themselves reminded that *Et in Arcadia ego*—"I am even in Arcadia": Death is speaking.

They say power is an aphrodisiac. Well, maybe, though surely a man who uses his status to compel Aphrodite is laughable. But also surely a want of power can be antaphrodisic, repellent: the stridency, the hysterics, the thrash-ings about, the desire to be at once sheltered and liberated, at once told and listened to, at once non-responsible and authoritative. What the weakly weak lack is the decision to follow the oddly noble injunction "Put up or shut up"—fight staunchly or yield gracefully.

Overheard, a young colleague to an elder: "I'll never trust your judgment again." Answer (that should have been): "Good, you're growing up." And when he has, he'll trust again, too.

Lovers of spontaneity don't seem to see how they're being orchestrated—especially students.

Institutional trauma: It's a factor to be reckoned with without ever quite achieving reality. People are licking their wounds and doing it with barbed tongues so as to keep the scab from forming; moreover the blood is totally figurative.

Dictionary of rebellion: We plan, he schemes; we trust, he's blind; we misinterpret, he lies; we have friends, he has cronies; we are firm, he's rigid; we consult, he conspires; we remember, he resents; we are flexible, he caves in; we share information, he betrays confidences; we mean what we say, he's legalistic. Poor president.

The vulgar maxims of the power alleys have some truth even in academia: "You can't make an omelet without breaking eggs"—but God help you if you do: all the eggs will be pronounced to have had embryos on their yolks and the omelet to be murderously inedible. "If you can't stand the fire stay out of the kitchen"—so we'll demand an air-conditioning system.

Here's a soothing diversion in one of those weeks-long crises: Put down-home English sayings into antique Greek. For example: The shit has hit the fan: *ho kópros enébale toi aerokóptri;* or into office English: The excrement has impacted the ventilator. Or into high Dutch: *Die Scheisse hat den Lüfter getroffen.* Wouldn't Jonathan Swift have fun!

Generation gap: The young want purity, the old survival. The former are willing to be beastly for the integrity of the ideal, the latter are willing to be base for a remnant of reality. The young are the devil in politics (where I mean by "young" not an age but a state of mind).

The vote: what a strange quantitative fusion of basically inadditive human wills! When we allow our noses to be counted and agree to stick with the sum, we are compromised in our human nature and confirmed in our political wisdom. And representation is equally strange: that another human being can be charged with making my will present in a place of decision by following his own judgment! The ways of democracy have a deep and subtle metaphysics, and in a small community it becomes almost palpable. I think if all students (high school or college) were asked to ponder the philosophical assumptions behind majoritarian decision-making and representative government we would have a citizenry awed by the bold subtlety and devoted to the salvational effectiveness of our constitutional framework.

Faculty opinion, like public opinion, works a little bit like a wave: The particles pump up and down in place, but since some are up while others are down the whole assumes an appearance of forward motion. And if there is a contrary order of up and down (that is, pro and con), the two waves might cancel each other and the impression would be that of flat inactivity, just when contrarieties were greatest.

The pleasures of speaking evil *about* someone are considerably greater than speaking it *to* them, as those charged with conveying and explaining bad news painfully learn.

One colleague wants to deny another a charge of responsibility because "he's too ambitious." *Tu quoque.*

Matthew 7:5: "Thou hypocrite; first cast out the beam out of thine own eye, and then shalt thou see clearly to cast out the mote out of thy brother's eye." Academic version: Let's call a meeting and have it out reciprocally. Fair enough.

A certain kind of academic is too bright to be nice and too intelligent to be nasty—a kind of characteriological brinkmanship.

There's often and suddenly a suspicion that study is a fronting activity, that it rehearses lines on a stage while truth waits behind the scenes. But it may be the best we—no, I—can do: march along pre-scribed paths, interpret given texts, analyze presented thoughts, preserve the continuity and communicability of a tradition of inquiry, plod on parallelwise, or maybe asymptotically, toward the waiting truth.

You can't cure vulgarity, a psychic texture, by education, but since vulgar souls are sometimes very good-hearted, you can take its abusive edge off.

A critical and an independent mind are not the same: The first occupies op-positions; it seats itself in cleverly formulated negations; the second moves ahead even of its own logical framework.

Aristotle rightly says that wonder requires conditions of relative ease, leisure above all but also creature comforts. It would be not impossible but almost miraculous if the scholars of Stalingrad, freezing in their libraries, drenched in never-ceasing martial music, endangered on their every errand, produced much differentiated wisdom.

If all the sheets of life came uncleated, the sails of thought would surely flap.

Rehearse desolation in the imagination: If all was gone, those we love, the communities we care about, our country—would we then continue (conditions permitting, for this thought experiment) to carry on with the life of learning? Would we say "Not now, when our world is gone" or "More than ever now, *because* our world is gone"?

It's folly to try to gauge working intelligence. Expect dumbness and you'll be surprised by sub-surface shrewdness, expect brightness and you'll wonder how dumb the smart can act.

There's dead seriousness and live seriousness, related as the letter to the spirit.

There are people who start their research with a meticulous marshalling (it used to be on index cards) of bits of information. This is methodical scholarship. The results will be competent, but they might be piddling. There are others who begin by futzing around, ranging hither and thither, conjecturing and retracting. This is free-form inquiry and the results might be interesting but they might be unreliable. If graduate school taught you how to get the two together it would be good for something.

From freshmen to seniors, students want to 1. "change the world" and 2. "make a difference." Who has the heart to ask them 1. "For the better?" and 2. "To whom?" Well, we the teachers had better demand some defensible precision, lest their fine afflatus dissipate in grandiosity. A student who answers 1. "Of course for the better; I want to get kids to read poetry," and 2. "To my village in New Mexico" has my instant admiring sympathy and the promise of a glowing recommendation.

It's a mark of good teachers that students trust but don't confide in them, that they speak in hypothetical, general, third-person terms—in the case of our students that they convert personal problems into philosophical issues. It's their way of showing respect for our common learning: They want from us not coddling warmth but serious reflection on their concerns.

The summery Phaeacia of learning (our Santa Fe campus): the balmy and heady air, the enchanting vistas, the fragrant campus, and moving within this setting, the easy camaraderie of young and old, the exhilarating pick-up conversations—and all of this is a second incarnation of our community of learning, its spacious Southwestern embodiment exhibiting the wonder of identity-in-difference.

Some studies are undertaken as a holiday of the spirit, a recreation of the soul; they refuel the imagination, re-ignite old passions, and above all re-illuminate old enigmas. For me reading about the Aztecs served that purpose, though I found myself wishing to serve them, that is, the memory of this terrifying, beautiful, and utterly annihilated people. And of course, they gave prime testimony on the most important historical question of modernity: Is the West merely a dominant moment or incarnate universality?

The academy loves marginalia. Unless they can flounce a text with commentary they won't look at it; not even then.

The ages of a teacher: In youth, playful withholding of one's cherished discoveries, hoping strongly (and fearing a little) that students will see it with minimal nudging, all in obedience to pedagogical reticence—and inexpertness in opening one's mind. In age, perfect readiness to tell all upon being asked, occasioned partly by the cumulative fullness of mind and a certain fearless nonchalance about one's "own" discoveries, partly by a fading taste for pedagogical fun and games—and not least from elderly garrulousness.

This "learning about others" is a suspect activity to me. It combines 1. a short attention span (learning the language is seldom required), 2. a figuratively prurient interest in strange ways (i.e., the more apparently outré customs), 3. no acknowledgment that unless you subscribe to an incredibly strong theory of learning transfer, knowing a little of one country leaves you in ignorance of some hundred and ninety-nine others, and above all, 4. it leaves the young with the weird notion that you can understand otherness without a deep knowledge of self. For most of these young globalists haven't got a clue—except such as is bred in the bone—about their own country. Ask them, for example, about the Tenth Federalist, that foundation-thought of our political well-being.

Curricular reform: Practical fate—months of uphill mentation by the few and an afternoon of (foreseeable) down votes by the many. Intellectual form—exuberantly nescient radicalism intent on instituting free-form rebellion, or highly theoretical ideology meant to "raise students' consciousness" (a euphemism for converting them), or cautious tinkering (usually the construction of interdisciplinary courses) designed for un-upsetting glamour. The truth is that faculties, so often liberal in their politics, are ultraconservative in their adherence to a disciplinary order of learning and a professorial mode of teaching. And that's where the problem lies.

As in monster movies a blanketing ooze comes in over the transom, so with writing on education. It's perhaps less scary but surely as suffocating. What's worse is that it spawns its antithesis: statistics, clear, precise, and unmeaning, and while the ooze envelops the status quo, the statistics incite action: make more practices quantifiable, that is, denature them.

Párturiént montés, nascétur rídiculús mus: "Mountains will be in labor, a laughable mouse will be born," says Horace (*Ars Poetica*). Had he attended an educational conference?

"The eunuch voice of scholarship" (Jon Stallworthy): What a perfect tetrameter-description! Scholarship prides itself on its neutered intellect which looks not for truth but circumstance: "context all the way down."

How strange that Plato's place should have become the byword for futility: "strictly academic," and that those "Groves of Academe" should have been pulped for professorial productivity.

It is gratifying to reveal the fruits of reflection to the enthusiastic young (more so than to the more restrained collegial age-mates who have their own budget of wisdom dearer to them even than mine). But it has to be done fleetingly, lightly: They think they sense an aura of something old and venerable that is nonetheless close to them—and then remember what you said for decades, all skewiffy.

Maybe humans obtain "a glassy essence" (Peirce) in time, but in youth it's more murky-like.

11 COLLEGE:
CORPOREAL COMMUNITY

A living community of learning needs rituals to signify its durability, traditions to save it from re-inventing the wheel, routines to keep its mind on the main matter, rules to put its essence into effect, discretion to keep the place humane, physical forms to embody its spirit, and festivities to recreate its soul.

A "sense of community" is a shifty, subjective thing. Don't trust it; trust the set spirit that carries on when "senses" fail.

Communities are not accidental accretions, nor instant bondings, nor created conveniences. They are mythically founded and naturally grown. In America, the land of utopias, it's often done backward: first the "intentional" or "planned" community, then the myth and the naturalization. This is a *made* country, and it conceives made communities.

The quality of a community can't be improved by "quality control," not that its goodness is so imponderable—excellence is perfectly ponderable—but that nothing gets better just by being tested (the huge illusion of the accountability movement in education). It's an open secret that tests make schools testable, period.

Citizen's Imperative: Always act as if you were then and there founding a community, be it of two or two hundred—in conducting conversations, in enacting routines, in mounting critiques. Plato's *Republic* is the model: While Socrates is constructing a mere pattern "to be laid up in heaven," he is founding a dialogic community of three: himself and his two eager young partners.

Ghost towns are "all but" places: You all but see the rawhide hero step out of the swinging doors of the saloon, right hand loosely swinging at hip height. Virtual communities seem to me "all buts" as well, except there isn't even a place. I thought human beings craved the actual, but maybe not.

The coincidence of conditions that make a happy founding possible is so miracle-requiringly improbable that those of us who have the luck to find ourselves members of such a community—be it America herself or one of her innumerable small progeny-communities—must wish to cherish and protect—and love—them.

The two communities that I love, the country and the college, have both had a founding and a re-founding, and I suspect it's always so. The first founding is bright, the documents are fluently enlightened, the negotiations are lustily assertive, the institutions are confidently devised. The second founding is a work of nostalgia for bright beginnings, sadness for-tainting tragedies; there's experience, sophistication, deeper delving into the philosophical and providential roots: from Jefferson to Lincoln.

Typical communities: Those you are born into or join for life and die out of (your country), those where you spend your working life and invest your public affections (my college), those you absorb unwittingly or even recalcitrantly (your culture), those you belong to by intentional choice (the Republic of Letters), those you cherish within (the worlds of the imagination), and first and finally, the natural private attachments (family and friends).

Communities form about aboriginally sacred topographies: the mesa of the Acropolis, pedestal of Athena's temple; Shiprock of the Navajos, where the gods live; etc. And sometimes it's a whole continent, from sea to shining sea.

Here's what a community is: a bastion of intelligible being and a safe haven for the imagination.

The car is America's confessional, that rushing cubicle of confidences.

Communities and souls have their festivities, the happy ones as complements and culminations of their soberly satisfying dailiness, the unhappy ones as a relief from dreary mundanity or as elevations of shared disaster.

Communities have a double seat: in their natural and in their human place; I mean in their landscape and in their country. Well, at least in the ones that get to me:

small towns, dinky or pretty, folded into the hills or plunked down on a vast plain, and feeling themselves to be America's epitome—"the heartland."

People have been bamboozled into embarrassment about saying out loud to each other what they do believe in their hearts together: that they'd rather call whatever made them a divinity than a natural force; that they can't help but love their country because, all things considered, it's good; that they trust their representatives because they're theirs; that they have a horror of unfaithfulness because it has victims; that they know better than their children who are, after all, children; that misconduct should be punished so that the world won't go out of kilter. Some people do say it brashly and crudely, but they're not the ones who know what they mean. Yet these subdued beliefs hold us together, and there might even be some special salvation in our common reticence. When you're on the road, a few words discover this community.

An age that exults in trashing truisms will soon be doing without communal truths.

The keepers of continuity are a band of comrades, the community of community-maintainers.

There's a slightly shoddy but also warmly human bond: indiscriminate, non-obligating, plain liking for one's fellow-citizens.

What's really wrong with a mutual admiration society? Now a unilateral admiration society—that's reprehensible.

Why *in corpore* communication is, after all, primary: People stay in touch by letters, telephone, e-mail. But, of course, "in touch" is just what they aren't—not within touching distance, not tangible to each other. Virtual togetherness is surely better than nothing but surely less than the actual thing. "Virtual"—that means "all but," "as if," abstracted from full existence, having the virtue of the event without its reality. It's a euphemism, really, for *ersatz* presence, for masking our distance-greed. But we are embodied souls, best together in body—why waste our way of being?

Why real communities are, after all, corporeal: There are some very old and wonderful virtual communities, for example, one I think I belong to, the Republic of Letters, and numerous new ones. But from the country to the college people in their place is what counts. Who can imagine America without its continent? No more can there be a community of learning without its campus, where take place the spontaneous encounters that give long-breathed friendship its chance, where we come face-to-face, day by day, year in year out. Intellectual communities especially need to be spatially compact and humanly physical; that's because they are so temporally expansive and home to so many disembodied presences, the authors of the works that animate them. A community of learning is people together in one place talking to each other about that which has gone out of time and beyond place.

Themistocles told his Athenians that the city was wherever they were, even if they were all in ships. By that desperate falsehood this man of patriotic guile recovered Athena's citadel and her Athens—the floating city wouldn't have lasted a month. The chances he took to win at Salamis were taken to save a sacred mesa.

"A" life—that's lived loyalty, steady love, among other things for a community.

Public sociability and communicativeness is a sort of civic duty, and Americans are, by and large, remarkably unabashed about taking it up. European children used to be brought up to be shy; blushing reticence and embarrassed contortions were signs of breeding in the young, to be succeeded by semi-gracious formality. Americans admire self-possession (maybe a little too much). But they're right in this: Shyness in adults is either pathological or a sign of excessively self-enclosed self-regard, refined sometimes, always a civic disability. Now stage fright is another matter—you owe that to your audience.

Of course we'll be all right in the long run, a rich continent with a vibrant people and a sound political system. The trouble is, we don't live in the sweep of history but in the nooks and crannies of the land and of time, and there more things can be broken in a tendentious decade than can get fixed for a good life now.

There is the "discretionary community" by which more and more Americans define themselves: choosily religious, expensively recreational, loosely educational. It seems pretty frivolous. But when the moment comes it's their work that brings Americans together in deeds of heroism, such as running up the staircase of that doomed tower to bring people down. And they think of themselves as Americans through those jobs—which turn out to be callings.

We are in this euphemistic mode now: Cripples become "disabled" (a *soi-disant* cripple said to me: "Do they need to grind it in?"), the retarded are "exceptional." I wonder if it's a gain in the long run to let the language-rectifiers have their way: to forego the warmth of sympathy and the dignity of acknowledged tragedy for a pretty forced normalcy.

There being too few of us, Jews aren't an official minority. But then, I don't even feel much like an American Jew—more like a Hebrew, albeit they were the bully-boys of the Lord. My folks in Israel are a secular, sloppy version; the non-victims par excellence, "Never again" incarnate. They're not very war-like, but they're pretty business-like.

The standard facile rebellion of Americans against the "thems"—government, corporations, whoever the powers-that-be may be: It rattles on like a cart on rails, trundling by all facts or circumstances. It is in fact American protestantism in the bloodstream, the routine of protesting. You have to give them this, though: They wouldn't do it if it didn't give them a warm fuzzy feeling, and that's sensible. And I do like their logic: "Three hundred thousand came out to protest against X; the people have spoken." What about the two hundred seventy-nine million seven hundred thousand who didn't?

The deprived envy the privileged (though usually not rabidly in this country) because they think that if you're well off you're happy and having amenities means having pleasure. They're wrong, of course, but by rights they ought to be right: If you're prosperous you have an obligation to belong to the band of the blessed, or at least to the communion of the contented. Who of us feels sorry, except in a luxuriating sort of way, for the miseries of the rich unless they are the usual human afflictions? Gatsby is a case in point. I feel for him not because "the rich are different" but because he's a boy in love who turns into a man with a love.

Community Building, Peace Corps style (1970s): some stacks of board and a keg of nails plus some hammers are delivered to the back campus. This was called "an unstructured environment." Then the assessment and accountability crew look on to see who will pick up the first hammer and drive a nail. This was called "showing leadership." Then they build some chicken coops. Then the hens arrive and begin laying. Then they had to wring a chicken neck. This was the final, and we were up into the night before graduation because some volunteers couldn't do it. They had learned a little Hindi but arrived in a Tamil-speaking region. This was called "culture shock." (Everything from a hundred miles offshore out was supposed to induce this terrible trauma.) Then they arrived in the village they were supposed to build up. As per letter from one of our volunteers, the locals thought that eggs give you a fever. So my volunteer announced that he'd eat three eggs in the village square at high noon. Which he did, with no harm. Then the villagers said:

"Oh well, *you're* an American." I think that's called "American exceptionalism." End of story, except my unforgettable encounter with the Minnesota Multiphasic Personality Inventory and the K factor. But that's another tale told by an idiot, signifying . . . ?

It is a test of a well-conditioned community that a moderately amiable person (well, even a good-hearted curmudgeon) who is well intentioned and decent can count on the supporting respect of colleagues. What a fearful thing is the foul breath from the caverns of backbiting intrigue, of subterranean exclusion, of whispering vilification against which there is no open-air defense. *Never* participate in such underground activity. If you must plot (and plot we must in the groves of academe) let it be toward swift action and a respectful aftermath.

Activity, the ardent pursuit of a well-composed soul, is a pearl that needs an oyster. A good community is such a worldly shell, and life within it has its daily irritations (well known to be needed to start a pearl) and its decadal contentment. And like an oyster, the community should sometimes open its shielding wings to the elements.

12 ADMINISTRATION: DEANING

"Leadership" is the quality apparently most desired by the faculty and in fact least tolerated. Its tolerable essence seems to be: first in to turn the lights on, last out to lock the doors. Or, more seriously: encourage all efforts while setting limits and preserving the point—the radii, circumference, and center of the dean's sphere of influence.

What *do* the colleagues mean by intellectual leadership? Probably this unlikely combination of activities: that the dean should express in every action a view of the school, but carry on in the mode of an unobtrusive *genius loci,* a sort of reticently serviceable sprite.

A dean should be worldly as hell so as to serve as a buffer between the—properly—inward-turned faculty and that potently intrusive fantasy called reality. It is loathing's labor lost to try to grind in what the rest of the educational world is so dangerously up to; the colleagues remain wisely and impregnably innocent. An occasional reproachful impulse ("How can one be so unworldly") is totally misplaced, since the contemplative peace of the community is much more valuable than the sharing of the storm watch.

Employ, when required, the various bureaucratic dialects, but only with that head-shaking hilarity with which we discover in ourselves a gusto for going suddenly and totally out of character.

Be continually on the watch to incur gratitude for the college from the outside. Everyone who so much as phones for information should feel our last-ditch humanity.

Co-opt fate; sit like a midget-Kutuzov waiting for that to happen which must happen. At most make channels for troubles to run off or for felicities to course through.

Small slips should be admitted with stupefying alacrity; big mistakes should be mitigated by the most industrious generosity.

Reverse yourself speedily and cheerfully. Compensate even unwitting wrongs.

A finger in every pie; and above all, a hand in every draft.

Try to be both motor and soul; work to keep the place serviceably purring as well as nobly animated.

This community lives between pervasive purpose and spirited aberration.

Embrace every new scheme that is well and truly born of the old stock or that bears grafting.

Motion: Institutional heaving, administrative laboring—a big nothing is extruded. Activity: A student asks a genuine question—a great event has made it into the world. Not believing this maxim of educational maxims makes deans into bureaucrats, those paper parasites with the power of strangulation.

Don't even dream of trying to leave a legacy. Sufficient to the day is the slippage thereof, and large is the scope of mere maintenance. A going concern needs preservation more than innovation, which is a substance-wasting sacrifice to that idol of drift worshiped as Change. As the old fates required to be apotropaically fended off, the new demons demand anticipatory resistance.

The point of getting locked into a fighting embrace with that protean monster, the future, is to protect the day-by-day present of the school, for as eternal life is a *nunc stans,* so life of learning is in the daily now.

Office-bound: The dean's duty station is the office, and the duty is to be a sitting duck; a sedentary dean saves a lot of grief.

Attendance: Appear at all functions. If you're there, no one notices; if you're not, everyone does.

Refreshments soothe the driven body and settle the savage breast; cookies are conducive to consensus. No meeting without its coffee service.

Fund as freely as possible both conviviality and intellectual initiatives. In this school, at least, the former is more apt to go over into the latter than the converse.

Document everything, for remembrance, law, and clarity. The days are so compacted with events that the whole inspissated plenum vanishes as one.

Classiness in office: return first the calls of those who want something—and have least status.

Power suddenly come into evidence betokens a history of neglect. Authority is nearly always merely immanent.

If "administration" returns to its meaning of a "ministering *to*," the officers of this college might be called administrators. But the term has a history of subverting its preposition and setting itself up as a final cause. Avoid it; even preach against it.

"*Ich dien*" is the motto of a British royal house. Nice for a dean.

When power surfaces, the affair has been botched. People exercising power are at once frightful and comical. And in general: "A man who uses his power only because he has it, against right and reason—he's cause for laughter. Or if he isn't yet today, he shall be so in the future" (Joseph's last speech to his brothers in Thomas Mann's greatest novel).

Resist the idea of constituent interests in this community. There are, to be sure, urgent bread-and-butter stakes that distinguish the parts of the college and must be acknowledged. But all will say—and mean it—that issues of the spirit matter as much. The dean, as the person having primary reporting relations to most of the non-teaching faculty, is responsible for signifying, by a meticulous and appreciative attention to the Associates' work, that it is the necessary condition for the well-working of the Program. Everyone thrives on being in the service of the central purpose.

When it is hard to find candidates for the Instruction Committee (which oversees everything) all is well. It means not only that the colleagues see nothing much remiss but that they assess the onerous distractions of the committee's work higher than the pleasures of influence.

The president and the dean represent respectively the existence and the essence of the community. The two are hand in glove, but as existence comes before essence in the temporal realm, so the president is first in the worldly locus of the embodied Program, the institution. No dean should forget that, nor, being a *ci-devant* tutor, how satisfying it is to be *merely* of the essence.

The local wisdom used to be that the dean's relation to the president was to represent the tension between end and means. But when the president is so attentively protective of the inwardness of the school, the opposition vanishes—an irresistibly relaxing moment with a hint of danger in the remote future.

People kindly ascribe the serenity of (beginning) old age to wisdom, but the apparent effect comes much less from life's lessons learned than from the wearing-down and filling-in of the soul's snags and fissures. This smooth imperviousness is neither quite reliable nor always adequate to the sorrows of the young. Yet who wants to quarrel with so pleasant an arrangement—being held in esteem for being more often comforable than not?

Self-admonition: Speedily turn all incipient pretentions into shame and shame into self-amusement. Ultimate maturity is, judging from my own case, unachievable. Every adult I know is, at least internally, part meanly vindictive, part playfully posturing child, threatening doom to opponents, exulting in their mishaps, strutting in the consciousness of position. The solution is to regard oneself as ineradicably funny. Oddly, the outward effect is respectable.

Try for prudence, the virtue of purpose-led good sense that puts principles into practice without much intervening theory—the royal lesson of the *Republic,* Plato's constitution of a community without administrative know-how.

Repeated surprise at expressions of respect is pretentious. Be grateful and say so.

Thank all and sundry even for the most irritatingly clueless advice. Even people utterly persuaded of their helpfulness often are.

Truth-telling in office: Suppress all remarks. Candor is ill-advised, truthfulness is of the essence. It is impossible to tell the whole truth because time runs out, memory fails, kindness modifies, and confidentiality abridges the story. Nor is it possible to tell nothing but the truth, since tact will always soften verity into verisimilitude. One rule is plain: Tell no self-serving lies.

People talk to discover what they mean. So even in the grip of an occasional wild desire to be done, let the conversation dribble on and peter out. Being allowed to run out of words is the specific for students who come charged with confusion.

Odysseus, the man of many mechanisms and long patience, is a dean's natural model: Readiness, even some relish, for listening to tales and resourcefulness in resolving imbroglios. My hero also has another facility, which I leave unmentioned.

Attract requests for advice by being reliable, quick and attentive. Make the office so helpful that it becomes a normal point of reference.

Preventive accessibility: Encourage people to come to you before you have to summon them.

Quandaries of the office interview: Why are the good often charmless and the wicked captivating (in youth only)?

Listen long enough, and at least some sorrows turn into projects. Listen long enough, and at least some complaints turn into self-accusation.

Listen hard enough to get at the point behind the gabble. Coagulate that into practicalities, especially in the face of real calamity. Send grieving students off to do one next thing and keep them coming back to report on that.

For miscreants and miserables, temper animadversions with precise advice and help.

Practice reserved kindness, such as students can take or leave.

The Open Door: Casual access complemented by purposeful conversation.

Warm sympathy and cool judgment.

Judge from principle without being in the clouds about persons.

The higher hypocrisy: Try to respect even fairly implausible claims to virtue, since the wish to appear good is not without grace.

Officiating requires absorption-in-scatter, collectedness-in-dispersion—a species of alert sleep-walking.

The life of action draws down the endowment accumulated in earlier reflection. There being a finite capital of pre-conceived opinions, the moment when action is no longer funded by thought is clearly foreseeable. Then resign, in both senses.

It is necessary to relax for a while the meticulous psychic housekeeping that keeps the soul a working habitat for reflection—not for lack of time but because of the contrary set of the officiating mind. But don't pack undigested soul matter into some mental cold chest; chuck it out altogether. One seven-year lacuna in seventy isn't fatal to the soul's salubriousness.

Study is, it seems to me, the busyness of thought, as contemplation is its activity. Together they constitute the life of learning—as I recall.

Teaching, conceived as applied learning, is much harder than administration. The timidities of officiating wear off; the stage fright of teaching never abates. The exercise of authority becomes habitual; the persuasions of pedagogy require ever-fresh effort. The worries of office are terminable by action; the anxieties of the classroom increase in retrospect.

"Getting things done" means curtailed deliberation and ill-founded decision. Why on earth does it tend to work?

No one, I imagine, is ever wholly "off" an engrossingly responsible job. The most wholehearted surrender to distraction will suddenly be rent by a welcome flash of recall to duty, a remembrance of the vibrant gravity of real life.

It is not so much the preempting of private by official life as the transformation of the imagination from a receiver of intimations to a designer of devices: scenes into scenarios.

Visitors rarely notice how full of escape hatches the room is. All the walls are breached by paintings to wander into for a glancing turn (an *Augenblick,* as the Germans say) in other worlds.

The springs of energy are forms of love: faith in the Program, affection for its people, appreciation for its forms, and a moving feel for the precariousness of all good things.

Define the faith with a latitudinal elasticity that has plenty of give without suffering permanent deformation.

Happiness is the soul's "being at work" (activity) in accordance with excellence, says Aristotle. He doesn't say how the quantity of work is to be compounded with the degree of excellence to find the intensity of the resultant happiness. If the *amount* of business is a permissible factor deaning is very bliss.

Having no time—shameful temporal ineptitude.

Clear the desk each day. Piles are incubi, and of the devil.

It is shameful to forget a task and burdensome to remember it, so do it now—clear conscience and mind together.

Some people take pleasure in efficiency. For me dispatch is a defense against the occupation of the mind by the Undone.

Practice anticipatory panic, so as to be cool in the event. Form concrete visions of looming evils, so as to be apotropaically prepared.

"Long-range planning" is schematized fantasy, but it captures the future for today's use.

Transform worry into work, and dissipate anxiety by resourcefulness. The great comfort of authority is the ability to act; those who have the means to confront life's offenses do not feel them so much as affronts. The extraordinarily irritable sensitivity of many faculties is largely the consequence of their "powerlessness," though good power is just endless work. Here is a perennial problem in school governance (that our Polity does much to address): People want to share authority but won't accept its work.

Is there, day by day, a whole that is *the* college? If there is, to whom is it manifest? Least of all to any of the three deans, each of whose offices attracts "cases," as does the doctor's.

The best plan is to frame a firm, ideal picture of the community, to act as if it were at any moment realized, and to receive with evident interest and inward skepticism all contrary reports concerning the current psychic state of "*the* student body" or "*the* faculty."

We must not be abashed to think that we are working at the world's veritable center. Those of our colleagues who, for the sake of modesty, labor to puncture the local afflatus seem to me to be multiply misguided—about the well-springs of energy, about the true sense of proportion, and about the real state of education. We need—and need so we may keep learning—our sense of working at the sources of intellectual life, of having chosen the difficult proximity of greatness, and of having realized in this tiny community a way of learning that seems to others like a utopia. "Utopia" means "no-place," but here we are—an actual place and what's more, a place of considerable consequence in the halls of liberal learning.

13 CONDUCT:
MORALS AND MITIGATIONS

Once you've made up your mind, you'd better bull on, wishing very hard (which is akin to prayer) that the world will turn right side up to align itself with your position. That "decent respect to the opinions of mankind" must cease to govern action after a certain point—not to speak of opinion polls.

A sense of humor is a kind of rejoicing in the contingencies of our finitude. *Sub specie aeternitatis* we tend to be comical.

The élan of accomplishment and a sense of limits should be complementary.

Inner life is so fluid, there's so much backing and forthing in it, that it's only by daring interpolations that we take each other's overt actions as continuous with themselves and with our nature. Moreover, it is also part of our character once in a while to go spectacularly out of character. The complementary conundrums of free will: Are we free in our consistently connected activity (which may be as chimerical as it seems jigged) or in our sporadically spontaneous behavior (which may be more antic than deliberate)?

The reason that bad luck lowers our self-esteem is that we have the sneaking, superstitious notion that our luck is, for good or ill, our desert.

Poke a modest person and you'll activate a nervous sensibility, puncture a boaster and some anxiety will well up. Stand-offishness and aggressiveness are both signs of excessive self-involvement, too much subjectivity. What's best is a coolly objective sense of one's worth. Then, when you get a compliment, smile gratefully and move on.

Whence comes the demon-charm of some desolate souls?

If you give up loyal love for large prospects in the world, you'll lose. Love's never well lost for ambition— unless you tailor your soul to suit.

How you receive generosity shows the magnitude of your soul; magnanimity is required for receiving as well as giving.

No good deed but it's on someone's back.

No good deed goes unpunished, they say—not because it's particularly culpable (everything's culpable), but because its recipient was mingy.

Self-deprecation is a very self-regarding mode: You get to talk about yourself and you take out a license for bad behavior. Listening to that stuff is like being asked to sign a release from liability.

You have to be morally deaf to listen to Bach and have ungenerous thoughts.

Swallow pride and preempt the first move; there's some dignity in being the larger, and some resignation.

The mundanities of life are best managed by a number of wise maxims, such as: 1. Dust ain't dirt (i.e., clean up moist messes but ignore circumambient sedimentations). 2. Whoever thinks of an idea earliest in life has thought of it first (i.e., if one of our kids discovers, say, that concepts deeply considered flip into their opposites, then he or she is the discoverer of Hegelian dialectic and has priority rights). 3. Futzing around is the best way to zero in (i.e., in thinking and writing start broad and draw in, emulating in reverse the nautilus, that beautiful realization of the logarithmic spiral which grows outward by proportional increments). And so on, *ad nauseam*.

Rigidity and indomitableness are practically indistinguishable in adversity, but they're practical opposites in prosperity.

Adherences we slip into with vacuous minds and placid feelings sometimes turn out to be the most steadfast.

I can't believe in *moments* of truth in moral matters; caught unawares the body shrinks and the soul cringes. What reveals character is whether we step up to the plate upon reflection. Similarly, spontaneous intensity is not the best index of commitment, but long-breathed loyalty is.

In a garden nature does the growing and you do the pruning and weeding and pest control. So leave your own moral nature be, and you just cut back excesses and root out wrongheadedness and restrain bad habits. The same with children, I think—train their moral character in accordance with their born nature.

I don't know about men, but for women—some women at least—sexual morality is just the assumption that sexual intimacy implies a serious, privileged attachment for decent duration, the breaking of which is an unforgettable offense. And since forgetting is the only really effective forgiving, it's unforgivable.

Isn't it odd that men and women, clearly each other's physical complements, don't jibe so well psychically. We do much better intellectually.

Guilt feelings are the conscience gone emotional.

How kind can kindness be if one wouldn't exactly want to be its object? It's a hopelessly condescending virtue. Try affection. Or justice. Or *public* charity.

The innocent bad manners of occurring intertwined in public and then stopping to talk in a friendly way to your teacher: It's like talking to a bicephalous creature.

Freedom : license :: Why? : Why not?

The index of our humanity is the ratio of behavior to conduct. Animals are all behavior; we turn the more to conduct the more we do what comes naturally—well, is supposed to come naturally—to us: think.

Spontaneity understood as programmatic freakishness, infantile friskiness, is a form of brat rebellion. Real spontaneity takes a lot of skilled control.

Principle leads to elegant simplicity of conduct (Jane Austen). Moral complexity leads to anguished experience (Charlotte Brontë). Now why is Jane Austen more interesting, finally? She works a blessed subversion of the general truth that variegated wickedness is more scintillating than intelligent goodness.

I guess it's OK, this occasional avidity for indulgent pleasures, for formless relaxation: hot baths, being wafted along at the bottom of the dinghy, guiding the tiller with a toe, pigging-out on TV, and shooting the breeze. It's the recreation of the zest for taut accomplishment. Sometimes I feel like a bottomlessly unfillable receptacle. Happily in fact the cup soon runneth over; I can't, in fact, take much of it.

Guilt feelings are moral unease without effective repentance; anxiety is fear without a determinate object; self-esteem is self-approval without cause, etc.—the moral modes I love to hate.

The inner philistine: I'd resent the Second Coming if it meant having to put out fresh towels.

What's worse? An affront to one's sense of propriety— outrage? Or a rebuff to one's feelings—hurt? Outrage over hurt, any time.

How heavy another's grace, how dull another's wit, how small another's means can make us feel! Why doesn't another's goodness do that? Why don't we eat our hearts out at another's virtue? Because we're rogues.

Not to be bored by intimations of paradise, not to grow tired of earthly contentments, not to chafe under reasonable rules, not to make ritual into routine, or the reverse, not to denigrate, from pure naiveté, the goods we have, not to lose the savor for "our daily bread"—that's sound-mindedness.

Selfless people are a little repellent. Self-forgetfulness tends to have off-putting side effects: an untended body and splayed sentiments. Besides people in self-denial have no capacity for embarrassment; they are loftily shameless.

The three sins of closeness: reproaches and accusations, demands and manipulations, complaints and maundering. These are like quicksand, easier to blunder into than to get out of.

The mean way: taking literally what was meant metaphorically and precisely what was meant hyperbolically—in sum frustrating laments with mingy rationality, the subversion of the hermeneutic "principle of charity," which says "Construe every utterance to its best advantage."

The innocently inappropriate gifts of unsophisticated people are particularly touching. Still, gratuitous gift-giving generally demands some adroitness: Find the present for which recipients discover a long-standing desire just when they open it.

To make people happy in their fashion, to find out what they want and to give exactly that and not something else—that activates intellectual and practical virtues at once: insightful sensitivity (ouch!) and shopping skills.

We are bidden to "let go"; people are proud of having done it, springily. Who knows what broke? Besides, it's probably good for children to do *some* serious battle with possessive love. They learn at the same time how much they matter and how to be cruel in self-protection, much-needed lessons.

Bad characters: They suck out of every act of care the convenience and leave the love.

Singles bars and similar stock exchanges of sex—sad.

Casual, merely adventitious human intimacies that are not developing events but passing happenings must, over time, decompose, scatter the character. People want pleasure to feel themselves alive, but they need permanence to hold themselves together—even the lustiest of bachelors, I imagine.

Does need act as a goad to response or as an antaphro-disiac? But people in need are in no mood to figure that one out, and probably beyond self-control.

There's a huge difference between making demands and being demanding. Under the natural law of reciproc-ity you can make nag-less demands. But if you're going to be generally demanding, you'd better have something your partner can't do without. These are the indignities of intimacy; gifts should come without asking.

Self-control is not indefinitely elastic; it can be over-stretched by mistreatment until it turns from a ductile virtue into the rigid strappings of dignity.

"I want you to be happy": accent on *I want*.

What are the ethics of mutual desire? Minimal, I should think. Desirous love is intensely selfish, since there's nothing less object-directed, more concentrated in its subject, nothing less to be shared than physical pleas-ure. And if it is reciprocal, that is a sheer lucky coinci-dence. So self-enclosed is pleasure that even "giving" it is only incidentally for the other. So it probably comes down to two commandments, one for both sexes and the other mostly for the man: Be maximally considerate, stop when asked.

Great rule: If you've promised to call at eight o'clock, do it or die trying.

There's pride, there's need, there's wisdom between.

Too much generosity is just recklessness and embarrassing. There's a subtle pleasure in the well-deliberated restraint of moderate gifts.

There's that deflating glimpse of my own smallness: Little, vermiculate anxieties, iterative dwelling on wrongs, tenacious insistence on getting what's mine; the whole ignoble litany. Luckily for my self-respect, I'm a believer in deeds over sentiments, and most of this doesn't have to be enacted.

Probably very large responsibilities often really do suppress personal smallness. But by then, you're no longer facing the other humans in their humanity but as large abstractions: the nation, popular opinion, the congress, agendas, what have you, and these objects are more apt to cause you headaches than heartaches.

It is moving to see a human being deeply preoccupied with non-subjective concerns, be it pursuing truth, making things, or doing good.

It is a humbling part of self-knowledge that one's character is partly pusillanimous, that it cowers before calls to public action. Well, I did it, but just. And then it turned out to be what Aristotle calls happiness: "the soul at work in accordance with virtue." I'd amend: "in accordance with conviction, or even love."

There are people with miseducated souls who turn sorrow into anxiety and grief into nerves and misfortune into offense. They make sympathy harder because they've subverted the dignity of their suffering.

The tolerance we can live with, not the teeth-gritting kind, should be an easy, even cheap virtue: undiscriminating, thick-skinned, and amiably indifferent.

Real pride is so deep that it doesn't show.

If you enter a family or community with strong rules of conduct and powerful faith, how do you accommodate yourself to its life without a false appearance of being in accord? Well, respectful candor, and if that's not acceptable, then get out.

Original sin, which is nothing to me as doctrine, is, however, familiar enough as an experience. You're always and aboriginally in the wrong, because you've always done too much or not enough or the wrong thing and done it too much with yourself in mind. This sense of sin is light-years away from that maundering sentiment called a guilt feeling. It is the perfectly objective recognition of human inadequacy, and, of course, you feel it only intermittently.

2 A.M.: I wake up knowing I've done wrong, multiply—against the human being I've knowingly left in the lurch, against the world I've selfishly appropriated to my use, against the depths of being I've blithely coasted over. 3 A.M.: The contrition was calculated to hold me harmless, and so I've compounded the iniquity.

Backbiting: since it is so warrantedly reciprocal, why doesn't it just die of neutralization? Perhaps it has a certain human value: It lacks the virtue of magnanimity but it also doesn't commit the sin of indifference.

The mechanical operation of the spirit is comical as a literary device, that is, as caricature. But it is scarily infuriating in life, even loathsome, especially when it takes one of the many forms of unconscious self-stimulation: twiddling, scratching, sucking. I think it's because the sight of somatic autism, the self-ishness of the body, is mortifying and the sight of a rampant habit morally injurious.

The purity-mongers don't realize how tainted they are by the sin of intromission.

I suppose you can grow virtuous by getting enough of vice in youth (I've seen that happen) or by remaining innocent all along, but a little, severely rationed vice seems to be of the devil.

Expressive children represent their internalized model (all too often some cartoon hero) with charmingly naive fidelity. Impressionable adults mimic an admired teacher (for instance) with comical adaptation. But I think almost all of us bear ourselves (at least sometimes) in accordance with an inner image of ourselves whose external original we've mostly forgotten. The saving grace is that our adult bodies are uncompliant enough to make the expression unrecognizable; if we could observe ourselves unobserved by ourselves, we'd probably not recognize our own representational intention.

If the gods gave us the gift of soundness by making us sad only for cause, would we be happier? Yes, except that their gifts tend to carry harsh provisos: Feel sorrow only for cause, but feel it for *every* cause. So we'd be sadder than ever.

Bread is appetizing every day, but what else is?

People who've had neglected childhoods, without love or discipline, fall to spoiling themselves; they're spoiled children in old age.

"Pride goeth before the fall," says Proverbs 14:18, and that's true with mechanical predictableness: Walk in the exaltation of facile competence and you'll take a pratfall. Guaranteed.

You must have a lot to say to keep talking in the anechoic chamber of indifference.

An object of injustice differs from a victim in self-conception. The one wants a wrong righted, a principle enforced, a perpetrator punished; the other wants a hurt relieved, compassion expressed, an oppressor pilloried.

Sometimes you need to make enemies, and you might even be a little grateful to them for helping you to define yourself morally.

Some people boast a lot—they mask it as a complaint—that they're overworked and too busy for doing what they claim to want to do. Give us a break: Why can't you distribute your life so that there's a piece left over for living? (Single mothers excepted.)

Pretentiousness is annoying not so much because the sinner thinks too well of himself—he mightn't even—but because he's blind to his own transparency, obtuse about the patency of his own pretending. Claiming to be greater than you are must betoken a helpless longing to *be* more than you are, and that part is pitiable, but the obliviousness is just irritating.

"Love thy neighbor"—well, try to like him; that failing, respect him; that not working, leave him alone. Why ask the impossible?

Sometimes spontaneous, sudden action will break a stuck situation loose, but usually it is the slow steady pressure, like that applied to a screw cap, that opens things up.

We sometimes say that people act like animals, but that's a mere figure of speech. Animals are neither innocent nor guilty, they just *are*, without moral predicates. Perhaps some fierce predators exult in mauling their prey, but they give no sign of that sadistic eros which constitutes human cruelty. Nor are brutes brutish, as are gross human beings whose sensibilities have atrophied.

Be nice, why not? It will grace your eminence, if you have any, and it will sweeten your ordinariness, if you haven't.

Hope: try again; wisdom: right away; luck: got it right this time!

That we bring ourselves to respect what we really don't like is the proof that objective judgment is possible.

Righteous indignation is to academics what current is to electric appliances: an energizing juice, to be switched on and off as needed.

For ordinary sins, forgetting is much better than forgiving, both for the perpetrator and the victim: The evildoer probably didn't really want to go about as one forgiven, and the victim shouldn't want to go around remembering.

Gratitude is more than a responsive courtesy; it's the aura about an object received that transfigures it into a gift.

Flaws: Pusillanimity—evading the enforcement of principle as long as is supportable and longer; dispassion-ateness—becoming icily unresponsive in the face of heated recriminations; parsimoniousness—hoarding my time for other purposes than human helpfulness. These are real faults of character to be mitigated but not eradicated—because they are also my *modus vivendi*.

There are heroes in the realm of passion. They are the ones who have the cool decision just to walk out, break it off, end it, cold turkey. How do they do it? Do they bear loss more bravely than the rest of us clingers-on? Or are they superior to the ensuing loneliness? Do they have hearts of pitch, which oozes slowly, but struck in the right way, shatters cleanly? I respect—and also suspect—them.

Human wonders: people who don't care about money and therefore don't pay their debts; people who have no sense of time so that they always arrive exactly twenty minutes late; people who are so tolerant that they harrass those who they think aren't; philosophical pragmatists who have no practical judgment; people who believe in the relativity of truth and lose their tempers when opposed.

In a position of responsibility you get to practice virtues you've mostly met in a book. Which speaks for study.

Resourcefulness isn't an extra added to good intentions, it's integral to them: The purpose both reveals and judges the way to fulfillment. The whole complex is what the ancients called *phronesis,* mindfulness, practical intelligence, the unitary knowledge of ends and means.

There seems to be a male type, resident in high-tech environments, who spends his time between calculating and copulating. What will he be when he grows up?

"Appraise" and "praise" are etymologically related— "to price correctly" and "to prize highly"—and they belong together in life as well: first value, then commend.

The courage of our convictions is on occasion circumvented by the cunning of our feelings.

Some people are being spontaneous and others get to pick up the pieces left by this chaotic arhythmia.

Nothing outwardly visible may change once infidelity has come between two people. They may live on discreetly (and discretely), yet everything is different. Integrity is gone and something makeshift, ramshackle, compromised replaces it. In this invisible cataclysm the ceremony of innocence is drowned and what is left is the labor of carrying on.

The vice of perfectionism: the frenzy of a perfectionist nestmaker who requires that everything must be tidied up and tied down before human matters can be attended to, and since woman's work is never done, human attention never gets paid: "Later, dear."

There are these macho types who think they owe it to themselves to despise others for their unwillingness to give pain to defend principle. They look too much like they're enjoying themselves.

If you spurn what life has on offer because you must have it exactly your way, you'll lose out—or you may get it exactly your way.

There's some ultimate profit in being shaken out of one's self-possession, in having to reconstruct one's shattered self-configuration, in re-collecting oneself. We pretty much rebound and come back together as we were in any case, though a little remodeled. Nonetheless: Never do it to anyone else. That work of destruction is double—the hurtful intentions and the havoc wrought.

You can manufacture a pretense of hurt out of a mere difference of opinion.

The ultimate stupidity is to allow yourself to despise a person who loves you. It's self-denigration with a nasty detour.

All human relations are going to develop flaws, and we had better learn the unwisdom of making the best the enemy of the good. Be it by tolerant compromise or by realistic resignation, we'd better learn to curb the unviable inflexibility of perfectionist desire.

Sometimes it's time to break open the old time-lock on the expression of affection. But it takes an uneasy couple of qualities: temerity and dexterity.

Self-pity, figuring oneself as delicate, easily bruised, and requiring respectful comfort, is an enjoyable *jeu d'esprit,* but if you don't start laughing soon, its fine fragrance turns into a festering sump.

Out in the world sins of omission generally count as less bad than sins of commission. In love they're the worst, because there it is: anything rather than nothing.

One manifestation of original sin: The strong are ever in the wrong: their deeds are acts of domination and their quiescence is a sign of insensibility.

Goodheartedness: simulating cheerfulness so that the other's grief can hold center stage.

What I say I mean as true. *That* I say it I mean for you.

Since the heart incubates its messages in obscurity, don't confound a person, who wants to confide, with obstructive cluelessness. It's repulsive in both senses of the word.

Imputing sins, reckoning up transgressions—all the wound-licking spleen—give it up and practice the gallantry of the heart.

"The hell with it"—that joyous kicking up of the heels of order—the unholy holiday of the dutiful spirit.

Why should being caught by surprise be the true proof of virtue? It's a test of one's quick mental reflexes. Whether we have courage, charity, or candor comes out when we've had time to be ourselves.

The righteousness that thinks its urgencies trump civility is self-convicted of self-righteousness.

I have a suspicion of humility. You must think your life is very bright to need hiding under a bushel.

When in doubt, have faith.

Insecurity and entrenchment: It's a piece of public psychology in this country that lack of confidence leads to inflexibility, that valuing the opposition without giving in to it is a sign of strength. The trouble is that saying so doesn't make people any more secure in themselves.

How can motives be pure when the mind is at work all day and much of the night, all week, every month, through the years? What is there that hasn't passed through it, good, bad, fine, ignoble? What contingencies and inevitabilities, what possibilities and necessities haven't crossed it? What matters is not what we consider but what we choose.

I seem to mind less about flaws of character than about natural defects of temperament, desiccation, coldness, obtuseness, crudeness. That's because for them there is no cure and therefore no responsibility: You can't blame people for being thus defective—and yet you want to.

Some people are like active volcanoes: If you live by them you can expect eruptions with antic regularity. What pressures are continually building deep in their soul-crater? Should we pity them, try to suppress them, or just run away? In their quiescent periods they tend to have an exquisite sort of sweetness.

People think it's hard-won discipline, when it's the free gift of zest.

It's true that good people are naive. They have rock-bottom souls; it's the immoralist who lives over an abyss. It follows that to be decent and deep as well is quite a trick.

If you're serious you're not earnest: Live seriousness, dead earnest.

Illumination while having lunch with a student who wanted to talk about the question: Why was freedom evidently not an issue for the Spartans? We discovered: Being contained is not being restrained if you find your community somewhere, somehow exhilarating.

Depart from your assigned role: It's exhilarating. Act outside your character: It's devastating. For your role is socially assigned and your character is largely self-made;

so escape from the one is a momentary liberation and from the other a consequence-laden collapse.

Acting superior is an impropriety for those who are superior because they are superior, and for those who aren't because they aren't.

Why are mixed motives thought to indicate that there's no single intention? Don't various perspectives prove there's *one* object?

When people fish for assurance or compliments it's a double rebuff not to take the hook: They are detected in an ignoble ploy, and they're left in need. So just play along.

Selflessness can't be called a vice but it is a love-repelling defect because we become real to each other through our passion, our effective selfhood. Sonya in *War and Peace* is the exemplar of selflessness, a cat-like clammy wraith, a ubiquitous nobody, asking to be used. The trouble is, how can you have empathy or sympathy with a non-being?

When our feelings rebel against the decisions of thought and thought insists, the result is cold action (a.k.a. duty). You can do that on occasion, but you can't live that way. Kant's Categorical Imperative—Be true to your rational will—is good for the knife's edge of moral decision but not for the continuum of daily life.

If you decide for prudence over principle, you'd better have excellent judgment.

Doing good is a dangerous business: "No good deed goes unpunished." That is because it's dominance if needed and intrusion if unwanted. And in retrospect it's often felt to have been unwanted: "Did I ask you?" (In fact, you did); "Just because I said . . . , you're looking and judging." (Probably true.)

So you have to know what you're doing. First of all, everyone who gives is somehow already in the wrong, because giving is an act of expansive self-assertion, and all but the most generous receivers know that: "It is more blessed to give than to receive" does bear that construction. Second, beware of this subconscious thought: "I can afford it, I won't even remember my benevolence to you—unless you offend me and then I'll remember with a vengeance." It's for gratitude as for an offense: much better than forgiving a debt is forgetting it altogether, pouf. Third, on your own part, be unabashedly grateful for benefactions received.

Polonius had it half right about "Neither a borrower nor a lender be." Why shouldn't I borrow if I'm sure I can repay? But never lend money, at least in your mind. Lend it ostensibly, if it helps your friend over the asking, but regard it as a gift in your heart. That way you'll have many pleasant surprises and no grief. I know people say that you'll be colluding with irresponsibility. So am I the moral enforcer?

If you know that someone means to hurt you it nullifies the substance but not the intention.

A man without integrity might think acutely, originally, even deeply—but not truly. But how can there be depth without truth? I think there can't be, because there are questions *and* answers. Deep and novel questions are framed by a subtle and penetrating intelligence. But formulating trust-inspiring answers depends on an attentive receptivity, a willingness to refrain from constructions, that is, the fabrications of the intelligence. Conclusion: a philosopher with bad character is a living contradiction in terms.

Imagine the divinity thus. It means us not to fuss much about our moral status: If you're about to sin, desist; if you have sinned, repair the wrong or mitigate it; if you're doing it now, abate it or live with it, but don't indulge in concurrent guilt feelings. Guilt *feelings* are from the conscience in its misty mode, when it evades hard-edged guilt and painful repentance.

Do always what you wish, and in a pinch wish to do what you must.

Life without heroes would be like star-gazing in the absence of stars with apparent magnitude less than 1 (the brighter the smaller the number, to make this simile intelligible). But my heroes aren't "role models." For one thing, I don't play my life as a role—it's the real thing, if anything is. For another, a hero is not a model to imitate but an adviser to consult. I might cite my heroes' words, but then I put quotations around them, I don't speak them in my own person. In short, I don't identify with my lifelong heroes, because I want to observe them, not be them.

People shouldn't lay reforming hands on what they don't love.

When on the verge of meanness ask yourself: *cui bono?*

One test of heroism is lonely coping. If you discover that's been going on, you've found a hero or heroine (in the sense of bravery).

I used to think psychological counselors couldn't possibly help people because they seemed to do a reverse kind of curve tracing, fitting all the points of complaint onto a grief-graph whose name was a catalogued syndrome. Then I saw that this was itself a comfort: to have a trouble others have, to belong again to the human race, to get standard, wisely harmless advice.

Here's a good kind of schizophrenia ("splitmindedness"): In public, to be on top of things, to act with sober judiciousness, with the élan of competence and the tractableness of confidence—in private, to be receptive, willingly in service to greatness, truly ancillary.

Purity is fragilely static; semi-purity is incessantly arduous.

Why praise unconditional love? Why should the suspension of judgment be a virtue (except in parents where love beyond reason is not moral but natural)? Even the truly bewitched become disenchanted in time with incorrigible corruption. At least they do in novels. (The worst people I know personally are only pitiably awful.)

Best: Do it right. Worst: Do it wrong. Mean: Don't do it at all.

People want their sins taken seriously, appreciated, so to speak. It's, oddly enough, unkind to say and unwelcome to hear "So what?"

There are strenuously disciplined people, but so much of their energy goes into being virtuous that the work done is sometimes lifeless. I believe in more weasely ways, like self-trickeries and self-incentives, since who cares how it gets done, if only it gets done? Of course the best way is the zest of love.

There are unsingable heroes who specialize in not making notable noises. For example, they never give offense and never take it, thinking it unlikely that anyone would single them out. They don't much seem in need of consolation, and they seem to absorb endless responsibilities. Or are they volcanoes waiting this long decade to erupt?

Honesty (tempered by discretion) is the best policy.

Grace under pressure is a gift not a virtue. To be sure, one should have a kit of emergency opinions handy, but sudden demands on our nervous system are hardly the way to bring out our truths. The character is not, like the body, trainable to hair-trigger responses. Still, if it's extended pressure, we should have the elasticity to rebound and recover ourselves. And that's a matter of surface remembering—without recollection of reasons and grounds—what must be our first responses: what's nonnegotiable, what's to be saved whatever else goes. In other words, our most thoughtful principles must now be to hand as mere opinions, unquestionable convictions. Thereafter the consulting and coping can begin. It might even look like grace, but it won't be. It'll be anticipation.

Every soul (I imagine) has its ape, a vindictive, resentful, whining shadow capering along, which vanishes at high noon, the moment of truth.

Our deviltry: that we can be so shallowly ashamed of and so hugely pleased by transgressions we get away with.

There's a cliché about not taking ourselves too seriously. But what would a community be worth that did not think that it was at the center of the universe, enclosing "the still point of the turning world"? I can bear a little comicality as the price of this pride in being close to the moving midst of a life that matters: the center-seeking gravity of my colleagues.

Don't let mulishness and inertia keep you from declaring affection—it's a crime against time.

For fulfilling a wish I apply to my imagination, for accomplishing my will I use my ingenuity.

In controlled amounts whining is good for the soul, better than raging; the tepid forms of self-indulgence are more reparable.

A socio-moral commandment: You're responsible for the air-tightness of your dissimulation if you think a social conversation is boring or clueless. America runs on intentionally pointless pleasantries. Do not subvert civility by an inopportune sincerity.

Simplicity of soul can go with a sophisticated sensibility, and conversely, naive tastes can go with a complex character. That's how we surprise each other.

Most speech is at its best when specific, but there is a realm of terrible things one should not describe audibly.

Ebullience, expansiveness is a warm circumambience to its practitioner but a crude intrusion to the onlooker.

Much apparent arrogance, especially American-style, is just heedless exuberance. When checked, the perpetrators feel at once innocent of any bad intention and guilty—of what? If they could tell it would probably be: guilty of taking up too much space—a very vacuous evil.

The worst temperamental composition: exquisitely nervous sensibility and the yearning for orgiastic excitement—probably worse for the possessor than for his readers, if he's a writer.

Two sorts deserve the disasters they bring on themselves: detractors of reason and demolishers of republics. Unfortunately, they bring it on their tradition and their nation too.

They talk of "giving people their dignity." But that's surely a solecism. You can't give or take what people have or lack on their own. If you humiliate others, it's your dignity, not theirs, that's lost.

Without some sort of transcendent reference the human virtues become as labile as our temperaments. Moreover, our moods go flat in their depths while their surfaces are hyper-excitable. Hence come the intellectual searchings for sophisticatedly absurd innovations, the pleasure-seeking for riskily extreme novelties. This is an observation, not a recommendation.

We keep advising each other to see the other side. It's actually only too easy to see the other side, since most human actions can be articulately explained, and explanations easily go over into justifications, usually by social situation or psychic necessity. What's hard is not to be shaken out of one's common sense by being co-opted as an insider to the other's world. And then there are actions so bad that we should not even wish for the ability to see the perpetrator from the inside out, that is, to empathize with him. For what would we have to become, such that evil would be understandable to us?

We owe it to human dignity to acquire the art of letting people down easy. It is shame enough to have failed in an appeal, we shouldn't add loss of countenance to the rebuff.

It is said that people direct their lives by making choices at the forkings of life's crossroads: "Two roads diverged in a wood, and I— / I took the one . . . ," well, whichever; that's not what befell me, nor did I make the choice of Heracles at the Crossroads: I never seem to have confronted either Frost's road less traveled or the hero's path of virtue. As I recall it, I grew into myself, surveyed my inward prospects, and luck colluded by opening viable byways. I figured incessantly and then let nature take it away. That's what Socrates' myth at the end of the *Republic* means: The main choice precedes life; the decisions within life are more like its realizations.

14 POLITICS: PRIVATELY PUBLIC

There is a coincidence of opposites in politics, such that one may pass through the extreme left to arrive at the extreme right and vice versa. Imagine a horizontal baseline as long as you please, a short upright upon it in front of you and from its top a line intersecting the base to the right. Rotate this line in the plane so that it crosses this base farther and farther out, and when its angle with the upright reaches a right angle the two lines will be parallel, or they may be said to intersect at an ideal point, a point at infinity. Keep rotating and the intersection will appear on the other side, as if it had passed behind the back of space to reappear on the left. So too the far-out right reappears as the far-out left having passed through an idealizing mental space. But there's nothing innocuous about this ideal passage, this going around the back of reality by means of an idealism that is radically removed from the finite human condition and is the space of *per-se* radicalism, any and all radicalism.

To be my kind of populist you have to distinguish between people's sense (pretty good) and their taste (not always so good).

Romance—the beauty of one's land and the grandeur of one's history; reason—the intelligibility of one's country's foundations and the decency of its politics: How perilous it is to live in a nation that is rich in the first and failing in the second respect, the nation that requires irrational love.

The burgher's contrary frights: the fear that an unsecured life will get you and the fear that if you're hunkered down it'll pass you by.

The real gain from our diversity is the delight of seeing sameness in difference, the human visage with differently disposed features. That's on the public scale. Then, in private life, it's the other way around: The type begins to be particular, personal. Much of love's delight is to discern the paradigm personalized.

Diversity is our latest nervous tic. I think it's a top-down ideology. Immigrants don't want to be diverse until incited to be. They want to be homogenized (or, more elegantly, assimilated) as quickly as possible; "finding their roots" is for the grandchildren. Americans, on the other hand, can't possibly be expected to show a professional anthropologist's interest in all the human tribes. The best thing is to make friends on common ground, where the hyper-personal differences add a fragrant spice to our common life. In fact, food is the most pacifying diversity-appreciation agent—who doesn't like ethnic cuisine? ("Cuisine" yet.)

The art of rhetoric seems to be this: to infuse public speech with personal conviction or—and this way round focuses on the art needed—to express personal conviction in public terms. This art consists of making the "I believe" the sensed but indiscernible undertone of the thematic tenor. Otherwise put: Your listeners have to sense your soul while they hear your argument. It isn't so different in private conversation: You find an objective formulation for your most intimate feelings.

Authority: People suspect you're human but they don't bet on it.

The social illusion: I talk about you but you don't talk about me. What's there to talk about anyway? I lead a blameless life (if the truth about my conduct were but properly explained).

In public action bad judgment is mighty close to immorality. What to sacrifice: the vulnerable human being to the sheltering institutions; careful planning to seizing the moment; one's own immaculateness to peace and preservation?

A sure test of politics (the sectarian sort): getting hot under the collar. You can always tell in a classroom or a collegial setting, and the thing is to retreat with alacrity.

Three configurations: active, receptive, passive, and their degenerated versions: busy, consuming, supine. Activity is fulfillment in being at work; receptivity is openness to world and soul; passivity (in the literal sense) liveliness of affects and passions. Busyness is motoric action, consumption frantic acquisitiveness, supineness mental inertia. Three by three they seem to me to be the possible configurations of life.

Should one trust an official who is all official, who has no private retreats and recesses? Action in the external realm shouldn't obliterate the life of our first and last world, the source of our humanity.

Discrimination has gotten a bad name at the moment. What a pity they couldn't find a more telling word for what is meant: invidious distinction. For we can't live without discriminating, discerning, making just and fine distinctions. But perhaps the word-legislators knew what they were doing, and the hidden agenda was not just to abolish bigotry but differentiation *per se*—between male and female, classical and popular, public and private, you name it.

Radical egalitarians mean to abolish liberal equality which is precisely the equity not of homogenous but of incommensurable beings.

By nature, or so it seems to me, the body is particular, private, forbidden, except for the parts custom allows us to expose (more, inch by inch). The intellect, on the other hand, is naturally public, communicable without remainder (except for lack of time and articulateness). There are always people who reverse that: Their bodies are quite publicly accessible to inspection and conversation (in the archaic sense) while their minds are their most private parts, gone opaque from suppression and lack of expressiveness. (Of course there are stupidly silent indecorous people, and also, as I know because one was once my landlady, articulately intelligent whores.)

It's a high point of honor to keep confidences and part of that is not to appear to have any to keep.

The best way to keep one's own secrets is either to seem not to have any or to be totally candid. If you're secretive you just concentrate conjecture on yourself. If you simply tell curious people what they want to know, half the time they cease to care and the other half they can't tell that they've been told something of consequence. Note: Friendly interest isn't curiosity.

Privacy really is a sort of privation. (Not for nothing is the Greek word for a private person *idiotes*.) It takes some deliberate retreating, warding off, withdrawal from responsibility. It's an indulgence, a small sin against friendship.

It's not a private act, a matter of mere private preference, to make private matters public; it has large public consequences.

"Revolution," as in Copernicus's *De Revolutionibus Orbium Coelestium,* once meant the steady cycling of the heavenly spheres. Well, the terrestrial revolutions turn out not to be so different: Things go round, then come round, by the decade or the century.

A social conscience is the moral equivalent of the warrior spirit: relief from boredom, escape from family, legitimized interference, and diversion from self-improvement. The only reformers I thoroughly trust are the ones who'd rather be doing something else.

Three kinds of radicality: axing the roots, cultivating the roots, exposing the roots—revolution, tradition, reflection. Which kind of radical is the most dangerous?

What we all know in private life, that impossible dreams inflict hurt, is just as true in public: Unrealistic expectations do harm. Fantastic daydreaming displaces energetic imagining, and hyperbolic hopes end in apathy.

In good and serious revolutionists rebellion is disappointed devotion.

The new class war of the sixties: the new little lords, whose social superiority was, as in the old Lady Bountiful days, expressed as social concern. And there were other lordly analogues: the lackadaisical willowiness and affected inarticulateness reviving the British upper-class stance and stammer, freakish dress, long hair and prankishness reminiscent of the Oxonians in the thirties, dilettantism and contempt for those willing parental wage slaves who had earned the supporting patrimonies, and a far too insouciant pacifism. But those older aristocrats died in the Battle of Britain, while these nouveau-nobles were merely "co-opted" as they grew past thirty. They have lovely children, though.

Four maxims of political morality: Never assist in word or deed in the weakening of a young republic (lesson of Weimar). Never introduce moral purity into political rhetoric (lesson of the French Terror). Never participate in a demonstration, since a. the individual conscience of a liberal democracy is inappropriately expressed in mass meetings; b. "demonstration" properly understood being the reasoned argument proving a proposition or an effective act confirming a feeling (as in: "She demonstrated her love by . . ."), and moreover, the corruption of verbal significance being a sin against the commonwealth, a pseudo-demonstration should be scouted like a false proof; c. since such demonstrations are also public theater, i.e., exciting and exhausting amusements, they sap the taste for the small, sober, private acts of politics, such as going to the voting booth; as the Christian Bible says "When thou prayest, enter into thy closet," so do your public duty privily first—and, of course, read, listen, and talk. And d. never suppose that your (or anyone's) announcement of anger gives you any moral claim; on the contrary, if your argument is "I'm very angry," then reply to yourself: "Then calm yourself down until you've regained reasonableness."

There *is* righteous anger, deep and long-breathed, and it only shows in deeds.

Many of the supposed novelties of the sixties student revolution were in fact repetitions of the European liberation of the twenties, unbeknownst, of course, to the participants who thought, as goes a Russian proverb, that they were "discovering America." But these features weren't news even then; they were the rejects of our tradition, well-known and feared; they were willfully resurrected old proscribed possibilities: the rebellious intake of forbidden stuff that makes experience vivid and evil exciting, together with the tempting of innocent partners (cf. Genesis 3); the joys of irrationality, recreational "experimenting" (a disingenuous co-option of a term of research), distrust of the elders, and so on. *Le plus ça change*. . . . I predict a high-tech version of the sixties starting about 2010.

In the sixties the students became a mob aristocracy: contempt for their own middle class, imaginary solidarity with the workers, affected languor (later "cool"), presumed inviolability from the law, and infinite leisure for imaginative high-jinks. Nowadays they're a hard-working lot, earning their expensive but evidently valued education.

Re-established order usually means a lot more rules, with opposite aims: to codify the expansion of rights and to suppress the next round of activism.

The three American temperaments: "If you're not part of the solution, you're part of the problem"—activist; "where there's a big problem, we need a big solution"—liberal; "if it ain't broke, don't fix it"—conservative. Amongst these we muddle through better than most, thank you.

There are party conservatives and there are temperamental conservatives, toughies and traditionalists, and they're not really very close, the latter being at heart conservationists, lovers of losing causes (which do sometimes serendipitously turn profitable).

There seem to be two sorts of utopianism—the radical, rational, ideological, totalitarian kind and the conservative, imaginative, traditional, local kind. The first is a social design which, even in its attempted realization, is dystopian; the other is an archetypal image which, being not a project but an animating reminiscence, is Edenic.

The bully conservatives know as little about conservation as the officious liberals know about liberty or the ranting radicals about roots.

During times of public stress, like war, certain mental illnesses and suicides are said to decrease. That's surely not an argument for the redemptive power of war but an illumination of the human condition in peace: Normalcy is the most stringent tester of souls.

Behold a briskly officious, incisively by-the-book person in the office and expect an agonizing ditherer at home (where you don't want to follow this one).

The exposed public life has its soft center in the private parts.

There's wisdom in Article II of the Constitution requiring that the President be "a natural born citizen" (or a member of the founding generation). Immigrants may be ardent patriots but in their dreams they often go home, and a soul once uprooted may not be capable of a second deep rooting. There's a test and a way: Amend the article to say: "No person not a natural born citizen shall be eligible to the office of President who shall not, after a decade of residence in these United States, have returned for the period of at least one week to his/her native land for the purpose of discovering where home really is. . . ."

The politics of a small community: You need a good ear for distinguishing the perennial and healthy grousing (the escape valve of a polity) from the brewing storm, the complaints that have substance or passion or both behind them.

As a public person one wants to be understood, as a private self, one isn't so eager to be comprehended, embraced (figuratively) by unauthorized personnel—though there is a keen pleasure in the swift, light penetration of someone who suddenly sees right through you.

Governing questions: How much indiscipline can a mission-driven community absorb before it loses itself? How far ahead should it look before it mortgages its present to a conjectural future? How far is compromise reasonable before it begins to degrade principle? Is there something that "the" American people, "the" faculty, "the" student body (some body!) "think," and how is it clued out? Is it safer to be sanguine or wary, and if both, how do you do it? Is it true or deeply false that what doesn't "move forward" must fall behind?

Why discretion is advisable in small communities even about creditable personal knowledge: because leakage waters avidity.

There's no such thing as hiding or revealing, as concealing oneself or giving oneself away on deep matters, not if you mean to talk about them at all. The perplexity of depth is just that it is at once obscure and plain, dark and luminous. Why would one, how could one, compound these difficulties? All esotericism, intentional secretiveness, bears the mark, not necessarily of charlatanism, but of some sort of misapprehension. "Nature loves to hide" rightly says Heraclitus. Why should we help her?

A small, long-lived community is the natural setting for comedy—if the essence of comedy is the mechanical operation of the human spirit. On this stage we act out our assumed roles and ritual habits, lovable (or not so very) and laughable, irritating and exhilarating, each to all. Here we are inevitably and comically ourselves. And then, when it's least expected—a quantum departure from our blueprint, as if to prove that we've still got the principle of motion within ourselves (Aristotle's definition of "being by nature").

Old colleagues become their own character actors, one is ever the *enfant terrible,* one always smells a rat, one is committed to continual non-committalism, one needs detailed expositions of side issues (especially around 6 P.M.), one specializes in righteous indignation, one in ardent unintelligibility. Me? I talk succinctly and sensibly, of course.

The two conservatisms: reaction vs. reverence.

The trick in maintaining a community is, it seems, not to be so fanatical about preserving its essence as to endanger its existence, nor so anxious about its existence as to compromise its essence.

"Thought"—take it, for official purposes, as the past participle of "thinking." Have thought fundamentals out so that in a crisis you're sleepwalking, calculating your tactics, and not worrying over strategic goals: the practical zombiism of emergencies.

Be utterly candid and next to no one will know what you've got in mind.

Discretion is not keeping secrets so much as leaving no evidential handle, so that suspicion flutters in a vacuum and dies of inanition. A real secret is what no one even knows you have.

There is a sober exhilaration—I think of it as having a pearl-gray sheen—in being a citizen on several levels: college, city, county, state, country.

Anything that *is* a being, human or political, is most itself when it is at its best. That is what the ancient ontologists knew, and it is a source of working love.

Three kinds of democratic spirit: vulgarly resentful egalitarianism that finds every distinction offensive; friendly camaraderie that rejoices in fellow citizens as fellow souls; noble idealization that sees all humans as infinitely valuable. The middle kind you can live with best.

What divides fellow citizens where it most matters, in daily life, are sensibilities far more than opinions. Our thinking may be on opposite ends of the spectrum yet in the same dimension, but our tastes can be hopelessly askew. Example: different levels of toleration for noise.

We want to preserve our privacy just because we do with it about what everybody else does. There is a deep Jewish explanation: Our Ancestors covered their nakedness after learning to distinguish good and evil. There is a deep pagan explanation: Privacy issues from a natural sense of shame. But I mean something much more mundane: our desire to be alone when doing what comes naturally, what is common in the lower sense. Before the public we want to be dressed in dignity.

How wrong-headed is the notion that the public has a need or right to know anyone's "life"! Cassandra Austen destroyed those of her sister's letters she deemed private. We should thank her for a good example, not blame her for destroying "documents." Why should the memorabilia that people preserve as aids to their memory be "sources" after their death? Whose business are a woman's affairs of the heart or the originals of her novels' characters? Now if you *want* to be posthumously known into your most intimate recesses (as for example, did Thomas Mann), go to it.

The art is to be utterly personal without getting personal.

The world is deeply recalcitrant to constructive human action. To wit: Human beings can blow up in seconds what it took centuries to make; mess makes itself and clean-up takes effort; time (as says Aristotle, who doesn't assign it any other powers) can deteriorate but not build things; a feast may take days to prepare and an hour to eat; and in general the effort in effecting even a little good is disproportionate to the lasting effect. This isn't just a mood: Nature is behind it by being entropic (i.e., it is self-degrading in quantifiable ways). What saves us from apathy is that action itself is exhilarating and local improvements are deeply satisfying.

When you see an event shaping up, you have to thrash about some, trying not to misread your role: whether to stay out of it (ostensibly) or insert yourself (tactfully). The latter is approvingly called exerting leadership and the former remains unsung, but it lets things get done.

An oath is the ultimate public representation of your steady intention and of the soul's dignity, which consists of the freedom to commit itself and the moral memory that keeps faith.

Promises are private oaths and to be cavalier about them, to forget them, is tantamount to losing one's self, for one's continuing identity depends on memory, and one's moral self depends on remembering one's commitments. So when you say "I'll send you . . ." or "I'll look into it . . . ," you're as bound as if you'd sworn. Bolt's Thomas More says to his daughter: "When a man takes an oath, Meg, he's holding his self in his own hands. Like water. . . . And if he opens his fingers *then*—he needn't hope to find himself again" (*A Man for All Seasons*). And that goes for your mere word.

The double whammy of political catastrophe is that when the years of oppression and persecution come to an end, when the hour of liberation comes and with it relief from the laborious miseries of surviving and the exalting terrors of resisting—that is also the last collected day for souls overstretched.

To talk a lot about honor is surely the sign of an amateur in the field of distinction, just as to be preoccupied by aristocracy is the mark of a natural plebeian.

As I would not be a do-gooder so I would not be done good by . . . I don't mean acts of grace by friends but deeds of benevolence by rectifiers.

Swords into plowshares: Refashion problems by minute attention to their detail; Defang directives by meticulous attention to their style.

"Understanding the enemy" is in some cases virtuous blather. Am I to see my way into the heart of a terrorist? I hope that's impossible. But even that call to "learn about other countries" isn't quite serious: all 200 or so of them? Here's what we can do: know our own and learn to learn; then await the occasion.

The bottomlessly unimaginative naiveté of the empathy mongers: We are to understand that we are rich and politically relatively sound, while the world that is said to hate us (it's clearly a love-hate relationship) is unimaginably poor and socially sick. What then? You want to know what hatred is? Try benevolence.

If I were education dictator for a day, I would leave everything strictly alone (unlike the D. of E.), except for three (funded) recommendations: Pre-kindergarten to first grade: every child to learn to dance the minuet, in culottes, jabots, and little (rubber) daggers; grades ten through twelve: everybody to read and discuss the founding documents; in between kids to build small-scale railroads or sailboats or harpsichords. Result: graceful, handy citizens.

Money: Everyone should have enough, I should have a little more, some people should be rich. It is a miserable country in which the poor outnumber the well-enough off, but so would it be a dreary world without large private wealth.

The most remarkable (implicit) teaching of Plato's *Republic* and to my mind the most useful: that ontology is a better preparation for governing a good community than management science, that knowing how flows from knowing what.

It's partly a temperamental matter: Some are revisionists, some conservationists; some take satisfaction in puncturing the present condition, others in shoring it up. The aptitude needed for either way is different. Those who collapse common opinion need to *know* what comes next; those who maintain the *status quo* need to *imagine* the ideal behind it.

Public activity without a strong inner base is centerless, privacy that doesn't emerge into the open world is without shaping circumference.

Freedom is an end, *the* end, for those deprived of it, but it is merely a means for those assured of it.

Why others' personal secrets become less and less interesting: because they are mostly human-all-too-human, and such attraction as they have is largely in one's becoming privy to the soul's classified knowledge and hardly in the facts themselves.

In bad times shortages make us comrades, in good times competitors.

Tolerance that is willing indifference is an enforceable democratic mode; if you try to ratchet it up into mutual appreciation it becomes a festering irritation.

Leadership is an intricate texture of pride and devotion, self-fulfillment and self-sacrifice.

These pairs are not really analogues, though they are intricately related: public-private, impersonal-personal, distant-intimate, objective-subjective. And they all cross-cut: Public matters can be deeply personally felt, intimate matters can be objectively expressed, private affairs can be viewed with a certain distance.

The power to act turns anxiety into deliberation.

Those who are in charge of a community don't actually live *in* it, but in time they will again—a most salutary fact to keep in mind.

One interpretation of being sensible: Be anticounterintuitive. Skewer perverse sophistications. Prime example: the claim that truth is a social construction; here that sophomoric clincher is irresistible: This one too?

Some people, taken as causes, are bottomless pits. You can labor mightily in their behalf without any discernible accumulation of good: The worst will be thought and no quarter given.

The practical details of governing are much more effective when not jigged by the advice of experts but loosely conformed to the dictates of wisdom.

Good governing—a combination of simplicity and cunning: simple faith in the ends, cunning construction of the means.

The rigidified language of bureaucrats is the camouflage for professional stage fright. They're afraid they'll forget their lines unless they rehearse them, because they've forgotten their meaning, if they ever knew it.

The paradox of position in a body politic: The head of a community is *ipso facto* out of it.

Whether we are inextricably social or radically individual beings and thus what our situation made us or what we make ourselves, whether meaning is inseparably contextual or ultimately atomic, that is, whether sentences precede nouns or nouns sentences—aren't these and similar questions of priority to be answered by way of judgment calls, framed to meet the excesses of the day?

When you're in authority you're in abeyance as a self, subservient to the office, genuinely absorbed by the task most of the time, now and then dutifully faking it.

"Having trouble with authority" turns out to be an official DSM (Diagnostic and Statistical Manual) category. Well, I've met a few of these would-be rebels. They're often lovably spirited kids, who are, *mirabile dictu,* in a rut and need an affectionate kick. In the adult world it seems to be true that those who needle the powers that be are totally clueless about how to be the power that is.

Like the kudzu vine that grows a foot a day and drapes itself over a whole grove of trees, the administrative function burgeons and blankets the communal purpose: Since it's driven by government regulation and parental demand it can, at best, be moderated. So much the more is it necessary for the administrators to remember and live up to their name: people who minister *to.* . . . They are adjuncts of some purpose, not absolute, autarchic sovereigns.

What a blessing Jefferson's crystalline shallowness was for this country! Who else could have declared politically usable and intellectually dubious truths with such passionately rational certitude?

The best defense against personal aggression: Remain impenetrably uncomprehending.

Sufficient unto the evil is the day thereof: Solve every problem on the very day if at all possible; don't let things brew and stew. But give good things time.

Listen the life out of zany notions; articulated at length, they often self-destruct.

Professed provos dream of announcing something startlingly new, when they are garbling something tiresomely old.

"Vision" is what governing bodies acquire when they want to evade their more expensive duties, such as maintaining what good there is in their institutions and paying its workers-in-the-field living wages.

Just as people's words when they've got hot under the collar are not to be taken seriously as to substance, so books that are written in the heat of anger teach us about nothing much except the writer's frame of mind.

Lord and liege: Those who govern with natural authority know how to serve with noble loyalty, now as then.

Tyrants, ancient and contemporary, prove over and over to be ingeniously efficient at deeds of devastation and almost guilelessly inept at works of salvation, even self-salvation.

15 INTELLECTUALS:
SHEEP IN WOLVES' CLOTHES

Intellectuals roar like lions, think like sheep, act like monkeys.

A rope will sooner pass through the needle's eye than a brilliant person will enter the gates of wisdom. Smart and wise are (practically) mutually exclusive.

Intellectuals sometimes talk like the wicked son in the Haggadah, who asks "What do *you* mean by this service?"—as if he weren't one of us.

Most golden surfaces hide some dark depths. But who gave one clan the exclusive mission of muckraking? Injustice should be exposed, but I trust the exposé most when it comes from solid participating citizens. Socrates says that those govern most reliably who don't want to, and I think those are the most trustworthy social critics who have come to it reluctantly, not with the professional's gusto.

Intellectuals are the aborigines of time-serving, studiously obsequious to their master, the Trend, sedulously assisting their Times.

How many words used in a cleverly critical article are really known by the author, really known in their denotation, connotation, etymology, history, in all the respects one might call the language's language? How much of such journalism is ritualistically neologistic twaddle, with new words for every piddling thought produced by the concept-engine? Walt Whitman speaks of "the union always surrounded by blatherers and always calm and impregnable" (Preface to *Leaves of Grass*). Let's hope.

Intellectuals are people who professionally saw off the branch they're sitting on—and the tree keeps paying them to do it.

Defining modes of social critics: Clarifying the historical situation by purveying apocalypse; playing procurer to the future by betraying the present; fabricating the excitation of self-spooking; exulting in the frisson of evil reports.

Intellectuals are driven into their particular corner partly by their rude and lusty counterparts the boor-scientists (my biologist-colleague's term), who move easily among those exemplars of second nature, the black boxes of the laboratory, but are out of their element with the black boxes of original nature, their fellow human beings.

Conceptual constructs: A puling thought with a neological label—presto! a theory.

Just as words chase each other circularly in a dictionary touching the base of meaning only in passing, so literary criticism often goes round in a circle touching the book only incidentally.

There's good sense to be found at either end: at the heights the wisdom of philosophers, at the base the sagacity of ordinary folks; in between it's the sophisms of the intellectuals.

There's a notion among publicists that ferreting out literary scandal and publishing it is an act of intellectual courage—a curious courage that dares nothing (except the mild contempt of unknown readers) and gains welcome notoriety. These exposés are totally *de trop:* We all know *that* every life, relation, institution has its underside; why would we wish to know *what* it is?

Intellectual arsonists—who with caustic intelligence burn to cinders the rickety structures we live in.

Fuss-potters and lit-critters: They demonstrate a flaw in the world's design. Why is it easier to expose a defect than to do a thing well and to deconstruct a text than to write a good book?

To congenital critics kindness of character is cause for suspecting constitutional naiveté, and simplicity of soul is explicable only as pathological obtuseness.

You watch some smart sophisticated intellectuals disporting themselves with their kind on talk shows or developing their theories on paper, and then you figure them spraying silicon into their sticky lock, and you think how humanizing American life is.

Intellectuals are the literal socialists of literature; they are much more interested in the social commentary to be gotten from a novel than in its imaginative world.

Some intellectuals are infinitely fascinating and infinitesimally interesting.

Reporting is that odd profession in which, if you actually do something constructive, you're being unprofessional.

It's nice that the Greek translation of journalism is ephemeralism: preoccupation with the fleeting day. News is by its nature a perishable commodity.

Watching reporters at a war briefing is like watching my two-year-olds at nursery school just before snack time: The need for instantaneous feeding with what they like makes them very cranky.

Why really is the fact of people demonstrating more newsworthy than that of people going to work? Because fewer do the one than the other and less often. So that's newsworthiness: what happens more rarely and involves fewer people.

The flockers: Reverence for great works is an intellectual virtue, but fascination by great men is a personal vice. A particularly shaming case is the flock of sheep around Goethe, and it seems that he was implicated. People felt a frisson at his demonism (I wonder if we'd be as vulnerable or if in this country it would seem more like brilliant willfulness). These poetic hangers-on seem to have been either diminished by a sense of inferiority or inflated by a notion of equality with this uncanny goblin. It is all testimony to their remoteness from an Anglo-Saxon sense of personal dignity, which admits hierarchies, once of birth and now of gifts, without relinquishing the original personal equality of every member of the species. Here's how it seems to me: It would be a reflection on our own boorishness not to honor (not to speak of love) those who make great works. But we are their addressees, and if we weren't in various ways up to their greatness their works would speak to a void. So occupation with greatness may be sometimes daunting, but it's not humiliating. Both the critic's flaunting superiority and the amateur's cringing subordination are false positions.

Homo academicus wears againstness like a uniform.

Those crybabies in an imagined wilderness, the very secure and protected groups like intellectuals and faculties with their continual seizures of *petit mal:* What can one say to them but: "You ain't seen nothing yet"?

If Herodotus had been to the university or Tocqueville to graduate school, would we know much about Greece or America?

16 PAST: HISTORICAL RELUCTANCE

Historians see epochs because people are perukes to them.

Three personal ways of absorbing contemporary history: 1. lap up the trendy froth knowing that in a decade it will invoke a mildly pleasant nostalgia; 2. take it in as the current manifestation of our master epoch, a retro-, neo-, or post-version of modernity; 3. savor it as an aura coloring the birth year of non-historical beings, like babies and books.

"Reluctance" in physics is the resistance to the establishment of electric flux, the lines of force through a current-carrying coil. To me it is an article of faith that we should be reluctant historians and mount resistance to the notional establishment of historical currents and forces, to the suprahuman flux of history, to impersonal "historical forces." These phantasms are the self-spooking of the intellectuals, lending a frisson of inevitability to their fears and an élan of irresistibility to their longings. Having foregone the suprahuman divinity, they evidently needed a substitute specter.

"Opinion" is a burden-carrying word for Socrates. It means people not quite knowing what they are doing or not understanding what they're saying or, above all, not actually thinking their thoughts. I think most of what goes for the Spirit of the Times is just people living off opinions. There are of course the instigators of these opinions (in historical terms, the incarnations of the Time-Spirit); their role proves that suprahuman history can't after all be left to its own devices—it needs human agents.

The whipping boy, Society: "I'm depraved on account I'm deprived" (*West Side Story*). Now does that mean I'm to blame or not?

Time advances continuously but history can't, or it would never be told. So it is treated as what evolutionists call "punctuated equilibrium"—stretches of stasis and points of eventfulness. And, we having ten digits, the events accommodatingly occur in decadal spurts and give each decade its flavor: from the conformist fifties through the liberated sixties to the greedy nineties, each with its defining moments. I know this much: Having agonized my way through each of them, I'm none the wiser. For example, aside from contradictory conjectures, I have no idea what in fact will come next, which, if history were intelligible, I should surely know. Perhaps the terrified century?

There is in fact one, and only one empirically derivable Law of History: More. Well, better more—more people, files, speed, you name it—than pouf, nothing.

If history has a moving force, my guess is that it's a contradiction in terms: inertial acceleration. People follow a trend—a trend being just people in the following mode latching on to something to follow, that's all—and do it more and faster, just the way amateur pianists unintentionally speed up the tempo as they go. Trendsetters tend to whip up motion; could there be one who led into quiescence? Yes, but it would be trendy repose—probably with a competitive component.

The believers in historical progress (not so many now) offer an odd syllogism: History is progressive. Things are getting pretty bad. Therefore the terrestrial paradise is at hand.

How strange is the process by which moving life turns into fixed history: Today real passage, tomorrow imaged past! But the truth is, it usually came to us already in image form: recorded. Few of us are the direct eyewitnesses of our time.

Prediction: Whole countries will declare themselves museums and charge admission for a nostalgia-trip; there will be schools of music composing in all the classical musical canons under their own labels; people in some lands will wear period costumes and maintain lending wardrobes for time travelers. Here's an aesthetic question: Is it in principle impossible for these researched renaissances to outdo their originals? And a hermeneutic one: Will a theme-park re-creation of the contemporary Eastern seaboard include our Williamsburg? And the one built three hundred years later, will it include a re-creation of a re-creation—recursion gone mad? For surely to a historically sensitive mind each re-creation will bear somewhere the stamp of its times; for example, the present costumed guides in theme parks are probably wearing underwear that would astonish their originals.

How will future ages come to deal with us, their past, who are privately and publicly so exhaustively documented? They will be excessively time-burdened; to rerun all the recorded evidence, reread all the documents and commentary, dig up all the ruins, would take up not only their lifetimes but all their real estate. They have these options: Give up archeology, which is grass-roots history, altogether or dig deep in small sites, which will surely give a skewed notion of our artifactual life. And historians too may either become minutely specialized or broadly abstract. Oh well, it's their problem. Ours is not to provide premature ruins.

Imagine our ancient heroes documented in their somatic peculiarities: an undersized Achilles, a bowlegged Odysseus (I keep forgetting they never were embodied), an actually ugly Socrates, a swarthy David. But perhaps their flesh and blood reality was even more captivating than their imagined memory?

I looked for Greece in the excavations of Attica and found America in its curators, and the Greeks came to life not in the excavations of the ancient marketplace of Athens where I worked but in the texts of a little college in Annapolis where I teach.

Shallow and skewed interpretations of history are probably more practically effective than the results of thorough and accurate research, for two reasons: The deeper you go the more the human beings of diverse epochs are alike, which rather spoils any specifically historical lesson, and also the more accurate you get the less it adds up: Imagine a small fracas in your college or firm or family; when it's over, who can figure out what it was all about? Now multiply it by millions of participants.

When imagining the past of a place don't omit the dreams investing them: Southwestern canyons dreaming of the Anastasi, the Old Ones; Great Plains towns dreaming of their European roots, as in "American Gothic;" medieval castles dreaming of Jerusalem; Athenian porticos dreaming of Troy; Babylon dreaming of Uruk.

The land of the soul is always in a past; think of the Mediterranean dream of Mann's *Magic Mountain,* of Yeats's Byzantium, of Rose Macauley's Trebizond.

Herodotus publishes his *Historía,* his Inquiry, "so that the things that have come from human beings may not fade out"—"from human beings," *ex anthropon:* His inquiry is "anthropological," an account of humanity, comprising Greeks and barbarians equally, and equally recording their "great and marvelous deeds"—lovely lessons in memorability, recorded in his suave Ionic language. This is my historian. For the most marvelous deeds in the most far-flung lands still come from the local motions of individual souls, and Herodotus never forgets that. His *Inquiry* turns up people thinking both with and against the customs of their countries.

Great deeds fit large venues, but the intimate motions of the soul fill our small private scenes and are just as worthy of being "recorded"—literally, "brought back to the heart." That's what I'm up to.

Don't let reality's recalcitrance prevent the imagination's revisionism: Re-envisioning what did happen as it ought to have happened, imaginatively falsifying the truism that you can't change the past, is what's called learning from experience.

Greece in six aspects: 1. *kephi* (merry-making) and retsina, vestiges of civil war and poverty, the kingly American currency and the colonial experience (fifties), local charm and the humblest language, drollish but live; 2. the American excavations, order, discipline, sobriety, fanatical organization and inhibitedly rampant romanticism easily outdoing the hang-dog Germans; 3. the dead (classical) Greece of scholarly reference books; 4. the vestigial dreams of the German philhellenism of my rebellious Brooklyn adolescence; 5. the texts, the true survivors; 6. the glowing red crepe of blown poppies by a fragrant footpath, an ivory temple pediment rising like a wing over far crests, spires of poplars in primordial landscapes—the real profit, deposited in the treasure house of unforgettables.

America in Greece: It was at the Agora excavations that I became an (Anglo)-American and learned how to ply meticulous scholarship without lumpish circumstantiality. Modern Greece was not much to my taste: the burdensomely gracious old hospitality of the peasants, the insistent physical familiarity of the city people, their exhausted need for party cheer (*kephi*)—I was too stiffly immature, too full of romantic classicism to try not to overlook the living locals, too poor at learning a third language not to despise their two-level tongue as a comic comedown from ancient Greek. But the crystalline air that made the idea of thereness visible—that got to me, better, into me.

The continuing question of historical time: Is the present just the cutting edge of history conceived as an extended continuum either trailing behind and pulling the present into the past, or coming up on it and pushing it into the future? Or is it all there at once, all its causative power and effect compressed into this latest moment?

Some things are just so, like it or lump it—it's *almost* a comfort, this relief from construal.

That unforgettably eventful night when, comfortably bedded and in no way insomniac, I received into the sight behind my eyes my past, a certain figure—hauntingly familiar and piercingly alienated, possessive and elusive, stripped of all the saving gracelessness of existence, faintly repellent and poignantly appealing, vulnerably essential and inescapably accusatory! So the hours go by as I mount a sterile struggle to capture the problem that's keeping me suspended 'twixt sleep and wake. At dawn it dawns on me: But you knew it all along! You've let dreaminess transform "Insolvable" into "Unformulable."

Facts are, speaking tautologically, *faits accomplis*. (Interesting: Latin *facta*—things done, prosaically; Greek *poetiká*—things made, poetically.) But maybe not so accomplished. You can supersede them by new action, defang them by resignation, refashion them by interpretation, or just plain forget them.

Am I (to revise the defective physics of Emerson's metaphor in "History") a particle pumping up and down in a wave pushing by? Well, that's one view of it: jumping up and down in place while things happen—except that this historical advance doesn't seem to be going anywhere (though doing it fast).

A pretty good use of history: as a kind of hanging on the walls of our present habitation—history as the still tapestry against which we are all business. My town, Annapolis, is like that.

Archeology has two major aspects: finding of treasures, sorting of trash—antiques and catalogue items. Oddly and wonderfully, once you hold the artifact in your hand, it's all the same, because oldness itself is magical. There's an innocuous little *kotyle,* a cup with horizontal handles at the rim—I'd date it roughly to that great century, the fifth B.C.—sitting beside me on the shelf; it's full of erasers and paperclips. I usually don't even see it, but when I do I'm flooded by a sort of veneration: "Thou foster-child of silence and slow time."

Personal history: Inspecting documents of bygones, dead loves, old honors, suspended friendships, abandoned places, is a pretty cool business. The heart isn't very responsive to archival collections; it's in the imagination that its past is deposited.

If you bulldoze the midden-heap, you're trashing the past or better, trashing the past's trash. If you keep the dump in use, you're burying the past with itself. That's why we have archeological reservations.

The crimes that began an epoch (the twentieth century) were great and terrible, the ones that saw it out petty and disgusting and much preferable. But then it started again: 9/11/01.

History condemns those who think she is a judge. They wait for a verdict, and it is too long in coming to matter, or reversible on error, or catastrophically negative.

Sometimes history does have an interpretable outcome: e.g., in South America where liberation theology turned people to evangelism, the religion of social justice to the religion of faith; the unintended consequence is history's chief trick.

Plato is said to have said that in his dialogues he presents a Socrates made young and beautiful. Of course, he's not beautiful except when Alcibiades opens the ugly satyr up, and he's young in only one dialogue (*Parmenides*). But I think what Plato means is that his Socrates glows with captivating vigor. "Not the historical Socrates," say the scholars. But don't our friends too lay aside their weary factual historicity to be youthfully beautiful for us? It's more a reflection on the historians' prosaicizing notion of history than on Plato's verisimilitude.

"He's history," says the American idiom—done for, done with. And yet America is the world's oldest republic and lives by the Bible and the Constitution. But that's not history, that's past-present.

The sacred practices of the present aren't justifiable or deconstructible by historical fact. They say the present Hindu prohibitions against eating beef are only half a millennium old and not in the Vedas, so away with sacred cows. Doesn't work that way.

There is a mistaken melancholy in reading fine historical novels—the people have passed, the epoch is time-expired. Well, the people never were, the author is a contemporary, and that world is alive in my fellow fiction-lovers and in me.

If you love a child, the horrors of history come alive.

They say that different perspectives make for depth, but I think it's due more to the distance than the angle if history ever does make sense. From far enough off everything appears "sortal," and human actions look like species behavior. Close up every deed is a choice conditioned by clouds of circumstance. Human beings live by minute particularities and understand in large generalities.

In terrible times our urgent wish is for peace and safety, and in calm times we long for significance and meaning.

When kings preempted history, evils had a grandeur that might catch the imagination. But contemporary horrors are not grand; they are rather huge and beyond imagining; the mind cowers before them. Are the notorious numbers that sum up for us our disasters devices of remembrance or concessions of insensibility?

The tactlessness of reaching for the horrors of the Holocaust to make some invidious political point! They can't be thinking, and they're certainly not imagining.

Anthropology seems to me a study of infinite significance which signifies no determinate lesson, except: They're just like us only totally different.

Some human characters are made to be more attractive alive, some dead. The former will have engaged in people-friendly activities, the latter in dangerous exploits.

The reason that historical conditions and social context are such dubious elements of account-giving is that no time is long enough to complete the condition and no intellect acute enough to specify the context.

History, and its static sibling Society, have as explanatory concepts forces, trends, times—which are abstractions from what is sizable, massive, motoric in human affairs—from what is best quantifiable and least free.

Was it Truman (my favorite president of the last century) who said something like "History is the news you missed"?

1976: The dining hall of our transcontinental campus in Santa Fe, July 4: We've sung the *Star Spangled Banner,* God knows no song to lift the spirit by its mere musical value: difficult and banal at once. I'm to speak on the Declaration, so I'm concentrated on the event. And all of a sudden there's a moment of sheer, wondering glory, the first time I've ever felt the spirit of history—in which on any other day I have no faith at all. Two hundred sun cycles ago, there was signed this explanatory document (two days after the political declaration of independence), stating in language too lucid for depth political axioms too basic for proof, axioms that are very doubtful to the philosophical intellect and near-sacred to the political spirit, and adherence to which makes me, an immigrant, "blood of the blood" with the Founders, in Lincoln's words. Here we were, testimony to the miraculous fact that over a whole continent and two hundred years, it had all become actual. For once history happened.

That some event "isn't historical"—meaning "has left no material evidence"—doesn't mean it didn't happen, to wit, the current denial by some historians of the Exodus. Now why would a raggle-taggle band of bedouins be expected to deposit archeological *realia* in a large desert?

17 MODERNITY: THE JUST-NOW TIME

Day by day nature turns into second nature, space into cyberspace, sources into resources, presences into representations. One might say that the world is on the way to being literally metaphysical, post-physical—a novel, non-transcendent after-nature. In tandem, our perceptions are more often literally unworldly, of delocalized places, disembodied bodies, derivative sense objects, absent presences, images for now (since before long the images that put de-realized objects before the senses will be deemed redundant, as the neural perceptual system can be stimulated directly)—a thingless perceptual after-world.

One comforting result of the multifarious multitude of modern movements is that their vectors cancel or decrease or divert each other's force; trend induces countertrend, opposed, oblique, or orthogonal: Globalism incites nationalism, secularism sectarianism, nationalism spiritualism, radicalism reaction, etc.

Man *en masse* becomes mass men, meaning that a human being in a crowd ceases for a while to represent his species, "the animal that has reasoned speech" (*zoon logon echon*). So stay away from crowds that are without children and picnic baskets.

When the massive conservatism of human beings meets the explosive power of technology, the results, in this country at least, are much more stable than one might fear.

When the original mischief comes from largeness, the reflex, to mount a big cure, is all wrong. Control megalomanias, like "changing the whole system." Start here and now, locally.

The unassimilable intrusiveness of our world: impossible to ignore and impossible to appropriate. Examples: the knowledge explosion, the profusion of options, the access to communication. Ignoring becomes a survival skill.

Rather shall a camel go through a needle's eye than bigness turn into grandeur.

The concept that became trendy was probably at its best in the months before publication, when it was yet a bright idea rather than a slick formula.

A mystery of modern psychological wisdom: that what has everywhere and always been found in hypertrophic abundance should be felt to be in such need of zealous defense: sex, self-esteem, irrationality, self-indulgence, sex again, and the rest of the therapeutic merry-go-round.

Surely the usual reason given for the default of philosophical, that is, pre-metaphysical, physics—that nature turns out to be more usably responsive to questions of "How?" than of "Why?"—is right. But I wonder if another practical reason doesn't play into it: An ever larger proportion of that nature which is near to us turns into second nature; given and grown *beings* turn into intended and made *things*. Artificial objects, however, don't respond to the old questions of prime philosophy, "What is fully achieved being?" "What is grown being?" Artifacts obey the laws of nature and the intentions of human beings and that, except in the imagination of science fiction writers, pretty well exhausts their being. Scholastically: They have no essence.

What the enlightened believers in the sure progress toward the ultimate relief of man's estate don't figure in is duration. They may well be right in the *very* long run, but this is what tyrants know: that terror is durably viable, that people can be made to live in hell indefinitely if it is properly calibrated, that human beings can be kept functional in fairly permanent depression by modern means.

The modern principle of equality can have the most diverse underpinnings: least-common-denominator conformity, everyone-to-his-own-taste relativism, and common-humanity, diversely-realized individualism. I think our Madisonian Constitution, that miracle of modernity, supports the last.

Let yourself surrender to that incantation about flexibility and complexity, and you are within an eyelash of sweeping doctrinal assertions.

Why is dignity of bearing not a strong suit of contemporary Americans, though the peasants and servants of

Europe were not without it? Because people talk of it as something that can be given or taken away, when it's rather an ingrained sense, not so much of having an estimable self as of having an integral soul. (The self is the soul in its self-intent, self-concerned mode; it is the ego underlying and monitoring other psychic capacities, while the soul is a human being's interiority; the self is an invention/discovery/construction of early modernity.)

Modern souls have given away the confirming gesture of their dignity: obeisance. Odysseus, repeating Agamemnon's message to Achilles, is large enough (as his chief isn't) to inject a visible gesture of deference into the verbatim speech: "My lord," he adds. Bach in the *Quoniam* of the B minor Mass works an audible obeisance into the words *tu solus altissimus*. And, of course, paintings are full of graceful genuflections. Well, we don't need to go that far, but a little practice in the generosities of self-respect would do us good.

"Decision process"—a dozen excellent little contributions that add up to one big mistake. Now "talking things over," that's apt to keep you from stepping confidently off the cliff.

In ancient days the gods took away people's wits; now we do it for ourselves. E.g.: Here's a person so besotted with non-judgmentalism that she can't summon any activating outrage even when someone makes her life miserable.

Students who have been in therapy sometimes talk of themselves with a fatalistic candor. They "have" a disability, syndrome, whatever, that we have to accede to since it's a professional diagnosis. They tell us very confidentially and then quite a few others conversationally.

Penis envy: I remember it vividly as a little girl, my adored older cousin having a directable nozzle. And that was, I'll swear, *all* there was to it.

Subconscious, certainly; Unconscious, no. There is surely more going on inside than I'm now aware of, just as my body keeps working away below my notice. But the very idea that I contain a reservoir of roiled passions, of vengeful, imprisoned desires, patent to an expert analyst and inaccessible to myself! The same goes for the interpretation of dreams; no one could possibly know better what they signify than I—or find them more suggestively enigmatic. To me the reason why dreams aren't systematically interpretable (supposing even the theory of wish-*fulfillment* was plausible, when so many dreams are just longing made visible) is that they manifest their meaning much more in their delicate and specific atmospheres than in their narrative (which is, in any case, mostly an *ex post facto* construct).

Although it is old wisdom that human beings are everywhere and always much alike, that, it seems to me, shouldn't mean real self-analysis must discover generalities. Introspection should be the most unjigged of inquiries, ready to find unclassifiably personal, indefinitely distinct, subtly unique conditions: We shouldn't be cases to our own inspection, or should be at most special cases. The crudity of psychological analysis consists in prescribing the patterns and terms of self-description, in turning a contemplative into a therapeutic activity, and substituting the absolution of sickness for the discipline of suffering.

And yet, the Socratic injunction "Know thyself" meant "Discover within yourself the parts and functions of the common human soul," but it didn't mean: "Search out the peculiar dispositions and motions of your particular self." That's a very modern activity to which psychological analysis has given premature categories. So avoid those; clue out (since you must) your peculiarities, but think most seriously about the common constitution of the sound soul.

Under cover of giving absolution for the secular sins of modernity, the social and psychological sciences are practical putdowns. Being bad is more dignified than being sick—and more directly curable; it needs no pill, only will.

People speak of themselves (and let others speak of them) as defensive, insecure, and the whole terminological litany of self-denigrating self-regard. These denominations seem to me at once trite and inadequate, and they've become backhanded insults when used by others. The trouble isn't that these aren't recognizably modern conditions (modern in the sense of being the natural concomitants of individualism) but that, as so often, the attention is on a subjective effect rather than the objective cause.

Proper reply to the sneak attack of "You're being defensive": "You bet, because you're being offensive."

The language regulation practiced for the sake of normalization has its dubious aspects. "Disabled, handicapped, physically challenged" are the successive polysyllabic officialese designations meant to bring people under neutralized categories that disallow condescending pity—but nullify pathos as well. The one-time cripple relinquishes a fate for a plastic tag. Is life really more bearable as a designated minority than as a marked individual, as a category than as a cross? One of my fellow members on the State Civil Rights Commission said to me: "I'm a cripple; euphemisms don't help." His point was: Mainstreamed I'm a liability to you, crippled I'm a hero to myself.

Almost all psychological theory, no matter how "enabling," has the effect of relocating self-control to expert control.

Self-expression, self-esteem—there are close to four hundred "self-" entries in my Heritage Dictionary, "self-absorbed" among them: luxuriating modernity.

"Modernity" comes from Latin *modo,* "just now." At first it meant what was just then current, at any time. But our modernity, Modernity as an epoch, is just-nowness made into a driving principle. The serene peace of the dwelled-in present is replaced by the running novelty of the Just-Now. Progress and obsolescence are complementary; the past is a junkyard rather than a treasure house. Of course, few people live in Modern times all the time; you have to be crazy to belong to your own time consistently.

Hence the above is merely the dim view, the slouching-beast vision of our times. It describes some salient phenomena but no historical necessity. You can take discriminating advantage of the goods offered and live at your own pace. So do that.

People look across town for diversity; look at your closest friend. I think that two persons living in the same house can be more strange to each other than two others living cultures and continents apart. Attention to diversity makes good human sense in a country as multifarious as ours, but as an insistent mantra diversity-mongering bears the marks of that modern failing Pascal calls "diversion," an external incitement to avoid being with yourself.

Why burden public obligations with spiritual requirements? It's hard enough to do your neighbors justice, why must I love them too? That's inviting backlash. Similarly for knowing them; whoever said that to know each other is to love each other got it half right: to know each other can be to hate each other. Why not preach unsentimentalized justice and common decency, and leave the fellow-feeling to the spontaneities of the moment? I like my reformers hard-headed, cool-hearted, and cost-effective.

"Words lost their meaning," says Thucydides of times of turmoil. Here's an example: I belong to a group too small to be a scheduled minority.

Innovation discourages cherishing maintenance (the mode I live by): Trash it and get a newer type. Children growing up that way are deficient in humanity's most humane habit: care. And yet: I became a liberated little

American the day I discovered (about week three) that not a soul darned socks.

You read yet another vigorous excoriation of this or that original linguistic sin or entrenched social iniquity, and you think: That does it; for good or ill, it's done for. No such thing. It's only been confirmed in its tough guerrilla life.

What is lost in the mood lately featured in modern life, the rights-minded, resentment-ready, "compassion"-ridden, therapy-controlled mood described by Nietzsche (who, let it be said, knows nothing of democracy but its ignobilities) is the mythic, heroic view of oneself that might carry youngsters into adulthood. After all, even the "common man" was once a grand historical type. (Nietzsche would hear with disdainful satisfaction that our supposedly more individualistic party makes a slogan of compassionate conservatism; why wouldn't cool-headed decency do?)

There is that decadal urge to assault yet more of the natural ways of being, to turn old virtues into trendy vices and normal reactions into unwitting execrations. But as the eras pass, you learn that anybody can do that to anybody. For human beings are by nature conventional, so that all virtues are constitutionally tainted with smugness, and all normalcy is infected with philistinism. Then you're more or less immune to these endemic aggressions.

Among the myriad of modern techniques for self-servicing is the borrowed injunction (from Buddhism, apparently) to empty your mind. Isn't it redundant? (Reminds me of my brother's reply to my threat to give him a piece of my mind: "Can you spare it?" And while I'm at it, when my mother in Brooklyn badgered us about eating up because of the starving children in Europe, he lifted up his plate to her and said innocently: "Send it.")

The engaged studies (women, gay, black) bring home the virtue of indifferentism: To sign up for a class because it's required, easy, still open, or on a random whim at least ensures a simulacrum of disengaged objectivity.

Mephistopheles tells Faust that he is the spirit who ever intends the bad and ever effects the good. Liberals do the reverse.

Conservatives, on the other hand, bear the name of safekeeping and do the deeds of bullying.

Our modern idiocies are really no worse than those of older times, only more ours.

The funny fact is that engines that spread intrusive noise and polluting nastiness abroad are so hermetically quiet and antiseptically clean inside (aside from the obligatory but inherently unnecessary drivel music). From train to car to airplane, those who are in transit are favored over those who stay at home. Pascal comes to mind: "The sole cause of man's unhappiness is that he does not know how to stay quietly in his room."

Why do those incarnations of rationalized process, machines, occasionally produce chaos? Because they are built-to-order efficient causes without built-in final cause. You can take a chainsaw apart and find out *how* it does its sawing, but you can't find out *why* it's cutting down this tree, and the person handling it may not know either.

Intellectuals and academics tend to be out of step and out of line with the country (though they imagine the reverse). Public opinion starts slowly moving, and they leap ahead, far out of bounds. There they're stuck, and when the tide begins to recede (as it always does), they are left behind. Ahead, behind, but not often in sync: These folks embrace the radicalisms of their youth and grow old along with them.

The rebellion against perennialism—not against stable answers but against everlasting questions—is a basic characteristic of modernity, whose founders in their search for certain and effective thought decided that ever-unsettled questions betokened reason trying, illegitimately, to exceed its limits (Kant). It's an old notion: Aristotle quotes a poet as saying that humans shouldn't search for knowledge beyond human matters; but this knowledge, says the Philosopher, is just what is most precious to us (*Metaphysics* I 2).

The modern argument cuts both ways: The fact that old questions have been asked and inconclusively answered over millennia might mean they are futile. Or it might mean they're indefeasible.

There are numerous ways to achieve newness: by a radical criticism of the tradition, by a naiveté that innocently reinvents the wheel, by developing an inherent hidden truth, by making the ordinary appear marvelous, by mounting a renascence of the past, and by the might-and-main production of novelty as novelty—all these have gone into modernity, and they issue in the last, innovation for innovation's sake.

Modernity is figuratively horizontal: complexity, extremes, quantity, limits, secularism—all these terms are extensive rather than intensive, planar conceptions rather than deep thoughts.

Some ways, simply incompatible with modern life, are beautiful to gaze at in the museum of the imagination and scary to contemplate as realities: ceremony at the court of Byzantium, the cult of the Samurai, a feast in a medieval castle, a voyage on a caravelle.

In pre-modern times, devout monks went among the poor and leprous from charity, to relieve suffering. Why do Americans so devote themselves? From moral expansiveness, to do sociological studies, to immerse themselves in a different culture, and undoubtedly to help. But the first three are at odds with the last. Never mind, mixed motives are the spice of morality.

I suppose zealotry was always the enemy of fervor, but zealotry plus ideology is a peculiarly modern depravity. Ideology is a thought-pill, swallowed down whole; it aggravates the inflammation of the mind that is zealotry and makes it the more infectious for laying a claim to rationality.

Children on the loose—that was the liberated subculture of the third quarter of the bygone century: a fecklessly cozy playing with fire, without subtlety, restraint, responsibility, reserve, caution, discretion—parochial in time and rootless in place. They were nice kids, moderately kind, humanly concerned, but bored out of their minds with the security of their lives. And when they met their causes they weren't quite up to them.

Permissiveness has a high theological ancestry: "If God is dead all is permitted." Our secular permissiveness is an evanescently mild descendant of that desperately jubilating notion: In the absence of acknowledged authority, who's to tell anyone what's what?

But we do have a mode left to us, one happily still much practiced in families and institutions: a large-minded liberality of governance which, perfectly sure of itself, sets the limits quite definitely for the sake of human containment, but also sets them very widely for the sake of human spaciousness. Permissiveness is its craven facsimile.

An old friend of mine, speaking of being a mother: "My function is to say 'no.'" Limits to children are as trellises to shrubs; they make it possible for them to grow into cultivated shapes. But it's not a universal truth: There are children that are allowed to run wild with indulgence who grow into nice adults from sheer good nature—quite a few.

Countercultural types are always "working on themselves," "working on their relationships," or just "working on it." Well, "work" means both an activity and a result, and it doesn't look much like either to me.

Discos—simulacra of inferno.

Conflict resolution, pain management, grieving process, support groups—I'm of two minds. One side urges that the technical treatment of the soul is demeaning to its dignity, the other says, "Whatever works." But does it work and at what price?

A mystery phrase of modern life: "being out of touch with your feelings." What on earth? Does it mean I have them but can't get to them, or I don't have any, or I won't acknowledge those I have? Are we being asked to breach the protective membrane around the heart, or to reveal our emptiness to ourselves or to unplug the inner volcano? Like too much soul-craft, this phrase is suspended between a slick assumption and a dangerous incitement.

Modern concept construction: either by cleverly formulated negation of an antecedent notion or by its sophistic elaboration—the systematic production of novelty. How used they to think? At their best they didn't "think about concepts" (which kind of mentation was called "second intention") but about beings, directly. That's harder now because most of the furniture of our life is second-intentional.

When all is said and done, it's better for people to be fluffily liberal and sloppily permissive than to be fixedly doctrinaire and fiercely rigid—if those were the alternatives for an aspiring participant in the *Zeitgeist* (charmingly pronounced *Zietgiest* by those of our kids who've heard of it, happily few). If rampant liberty or rabid substance were the choices, as zealots make out, then far better to opt for the side of vague possibility. But of course, there is a third, best way: We preserve the content we care for by self-discipline and the freedom we want by legalities. As our runner-up national anthem exhorts us: "America! America! / God mend thine every flaw, / Confirm thy soul in self-control, / Thy liberty in law!"

There must be something wrong with the claim that we appropriate great works through cultural context. Why do naive young lovers of classical music usually land neither on plainsong nor on contemporary composers, but somewhere between Bach and Beethoven? Surely because neither history nor contemporaneity draws them but greatness. Not: culture gives access to works, but: works incite cultivation. Similarly for painting; explain why a first close look ever at a Chinese brush-painting of a branch of a plum tree in blossom can totally captivate an imagination that is clueless about the symbolism?

The converted obverse of Socrates' dictum "Virtue is knowledge" is equally true: "Ignorance ends up as vice." That fact was sadly demonstrated by the kids who were, from sheer ignorance, seduced by vicious adults into mind-altering activities. Haight-Ashbury came in as bliss and went out in murder.

Our enlightened modernity, sinless, self-confident, coolly benevolent, may not have, in its easy rationalism, much depth, but when you consider the obstinate, exclusive, willfully imageless, dyspeptic devotion of my ancestors to their God, it seems purely luminous, sweetness and light itself. (I really wasn't made to be a good Jew, though perhaps a Zionist.) And yet, the Seder, the lighting of the menorah, verses from Genesis and Psalms . . .

"Righteous indignation" and "thinking for yourself," the moral and intellectual mainstays of enlightened politics, are both redundancies: Our capacity for indignation (which the ancients called *thymos*) is *ipso facto* righteous, and thinking is *ipso facto* by oneself for oneself. Is there a significance in this loose talk? Yes, it means that people are captivated by these notions but disinclined to consider what's behind them.

Human beings seem to me to be alike on the lowest and highest levels, as animals and as thinkers, and different on the middle level where food, hygiene, humor, gesture, customs sexual and ceremonial, and sensibility in general is located. The modern social disciplines tend to overlook the former and denigrate the latter, which leaves them with a theory-induced sense of radical diversity.

Religion being—against all modern expectations—the deepest and most rousing human adherence, the great question of our time is whether all religions, Western, Middle Eastern, Eastern, worship the same or different divinities. The trouble is that those studying it secularly are *ipso facto* unable to deal with it, and those who are believers are *ipso facto* unreliable respondents. That's of course aside from the problem of discerning who has kept the faith most purely.

Those gently banal, formulaic popguns leveled by Westerners against the West seem often to aim where there is little left standing, e.g., faith in progress, suppression of the emotions, a sense of superiority.

Novelty is to newness as frisson is to feeling: Novelty is a bit of contrived newness, the taste for which is a kind of condensation of the modern mode. (Since the appearances which we live among are full of variety, novelty is in one sense the given order of our day, but that natural novelty doesn't cause much excitation.) The newness that moderns long for with depth of feeling is in fact pretty rare in our "just-now" times. One trivial revolution follows the other, and the nugatory parade masks the fact that we have lived for over two hundred years in a truly new era, in the *novus ordo seclorum* engraved on our dollar, the American political framework of 1788. But no, that's wrong, for the Constitution, itself the consequence of a great Revolution, institutionalized the production of little ones; it stabilized novelty as a settled way of life.

How dreary the exciting life is, the competitive sociability, the frantic jetting around, the discretionarily risky amusements, the savvily classy consumption!

I know people who make a virtue of rootlessness, regarding it as an expression of the flexibility they cherish. It's an old and prime mark of modern humanity; see Pico della Mirandola, *On the Dignity of Man* (c. 1487), God speaking: "We have given you, Oh Adam, no visage proper to yourself, nor any endowment properly your own, in order that whatever place, whatever form, whatever gifts you may with premeditations select, these same you may have through your own judgment and decision . . . Who then will look with awe upon this our chameleon . . . ?" Half a millennium later, would *we* say that this chameleon-man has much dignity? Much premeditation or judgment? It's the usual fate of very acute prognostications: It turns out just like that only different.

How peculiarly and significantly the philosophers of history (a contradiction in terms, but let that be) diverge in their judgment of our condition! Some think we are at a height and still going forward, others expect, even invoke apocalypse. The funny thing is, both types seem somehow to rejoice in their prognostications.

The humanities in our universities: a friendly, mildly excited interest in the bygone and superseded just because it happens to have happened. Humanities teachers (*of course*, not all) think the tradition is pretty nonsensical by modern standards but they don't hold that against it: they are well inclined to what is out of commission. If it were to be shown that this old research fodder had present force, they'd be fiercely against it.

Pessimism as preemptive panic: Put yourself into permanent expectation of the worst so that the bad that comes won't hurt so much. Some people do this on a cosmic scale. Pessimism seems to me a modern affect because implicit in it is a sense of a linearly directed tendency (i.e., negative progress), whereas the ancients thought that what goes round comes round, down today, up tomorrow.

Sober pessimism: to live as a cannily reserved participant of modern times and for the rest to choose your own age.

It could be that the moral limits that moderns have talked themselves out of subjection to will be re-established by brute catastrophe: the price of sexual promiscuity, economic profligacy, substance abuse—all the practices that, people persuaded themselves during the last century, carried no defensible prohibitions. But brute facts are a bad argument for morality. As soon as technical controls and protections are devised their force is dissipated; nature's lessons just incite human ingenuity.

All those eager beavers wanting to "raise my consciousness," force me to "rethink," "change with the times," "be innovative," and all that intrusive trend-talk! In Brooklyn we used to say: "Mr. Buttinsky!"

There might have been a sly agenda in the permissiveness movement: that what is freely permitted will cease to interest. It doesn't work that way; the appetite grows as it feeds.

Sociology was once, in the last century, going to save society, probably because it was overtly a science and covertly an ideology—a good, safe way to make revolutions. It didn't work, because the ideology, that of class oppression, wasn't very plausible to a country that still thinks of itself as predominantly middle-class or would-be middle-class, and the science, that of socially determined thought, couldn't deal with independent minds.

Ubiquity is the squishy juggernaut of modernity.

"We now know . . . ," "We've learned that . . . ," "We live in an age that . . . ," and so on: Who "we"? Not me.

The ancient astronomers "saved," meaning "saved for reason," the heavenly appearances by undergirding them with mathematical hypotheses. Modern social scientists and historians try to do likewise. But the human world is no cosmos.

Sometimes studying up on the analyses of modernity and its satyr play, postmodernism, feels like listening to patients in a waiting room who've all been stricken by anomalous forms of the same chronic disease for which they've taken a variety of addictive drugs that are beginning to reveal deteriorating side effects.

"Question everything." The Germans say: "*Erstmal können vor lachen*," meaning "You'll die laughing."

The victory of method over matter, as in the oddly named "material" symbolic logic, in social studies, in bureaucracy, etc.—this replacement of natural being by rationalized doing has one region that might reconcile one to the rest: procedural democracy, our political salvation.

Could it be that the sexual revolution is a Darwinian trick to prevent propagation, that the natural evolutionary checks failing, a social preventive has established itself?

Who does more to frustrate normal development— the old-style obstructionist reactionaries or the modern-minded, future-facilitating progressives? The former stand staunchly in the way, yet in so doing act to screen out all but the really needful; the latter "prevent" the future in that lovely Biblical sense ("I prevented the dawning of the morning," Psalm 119) of anticipating it, yet in so doing keep it from finding its natural shape. And then there is the tribe of prognosticators, who, by telling what the future must be, are really issuing self-confirming predictions—if they are believed.

Aristotle calls the tool an inanimate slave, to make it clear who's master. If we could only remember who's in charge and exploit and discard our technology, be it an instrument for work or a medium of communication, with sovereignly appreciative contempt: unplug, turn off, when we've had the service or entertainment we want. Instead those things—and that's all they are—tend to run us, and like the sorcerer's apprentice we are danced by our brooms. Could it be that somewhere in our hearts we believe that technological objects are animated and have a claim on our allegiance?

When the center doesn't hold then eccentricity is the common fate; to wit: fashions in dress.

My gadgets have enough functions to make me dysfunctional, so many new modes that my blunt senses and limited desires are overwhelmed. My new 35-dollar wristwatch came with four closely printed panels of instructions (and then in six languages). Options! Hell must be the place of unlimited options, where you can't find the on/off button.

Until the last century hardly anyone ever lived alone: Rich ladies had paid companions; everyone had servants;

servants had siblings to retire with, and if you read that masterpiece of descriptive sociology, Mayhew's *London Labor and the London Poor,* you'll see that even the most helplessly destitute found a companionable landlady. Now we live in "apartments," apart and separate. Well, when you read, say, in the life of the Brontës, of the hell they made for each other living together, isolation seems heavenly. The point is, though, that while in some respects we're pretty coddled, we probably have developed more psychological and practical (though not intellectual) self-sufficiency, more taste and capacity for living apart than people of previous times had, to whom our liberated privacies might seem pretty desolate and our do-it-yourself ingenuity pretty demeaning.

We have two routes to uglification (an *Alice* word), accident and design. The accidental ugliness is just incidental to convenience: strip malls, highways, offices. The designed ugliness results from creativity: highly designed architecture, creative furniture, collectible paintings.

A day is imaginable when the sciences die of boredom, the research is more and more just number crunching, the global theories have either failed—or succeeded, and the major applications are socially proscribed or commonplace. After all, a number of grand endeavors were dead before they were gone: the Roman Empire, scholasticism, social science, musical styles.

Prime axiom: Every bit of progress makes things a little worse. Well, anyway in education.

Some moderns, the apocalyptic types, foretell secularized versions of the Rapture, the Tribulation, the Second Coming, of the end of History, of Civilization, of Time. But the first and the second millennium went by eventlessly, and even if the Beast were slouching ever so slowly it would have got to Bethlehem by now. There's a frisson in foretelling the coming End Time. But I think nothing is coming and nothing is ending and if it does it'll just be a huge, preventable accident.

A very characteristic modern euphemism: "experimenting," which really means "indulging." A scientific experiment doesn't fail; even if it's negative something is learned. But "experimentation" can fail and wreck or take a life. Experimenting in the counter-cultural sense means ratcheting up experience by illicit means. It is humanity's first temptation all over again:

> Greedily she ingorged without restraint,
> And knew not eating death. Satiate at length,
> And hightened as with wine, jocund and boon,
> Thus to herself she pleasingly began:—
> . . . .
> . . . Experience, next to thee I owe,
> Best guide: not following thee, I had remained
> In ignorance; thou open'st Wisdom's way,
> And giv'st access, though secret she retire.
> (*Paradise Lost* IX)

Eve is humanity's original experimenter and rebel. But then, her father and husband, "domestic Adam," is a klutz.

The more diffident people are badgered into creativity, the further their imagination retreats; it doesn't like willful interference.

Creativity was once God's prerogative: making something out of nothing. Now it's humanity's arrogation: making nothing out of something. I once visited a pottery workshop in Attica. There was a row of lovely *oinochoai,* wine-decanters, in the clean classical style. The old potter went by them punching each one in the belly. "She makes me do it"—"she" being the creative owner of a classy boutique in Athens.

Select Dictionary of Recent Modernity

> Writing = Word processing
> Bad for you = Impacts negatively
> Self-control = Repression
> Beauty = NA
> Worth = Value
> Passion = Emotion
> Messing around = Experimenting
> Desire = Need
> Imagination = Creativity
> Work = Operate, etc.

I put equal signs but not to betoken identity of meaning.

Maxim of Meaning (gleaned from a statistically significant number of cases): Communicated significance varies inversely with the number of syllables used.

On TV, the wife of a public figure who had gone through what used to be called a "dark night of the soul" explained: "He reevaluated his priorities and rescheduled his activities." Well, it's nice iambic near-poetry, but isn't the diction more than that of a manager restructuring his job than a man rethinking his life? A serious question: Is this merely linguistic ineptitude, these current clichés that sometimes take over in the face of human distress, or is it a mark, even a cause, of the debasement—so to speak—of human profundity?

There's the wicked pleasure of leading the world by the nose-ring of candor. "Unless you tell me I'll never know," they say. Well, sometimes it's the other way around: Practice candor and no one catches on. That's another sense of "open secrets."

2

INWARD PROSPECTS

18 SOUL: SHAPES

An incurable deformity of soul in someone we actually know is next to impossible to contemplate. It keeps looking like a character defect correctable at will.

The soul's water table rises and falls: We are awash with the flood of feeling or arid with the drought of indifference. Await the season.

The body is the soul's publisher—a truer metaphor even than Donne's: "Love's mysteries in soules doe grow / But yet the body is his booke." But it's the converse figure that is the real enigma: The soul's uncircumventable bodiliness: It can be bruised, benumbed, flooded, desiccated, deformed. It can dance, cringe, expand; for Yeats "Soul" can even "clap its hands and sing." And it can certainly be wounded and certainly healed.

I can think of some reasons that we figure our soul to ourselves as a body: It seems to be within the body; at least the body is its means of locomotion, so by an absurd but natural leap we think of it as fitting itself into our physique. We seem to have a duplicate set of pleasures and pains, somatic and psychic. (Think of the time when in the throbbing vise of a migraine headache your soul soared free with the joy of a letter received.) So we attribute to the soul a sensitive psychic body. But the curious thing is that, though we have a figure for our soul, it only appears in speech; I doubt that people see their own souls in their imaginations very often. In fact, when philosophers and psychologists figure the soul they do it as a territory—a spatial topography—though when painters do it, it's a lady in a nightgown.

More evidence of the body-likeness of the soul: It is elastic, very elastic, to a point—and then it's over-stretched and doesn't snap back or it simply snaps: We cease caring or just lose it.

People talk of "being out of touch with their feelings" as if those feelings were in attendance waiting for the psychic phone to ring. But there's something in it: the debris of past destructions, the accretions of daily business, can clog the springs that irrigate our psychic soil, and then we go dry. We are obsessed rather than devoted; we rationalize rather than think; we are objectlessly anxious rather than focusedly fearful; we fuss rather than care, are rigid rather than strong, pessimistic rather than realistic—and so through all the substitutions of the desiccated soul. Is that what the silly cliché means?

Observation and reflection can't well be simultaneous. Thus the soul, delightedly feeding on what it finds delicious, needs distance and time to digest its feast. Otherwise put: The sheer thereness of an object that draws our intense observation is overwhelming, distracting, numbing; we have to stop looking and get away, so that we may reflect and so properly appropriate the object of such an acute interest.

We may wish to be above it, but our soul rebels at receiving a shabbily meager return for a noble offering.

The soul's like a bat flapping around in melancholy restlessness when it has come out in the evening and the presence it seeks is absent.

What worldly territory the soul doesn't claim the body will quickly take over; absent-mindedness is a major cause of physical excess.

If through the years you didn't neglect to exercise your soul, your heart will move with lightning-swift sureness when its moment comes.

"The soul," they say, "is a prescientific concept"—and they're quite right: It precedes all science.

The depths of the soul are dredged up in remembrance of things past; the roots of the intellect are pulled up in recollection of things atemporal. Bygones recovered extend us in time; truths discovered retract us from time.

Our psychic interior and our physical exterior alike are in constant need of cultivation—as in a garden, where nature does the growing and we do the pruning. Inside we want ourselves to be clear and ready; outside we want our possessions to be clean and shipshape. Well, some of us do.

As we run from coming into being to going out of it, our nemesis is deterioration, which is to be held at bay by labor. "But the labor that keeps us up runs us down." "No, the flesh wears itself out *so that* the soul may stay fresh."

The tasteless tears of the soul are more fervent than the salt tears of the eyes. We weep in public not only spontaneously but also demonstratively, whereas within we just cry.

At crucial, high moments the soul goes plain and simple in its affects, however subtle its wonted modulations, however sophisticated its mundane *modus operandi* may be.

Some souls are like large sailing vessels, moving with stately steadiness over the seas but hard to bring about and impossible to bring to.

Even desiccated souls can bloom at a drop if the season is right. But the woman with the watering can has taken on a *big* responsibility.

There is, *mirabile dictu,* a psychologist to whom our animating principle is not a psyche but a soul. He says: "We should save the phenomena just as they are, untreated, uncured" (recall that "saving the phenomena" is the Platonic phrase for making the anomalous revolutions of the planets intelligible by rational hypotheses) ". . . through our depression we enter depths and in depths we find soul . . . *The true revolution begins in the individual who can be true to his or her depression.*" And when we see through ourselves to our mythic depths we find that "*soul is imagina-*

tion." This collage of quotations from James Hillman contains the three truths we need: That our despondencies are to be seized as opportunities for descending into our souls; that the soul we can live with, live *in,* is not to be imagined as a small ego but a large landscape; that we must follow Plato's injunction, to solve the same problem he sets the student of the heavens—to make our irregular ways intelligible to ourselves by hypotheses of regular motion. What a lovely thought, that we are called to become astronomers of the soul, making sense of our abnormal paths. (Long before I came on the Hillman quotation, I called this collection "Dictionary of Depression.")

To be sure there are clinical depressions that require therapy and medicine. But the normal dejections of our days are amenable to the discipline of introspection, especially to the effort of articulation: A confusion formulated is pretty nearly a confusion overcome, and a sorrow put into words is almost a comfort. But stay clear of the terms of soul-technique; better to swallow a pill than be in thrall to a theory—for my money (and money has a lot to do with it). Still, if it helps. . . .

The soul may have parts but it is also all one: a taint stains the whole—thought, spirit, passions—and a wound to any of these hurts in all. Example: Do something shameful and the intellect turns in futile circles, pride loses its élan and cowers, feeling writhes and withers.

The soul contradicts its contradictions: What is antic self-contrariness on one day, is a whole in a sound tension of opposites on another.

Piddling insight by piddling insight, the soul's labor can attain a certain magnitude.

The soul takes a secular holiday, waiting for its reservoirs to fill up, that is, the body makes the arrangements—a bag of glazed doughnuts and a middling good novel—and the soul comes along.

The closed, encapsulated soul breaks open and flowers in the climate of measured delight and numbered glory that is music. Generosity is its first ethical effect—I mean the music of worship, not of self-expression and excitation. Why beat around the bush: Bach.

"A friend is another self." If so, why bother? One of me is enough. No, it's just because souls are never transparent to each other without remainder that they see each other at all. Mutual opacity keeps us two, together but unmerged.

The soul that digests each event and sucks out its lesson will be least prone to sourness or bitterness—though not immune to sorrow and sadness. Besides, bitterness and sourness are diagnostics of ill health. If you can't stomach life take the cure, which is to remember that cynicism reflects more on the cynic's dyspeptic constitution than on the world's badness. Now if someone's soul has been stretched beyond its limits by misfortune, that's a different story.

Here are three ways to think of a well-constituted soul: concentric—centered about an inner sanctum; balanced—having well-adjusted parts; hierarchical—ordered to an affirmed summit.

The soul as a sack: only the world's impressions; the soul as a tube: intimations from beyond as well.

Our souls' depths send up signals before we have gotten to ourselves. For example, there is a sort of dry, taut, humming, a tense, desiccated excitement that tells us we're guilty before we've quite become aware of what we've done.

Much happens sub-consciously that I learn of late and by a lucky association—of course. But that I should carry about a hermetic "un-conscious," closed to me in principle but open, of all things, to an expert in analyzing the psyche—that is just ludicrous.

In those futile disputes about whether we have souls or brain centers the best thing is to leave the brains to those who want them and the souls to those who can't live without them—in disputes, that is; the *inquiry* concerning the relation of neurology to consciousness is uncircumventable. And so is the question whether the naturalists of the psyche live a different life from the spiritualists of the soul; it's got to make some sort of difference.

19 INTERIORITY: LOOKING WITHIN

You can calculate while you're in action, but you can't think. Therefore efficient action is sleepwalking. All the thinking got done in the light of leisure; the murk of action requires a certain automatism. People who've looked all their lives into the world and hardly within should not be in charge.

It's extremist to require that the inner household be totally tidy before you issue into the world of action, but it helps to have kept on top of things.

There comes a deflating realization that the interior conversation was in fact a self-deceiving monologue, that proud declarations of independence were in fact veiled offers of submission made to a stone-deaf idol.

Interior battle: between the wish to get behind the scenes of myself, to be illuminated (albeit in a waking dream) about the bottoms and bases of my being, and the desire to dissolve dis-ease and confusion by a sensible side-slipping into my normal daily ways with their assumptions of practical mastery—to solve problems rather than plumb depths.

Daydreams, stage sets purposefully constructed to rouse desire in the frontages of the imagination, are worlds apart from the spontaneous images that the fullness of feeling brings forth from the depths of the imagination.

The soul's fraudulent independence: In the security of health, prosperity, and possession of love it sometimes seems as if one could as well do without. Even a breath of peril will teach you better.

Is disinterested introspection diverted by the ubiquitous calculi of desire? Not when it is directed straight at them.

The heart's a copycat: Show it a feeling and it will feel, passion and it will grow impassioned, tenderness and it will respond. Say to it, "I care" and it will say, "Likewise."

It is a compliment to the delicacy of thought that it can make passion its subject without quashing or even dimming it. Of course, there are those formulaic assaults, bent on therapy rather than illumination—but they can't wreck anything interior because they don't reach anything.

Others are strange chimaeras, oddly composed, queerly fused. Me? I'm a piece of nature, normal as the day is long. Ha.

The bounds of self-revelation are pretty soon reached. We may be inexhaustible to ourselves but to others we quickly begin to run true to form. That's friendship: actually rejoicing in the other's being inexorably self-same.

We understand each other—know our stories and histories, recognize preoccupations and patterns, divine the intended significances of our throwaway remarks. Then, the next thing you know, we're once more utter mysteries to each other. And when that's ceased to happen, we're finished with each other.

When events and experiences come too thick and fast, feeling goes numb and reflection shuts down. Lesson: Don't try to kill several birds with one stone (a nasty thought in any case). Don't try to be efficient with the life of your soul. Don't fill up its calendar.

Here's a strange thought: I sit in my inside looking out. What do you see, whose looking stops at my face and is reflected, not admitted, by my eyes? Well, you see what I've never seen, this face of which the mirror throws back at me only what I take to be a defective image, ineluctably posed, and perforce staring. So you know something about me that I can't know but you learn it by being stopped before you get to me. And *vice versa*. It's not a strange thought—it's mind-boggling: I can look out and you can't look in; you can look out and I can't look in.

I know for a fact that "I need you" is only an urgent way of saying "I want you." Children, to be sure, *need* love, adults only want it.

The heart's inconstancy seems like a blessing in the long run. Yet it's just in the long run that time's operations are set at naught: The heart is a veritable museum of preserved feeling, each love like a fly caught in amber—and suddenly it beats its wings.

"The heart has its reasons which the reason does not know." I don't believe Pascal. The heart's reasons are well known to me and to my thinking self, but we are both too tactful—or too inept—to articulate them.

Coming clean to oneself, practicing total candor within, is an absolute duty—though not really a duty either, not a self-imposed task, but a simple necessity. Why? Things are mysterious enough without me being misty to myself.

Luxuriating in the swampy stuckness of a weepy grievance, delivering internal orations eloquently laying out the wrongs suffered, indulging in deliciously iterative recitals of the whole sorry brief: good for the soul—in moderation.

The soul externalized: Dithering empathy comes through as considerate decisiveness, overt ambition is disciplined by canny pride, hatred of business shows as eager efficiency, inner distance transforms into public kindness, wild romanticism goes into the world as practical sobriety. Inner dispositions wear strange masks in the outer world.

From where I sit, most of my doings are both spontaneous and consequential; from where those not privy to my inner counsels stand, they are at once typical and impulsive. Who's right?

When you are tempted to see yourself as the center of a tragedy, a being of pathos and high dignity, make sure the satyr play, the comic relief, follows soon after. N.B.: "When you see yourself"—those who are really in that condition have no mind for drama.

To ourselves we seem at once natural and unique but to others we look more like aberrant facsimiles.

Do my colleagues see themselves, *mutatis mutandis,* as I see myself?—a being of dubious gravity, urgently perfectionist about small things and dilatory about great ones, an everlasting amateur frivolously suspicious of expertise, kept callow by the luck of life that has preserved me from chronic tragedy, extensively introspective in leisure wrested from responsibility—an old woman with an unconscionably young soul?

It is now the thing to ask people whether they like themselves. Well, I wouldn't know: I leave myself and myself leaves me alone on that score. But that's not quite it. The truth is that to myself I'm not an "I" so much as a landscape under changing skies peopled with very vivid figures. I may meet myself among these, and if I appear in these "fields and spacious palaces" as doing something shameful, of course I turn away in dislike.

And occasionally I figure myself to myself more particularly—as slightly but not excessively absurd, serene in perfectly undeserved physical normalcy, with no illusions of cutting an elegant figure outside, and certain that whatever bearing I construe for myself internally is unlikely to survive translation into the world. That is what I *see*. And I *think* of myself as on many occasions more estimable than lovable, but also—and this I do rejoice in—as plying my man's intellect in a womanly way. And I'm far less rigid than my old friends know and far more limited than my new friends think.

There are things in my inner sanctum—and I suppose in everyone's—that I would never tell, not from pride or shame, but from a simple aversion to being known, the fear of dissipating my substance, you might say. Well, I'm sailing pretty close to the wind, but that's always been my favorite sailing position, heeled over and hiking out.

How different people look to themselves and to others: passion—fanaticism, tolerance—vagueness, tact—dishonesty, spontaneity—unaccountability, earthiness—dirtiness, immediacy—thoughtlessness, privacy—evasiveness, and the whole polar litany. The critics may be perfectly right but the criticized have an unbeatable argument: They got there first and have the right of way.

You're worried about me. I'm touched by the attention but unimpressed with your take on my situation.

There comes a moment when, irritated by the midden heap of unassimilated experience, there's to be a great spring cleaning: Be clarified or clear off. But unlike solid stuff, impressions aren't really disposable: Memories are even less biodegradable than the plastic in the town dump. So they'd better be analyzed into oblivion. This metaphor is not as strained as it seems.

People who don't know themselves are really unknowable, not only because all we know is what we're told (since both expressions and behavior are very deceptive indices to internal life), but above all because the unarticulated soul is purely potential, unformed matter; it has no essence or rational formula, as the Aristotelians would say. That doesn't mean they aren't lovable. Who after all is more lovable than a child?

One's character and one's nature being often at odds, the art of living includes when to give which its head—when to let my moral agent go to work and when to let my being be. But that means there's a referee between my acquired and my original self: Well, of course: thought.

How does the heart bear all that has come, eventuated, gone? Sometimes it seems that the incessant repetitions (because after three-quarters of a century, it is mostly the same thing, though to be sure with riveting variations) carve their mark ever deeper, and sometimes it seems as if three score and fifteen years had simply come and gone leaving only evanescent tracings.

The heart isn't very good at solving problems but it is great at premonitions of trouble.

There are uncultivated hearts, rank with lack of pruning, weeding, and sweeping, which one shudders to see opening.

Even reserved people suppose that much about them is tacitly assumed—and then are shocked to discover that they were in fact presumed to be blankly innocent. They wanted to live incognito, and now they're a little bit insulted.

Our life as externally observed: anecdotal, episodic, and skewed; as internally lived: epic, continuous, and artlessly fluent.

What irritates us most about each other is that we are forever being ourselves, expansively, unstoppably. It's also what we love.

A willow has no re-flection, it casts its image on a creek, and there it stays. A human being looks in the mirror and its image returns to the looking eyes—and so, or even more so it is in introspective reflection; here we and our reflections are one and the same.

The faint tedium of talking about oneself: Been there, done that. People who are in frequent self-communication are used to a partner who knows without being told, but if one's talking to others, candor requires impermissible exhaustiveness, and modesty demands unsatisfactory abridgment.

If we could be perfectly tolerant, accepting, fluid—but that's just what having a character forestalls. We have limits, and behold! they trump longings and the need to keep in moral shape wins out over desire—in the long run.

Teutons: cumbrous and undeft. (Some French literateur said—forgive the repetition: When I see a German trying to be graceful I want to jump out of the window; well, French *tournure* has its irritations too.) Anyhow, to the point. Am I German? I think I revert in my off-moments. By a happy fate I'm mostly an American, that is to say, an unbuttoned Anglo-Saxon. And, of course, a Jew, a Maccabee. Yet also a pagan, who is not scandalized by visible gods and has a certain care for the question asked "of old and now and forever": What is Being? (*Metaphysics* VII 1)

Self-lucid people are, within limits, flexible; balky mulishness is the self-assertion of the self-obscure.

The heart's a brat and the soul a permissive parent.

Isn't it a sign of conceit to tolerate as a cute caper in another what you censor as a shameful slip in yourself? Well, that's how our national virtue works, if truth be told.

There's the delight of watching a future friend gravitate toward oneself and of feeling a responsive motion within, a rising disposition toward commitment.

It is moving to see another moved. Unmoved movers may move the stars, but not us humans. Oh my God, I've just undone Aristotle!

Some things make one writhe, for example, the emotional life of ignoble females: cravenly aggressive, idiosyncratically common, calculatingly emotional, and opportunistically offended. A man might be equally awful, but he would be rank as game rather than rancid as oil.

In love, in study, in introspection, intensity and concreteness are complements, as are diffuseness and abstraction—and of course, in philosophizing.

There is a recalcitrant little devil in us that won't respond to furtive, oblique, uncandid demands for help but turns into a ready angel when it hears a trustful, lusty appeal for comfort. Sadly, that goes sometimes even for crying children.

Our anger gets ratcheted up when we are in fact colluding in the condition we're righteously angry about, especially in demonstrative politics, private or public.

What a reflection on yourself it is to despise those who admire you! That said, one's usually of two minds: 1. You're ludicrously overdoing it; 2. You don't know the half of it.

Two kinds of loners: Those who slip easily in and out of company because they are in company when alone, and those for whom re-entry is painful because they were seeking to be lonely, so as to savor their bitterness.

Sympathy from an anxiously self-involved person is clammy; it might come off on you.

It's easy to be generous in safety, but let your territory be invaded: instant meanness.

An other human being: just like me and *therefore* impenetrably strange.

Why does our whole inner world grow ruddy with shame when we are denied common respect? Because we should be such as to compel it.

There is no thought *sui generis,* and if no one now on earth thinks as you do, someone among the dead will have done so. Here's a curious but unsuppressable irrelevancy: The Romans spoke of dying as going to the majority, but we the living are now very much in the majority, I've heard. It's curiously unsettling, a kind of top-heaviness in human existence and nonexistence.

Tacitly, to an acquaintance who is belaboring me with arguments: If I thought what you think, I'd be what you are, and that wouldn't suit me at all.

Speak heart and tell me your thoughts! My thought has heart enough to listen.

How would we know others' unspoken minds except by consulting our own? But that requires not an average but a normal mind: The question "What would I think" should be addressed to a mind that thinks as one's fellow humans do think, not to a machine that grinds the lean and the fat into a notional hamburger.

If you're too much admired for your wit, you may be the less trusted for your wisdom.

Your chief influence on yourself is yourself, who else?

An eye-opener: I'm in full spate of fast-moving activity and people around me are harried by my pace, my efficiency, my very absorption. Am I innocent? No—for humans, being fully at work (Aristotle's *energeia*) is indeed a kind of self-absorption. Take heed.

Sober self-assessment is not without its satisfactions; the dignity of oneself having marked out one's limits and the comfort of having come to terms.

Can I learn anything new from myself? Is introspection like observation? It seems so, but only if the soul is a great palace with reception halls, labyrinthine corridors, several floors, some secret chambers, and of course, a foundation. It will have doors and windows fronting on our world, and the great question is whether it has exits and entrances to the rear into an other world. If it were so it would not be *from* myself that I learned truly wonderful things but rather *through* myself. Philosophical fantasies!

Since human interiority is neither literally spatial nor altogether temporal, human complexity can't be quite the same as logical complexity (elements involved with each other in a rule-governed spatio-temporal system). Perhaps one should say that the soul is complicated (involuted to its depths) rather than complex. In any case, although many might quarrel with the soul as a subject, no one could doubt human twistiness as the predicate.

Trust in others derives from faith in oneself.

Being complicated and thinking complexly don't imply each other. One person is simple-souled to the point of boorishness but he evolves very complex thought structures, another is complicated enough to seem incomprehensible but brings forth thoughts of crystalline simplicity.

I'm to put myself in another's shoes. So I try hard and now I know where's the rub. Is my sympathy therefore the greater? Sometimes to know each other is cordially to dislike each other. Justice is more reliable than empathy.

The two defenses of my youth: implacable resistance and compulsive excogitation.

Why might an expression of natural and true feeling sound awkward and look artificial? Because utterance, which issues magically through the looking glass from the inside into the outside, requires much thought to be natural. We learn, largely from reading, the words that are adequate to our intention, and we gain the poise which keeps our limbs where nature wants them.

We may be definable as featherless bipeds or rational animals, but to me it is a continual source of wonder that we are the finitely solid organisms that nevertheless have an illimitably spacious inside, wide inward prospects, that are, moreover, ours and ours alone to open to fellow humans. We are the bodies with an astounding topology: Our interior is not a body, and so it is somewhat transparent to ourselves, and opaque at will to others.

I suppose we all have our moments of sore-heartedness at the unceremoniouness with which life leaves us to our own devices, the desire to run into shelter and to perfect repose, to rely no longer on our own able-bodiedness but to go to bed and be served. That lasts about one half-hour.

People would feel easier in their skins if they learned that being ambivalent is not being "conflicted." Double-valuing is a perfectly sound, stable position.

Sometimes I wonder if this absurd accumulation shouldn't be entitled "Me, on a platter"—which makes me think of Salome.

Eighteen hours of waking mentation: Mostly it chases itself on the surface, but now and then something wells up from within.

If someone entitled to know (who could that be?) asked me what I think of myself I might answer as follows: I think of myself not as good (since goodness often implies self-denial) but as sound (meaning sane within reason, so to speak). I get wildly and not always silently annoyed when my privacy is breached or my time is futilely occupied. I can eat my heart out over not much and lose my temper at innocent functionaries. I'm all too willing to evade sorrow or discomfort and sometimes complacent in thought, letting verbal wit carry the day. I'm a control freak in my immediate surroundings, who has to have the decks clear and scrubbed and all the stuff done right now, even at human expense. I'm capable of inventing wonderful scenarios of revenge and have twinges of *Schadenfreude* (joy in harm to others, for those who don't know the charming German language), which moreover I express as sympathy. And I don't even take my defects seriously, levigating them by means of self-knowledge.

There's a flipside: I don't (much) lie to myself and by preference not to others. I feel keen gratitude to the known agencies of my good life, my country, my college, my friends and lovers, alive and dead, and to those unknown, those mysterious guardians of psychic health and zest for work. I have a ready reverence for high and excellent things, and the capacity for not being bored by perfection—in short, I am grateful for being one of Eden's bottle washers. Finally, I combine a working respect for almost all of my fellow humans with a sound sense of the hierarchy of souls. And there are lots of modifications to this *nobody* needs to know.

We conjecture beyond the self-expositions of those we despise, while we respect the self-revelations of those we esteem, both as telling truth and as setting limits.

Inside a human being an anthropologist or sociologist (who perforce has to establish categories and join them in theories) would be out of business. All is too fluidly potential, inchoately type-less, idiosyncratically all-human. It's when we behave as *anthropoi,* humans among humans, and as social beings that we become specimens.

How much of inner life is inexpressible not because it would be shameful to expose but because it is so atmospheric, so subtly fragrant that a treatise could not specify it—though it could kill it!

Every night—no, many nights—we wake up into a second world. As Descartes rightly says, it has place, number, configuration, and motion sortally in common with the waking world. But we've never seen this one.

What would keep the inner world from yet being what the outer one once was: a cosmos, a harmonious whole?

I've never come to grips with the philosophical notion of a Leibnizian monad, but it surely is a plausible figure for our souls: inner world theaters, isolated from each other but in harmony by reason of containing the same scenery from a slightly different perspective. That's just how we seem to be with each other—so maybe it's not a figure.

I wonder if eccentrics aren't just more unguarded about letting their behavior express their inner life than the rest of us, whose anomalies are moderated into personal style. If all one's nuttiness found expression—!

A body is accessible to touch—what is tangible can be touched. The soul is intangible and untouchable. Therefore it is the body that needs to be concealed under clothing. The soul is self-concealed.

The soul presents itself in the image of a body. One token of the soul's body-likeness is its desire to hide from intrusive stares, to conceal even, or even especially, a point of pride, an inner treasure. The soul can be made to shudder by an uninvited touch, just like the body.

Shame is the affective acknowledgment of the figuratively somatic character of the soul. Shameless people are self-exposed; though they don't cringe, it is repulsive to see. Shamelessness is the breakdown of that delicacy and distance that makes psychically modest people draw in on themselves after a psychic mishap and sensitive people look the other way.

We're ornery. First we're hell-bent on keeping ourselves to ourselves, and then we want to know why our friends pass over our inner celebrations, anniversaries, and commemorations with cavalier casualness. How are they to know that a spot, a date, an object, has epochal significance for us if we don't say so? And we won't say so because they're supposed to know, though if they did hint we'd make short shrift of their approach. The same goes for those cool little accounts that are really *sub rosa* confidences. But here's the kicker: They do often know and receive signals in just the right way. And so should we all.

People have an essence; I mean here not in the sense of a metaphysical nature but in the sense of a personal extract, a fragrance. Proud people have the most delicate essence because they remain unfingered.

Our dignity lies first of all in how we address ourselves.

In respecting, that is, in extending our regard to others, we enlarge our own self-regard. And in admiring them openly we evince our generosity—"freedom" in Chaucerian English—the liberality of soul that allows our sense of another's worth to overflow in expressive words or gestures.

Praise from others is, it seems, always at once above and below the mark. For it tends to overstate the grade of excellence of the accomplishment while it fudges the details we're so proud of. But the ambiguous feel goes deeper: on the one hand embarrassment at being exposed to falsification, on the other hand the arrogantly stand-offish thought: "To you, I should be invaluable."

To myself: Don't let yourself be borne off on the billows of imagining when you're supposed to be traipsing up the rocky road of thinking.

20 PASSION: LOVE'S LABOR

Love's complaints are really more plaints, lamentations, than protests. Serious accusations of fecklessness or meanness are no longer within love's discourse.

Miscarried love is a bone-wearying enterprise.

The firsts of love are the most unforgettable but not the most satisfying. Contentment comes in the follow-ups.

Disaster: when one cannot go on and the other cannot give up.

How love gone wrong crudifies everything, pushes us past delicacy, pride, shame, into the withholding of the generous affection that would at least save the friendship, into fruitless reckonings, into baneful explicitness, into the extraction as debts of what ought to be free gifts.

Why this one? That's the mystery of mysteries to which love pretends to have an answer.

"They that have pow'r to hurt and will do none"—they are the ones who infect others and make them ill while themselves staying hale.

Around love is spun a complex and delicate web of hopes and expectations. One word unfitly spoken, say a cagey but quite clear declaration of independence, shows that one's cocoon was the other's prison: a horrid breath of truth in a fool's paradise.

For the young, love is a hobo seeking a migrant's employment.

Love is the juncture of repose and excitement.

The paired boons of love: delight and duty, protectiveness and protection, company and solitude, camaraderie and lovemaking, world-access and lair-building, conversation and silence.

The two phases of love: Contractive—there is no world except as a venue, no time except before and after. Expansive—time has reopened for work and the world is host to continual excursionary delights.

How so evidently delicate a spell can be so sturdily durable! But then, its casting was a contingency while its undoing is a work of will.

Is disproportion in love a human norm or an offense against nature?

Happiness: Discharging daily duties, living life's mundanities to the descant of love's delights, from blithe banter through earnest confidences to closest encounters.

Give me a break! I'm supposed to help you mourn your last love?

Vacation from passion: back to the unroiled flow of life, relieved from the watches of love. Let-down or relief?

The distractedly watchful hypocrisy of incipient love: carrying on a sensible conversation while scanning the face for indices.

The inspections of love raise that famous philosophical "one-over-many problem" very acutely: How do so many confoundingly enchanting details make up one infinitely familiar face?

One request can't be fulfilled in love: "Tone it down." Sooner can the rich economize than the heart retrench its expense of spirit. The offer of aid, "Let's be friends," is a cruel stupidity.

Why is it just the ravishing particularity of anything—people, nature, works of art—that can't be held in memory, so the acute cause of love is first to be lost? It's because in love we are well and truly caught in appearances and neither our speech nor our memory is up to their vagrant infinitude.

Presence has a plangent message: We wanted to take possession, here and now, by eyes and arms, and all our preoccupation with the soul was only the makeshift of absence. But that's a half-truth, a truth compressed by the pressure of passion.

When a newer love has sapped the savor out of old haunts and companions it's time to bring old loyalties before the imagination. Well-conditioned love doesn't degenerate into centripetal folly.

Over and over: In full spate love sweeps over all obstacles, and as the tide recedes all the rocks and snags emerge, those old facts of nature in general and in particular.

The limbo in love is closeness without clarity.

Absence is the acid and the stretch test of love: Can time eat through the brittle bonds or distance snap them? If you can take right up where you left off six months ago, you're in it for the long haul.

Being in love is like being in the gondola of a balloon: Unless you keep the burners going and the flames heating the air, you'll be coming down with a big bump.

In first love the sensibilities are so tender and the imagination so vulnerable that the inner world is like a balloon that a pinprick can collapse. And when the inner world is limp rubber on a string, the outer world is about as much.

I recall as a child coming home to my Peter, a doll that I loved, and sensing, for one abysmal moment, that I was lavishing affection on a foot-high bag of rags with a plastic head whose eyes opened and closed with the click of a mechanism. But a night's sleep restored the vigorous oblivion that is one of the imagination's great works. Was it much different with adult love?

Love is philosophy's laboratory. If Terms and their Relations, the Same and its Other, Being and its Appearance are the topics of research, in love all these are found in condensed, isolated, eminently dissectable form.

When the soul's engaged all things have a comely shape and a mat luster.

In mature love the limits are well in view, the object quite perspicuous, the sensibility properly toughened— and yet the ground will shake.

"It is more blessed to give than to receive" (Acts 20: 35). In love, that's gospel. It hurts not to get, but not to be allowed to give is very hell.

One feature of our West (as distinct from the Buddhist East) seems to be our division of time into mundane and festive, weekdays and holidays. That defines love's abnormality: It is a continual festivity.

In love the burden of gratitude is on the side of the giver.

Being loved wholeheartedly and being loved to the top of someone's capability: The first is full of promise, the second full of limitations.

Love is externally induced bipolar disease; we become pathologically attuned to the reversible states of another's psyche.

Get involved with a lover of brief intentions, shallow execution, curtailed affects, and you have nothing but liabilities. Love without generosity or reliability builds no psychic deposits to draw down. Such loves are like insurance companies whose inflated rates you pay for decades without building any credit. Let there be an accident, even a mishap, and you're back at the beginning, without brownie points. So too in these affairs: You have to be watchful all the time because one failure and it all comes down. Not the company you want to keep.

Love can be utterly selfish: It hopes for a chance to give comfort.

A first thought: Love depends on nearness; absence obliterates concrete attachments—you can't love what isn't in your neighborhood or what disappeared before your feelings were fixed. A better second thought: You *can* be strongly bound to things far away and long ago.

Certain loves are prisons: constricted spaces with occasional shafts of light through a barred window, dreams better than waking, and a jailer equally loved and hated.

"'Tis better to have loved and lost," etc. Yes, in the very long run.

In what other human relation is indifference power? Well, perhaps in diplomacy.

For love's sickness the treatment of choice is homeopathic—the cause is the cure.

Aristotle's definition of a natural substance as that "this" which has the cause of motion within becomes perfectly vivid in love: *this* particular human being in its moving independence.

"Who, moving others, are themselves as stone, / Unmoved, cold . . ." Aristotle's divinity, the Unmoved Mover, has his human versions. They incite love once by their attraction and once again by their indifference.

Sometimes a human being seems to achieve an epiphany: essence and accidents in simultaneous view—the embodied soul in full sight.

The labor of love is an exercise in complete description. Can words, if used with plenitude and precision, capture the one being whose particularity we want to articulate and fix in memory? The lesson of love repeats more acutely the teaching of philosophy, that appearance in general is inarticulable and a particular appearance is doubly ineffable.

Love is a hermeneutic labor, the work of interpreting the infinite significance of a gesture, a line, a hue. The spur for this activity, traceless, passing, unrecorded, is the fear of oblivion, the oblivion not only of forgetting in absence but of not fully taking in the very presence.

The saddest realization: that there is no debt that hasn't been repaid over and over.

Love meagerly fed first becomes insatiable and then dies of inanition.

There is a bittersweet coda to love when the main music is over and there is a last reminiscent crescendo—a last adieu of the heart.

It's over when the daily images are consigned to memory and to the night, when the imagination withdraws from active visualizing to dreaming and spontaneous remembering.

The acute delight of clandestine communication at a party, especially on the first night of the first day of love finally declared—but all that's in *Persuasion,* Chapter XI.

Frequent ritualized expressions of gratitude and self-deprecation are ominous, the foreswearing of responsibility and a casting loose of the bonds.

People speak of being "involved"—implicated seems more descriptive.

For old-fashioned romantic love, who can answer this question: Is sex a culmination or by-play? It surely is neither beginning nor end.

Some affairs are indeed just the coagulation of subjective readiness about an object (Stendhal's silly theory of crystallization). But the real thing is altogether compelled by the object—it could be a human being or place or an artifact or a vocation. Real love is objectivity itself, in accordance with Socrates' saying in the *Phaedrus* that beauty is visibility itself.

If the sweetness of love makes the world insipid, that's a portent of disaster.

Unconfirmed love makes archeologists of us: We sort, fit, reconstruct (and invent) until we have the shape—which a plain word might shatter.

I wonder if the occurrence of romantic love, that intimate festivity, rises and falls inversely with the institution of public festivals?

Can nudists fall in love? Can people who think sex is natural?

Desire fulfilled is delight, need assuaged is contentment. To be freed from need is a relief, to be freed from desire is a letdown.

What if the flesh is sound and the soul shallow? Then people have an "affair"—that curious flare-up of passion in the absence of the soul.

It's a melancholic satisfaction to be proved right in love's battles, since vindication involves depreciation of another's being.

Love's R.I.P.: these famous manumissions—giving and wanting one's freedom. Lovers and logicians have this in common: They know that they are in bondage and that's how they want it.

In the third year of love the dredging's done and the channels run full and easy.

Since in acute love a blemish becomes a point of passion the uncensored language of love would be quite offensive: "I love you because of your ugly . . ."

Two types: radical and reasonable love. The first goes for all or nothing; it tries to force the gift of counter-passion by mere assertion of need and then despises the response for lacking spontaneity. The second is satisfied with a compromise; it is willing to content itself with *de facto* possession when available.

In love every scene is but a setting for one figure.

How strange that when the distance between our bodies has closed and they are one, our imaginations go separately off into the wild blue yonder!

All our attention is retracted into one human being, but that being is, contrarily, diffused into every landscape.

What demon keeps pushing for proved reciprocity when pleasure depends on keeping up the illusion of ardor's symmetry?

The carousel of hurt in love goes round and round and up and down, as the steam organ drones its merry-go-round music—but the whole rickety round can stop at a touch.

The world-without-end hour: "Waiting for" is "attending to" with a negative object. The heart beats on but time stands still. The mind vibrates but doesn't work. A letter, a ring, and it's from rack to ruin—or release.

The office romance is the most banal scenario—and yet! To find love *in situ,* in the place where we're mundanely fixed, is serendipity itself, provided the arcane bond does its little world more good than harm.

In the beginning: the golden-green sheen of open possibility not yet fettered by established passion, a wanton sense of delicious indeterminacy blithely reckless of the entanglements to come.

Love makes vulnerable, friendship confident.

When the inner bond is absolute and its outer recognition simply absent—that's invisible slavery.

The stage fright of first love constricts speech, makes it stilted, over-rehearsed, freighted with coagulated feeling.

The wit of love is, like Eros, winged, and darts about on the winds of passion, while its wisdom is, like Homer's "wingless word," settled in the calm of the mind.

Love wants access, to the body to be sure, but above all to the soul, and (the pass once obtained) coming and going, without rebuffing restrictions or disconcerting revelations.

What used to be the Anglo-Saxon mode of love was made for the novel: in its undeclared stage condensed by containment and heightened by silence, after the declaration, expressed in poignant courtliness and rising to shy liberties. Thus the novelist had intense hearts and shapely demeanors to work with—well, Jane Austen anyway.

There is a literal catastrophe ("downturn") of love when our sense of serving a glorious sovereign is clouded by a hint of sub-alternity in our Lord. For in love it is lovelier to be liege than lord. Well, we recover and reconstitute our allegiance in tenderness and pity.

Life in the ambience of the deity: daily danger.

Why does the image of love's object cause high excitement by day and aid soporific relaxation by night? Well, love's multipotent.

"Being your slave, what should I do but tend . . .": Love engineers the day as an off-on setting, vacant or full and nothing in between.

An affair of the heart is confirmed, given objective status, by a well-wishing observer.

What do we think of a person who walks away from love's imbroglio? Not much.

Love's loveliest moment is the pre-passionate élan, when banter is jauntily brisk, every gesture is crisp and every motion deft, when one walks securely on air and failure is far off. If we ever learned anything, our hearts would constrict in fear.

The moment we are secure, Eros's bowstring goes slack and his arrows don't reach us. This young demon is perverse!

Eros is a boy and cupids are babies: Love is lithe and flirtations are roly-poly.

Repression, in putting the heart under pressure, gives the soul definition. Love gone incognito makes us known to ourselves.

That perpetual, unfailing delight should emanate from one being! And then cease!

Those "That do not do the thing they most do show": When Eros, the great tyrant, refuses to exercise his dominion—that's the ultimate rejection.

Absence contracts the whole world to that salient point, the moveless clock. Presence makes the world expand and the clock a racing irrelevance.

Grief's two modes: The gorge rises or the heart plunges.

It's a cold but salutary moment when you realize that there's no fault to be found and no blame to be assigned: You're simply involved in a mistake with two victims and no perpetrator. Isn't that the silent message behind the moaning and groaning of Country and Western music?

In love, the imagination takes its Edenic epiphanies into the world and its paradises occupy terrestrial ground— for a while.

The endless labor of reasoning oneself out of hope and tricking oneself back into it, the bone-weary battle between resignation and resentment—and they say it's better to have loved and lost, etc.!

The pointed passion of love will make you into an observant nominalist, one who has experienced the primacy of the contingent individual existent, a knowing believer in the ultimacy of the atomic fact: the object of love.

The best love does not minister to a pre-existent condition but calls forth its own specific need. Anyhow you deserve love not by needing it but by falling into it gratuitously. For love adds a supererogatory sweetness to life; it doesn't give life itself. It supplies a surplus of being; it doesn't repair a deficiency.

People in need (they call them "needy" now, yech!) tend to maunder, inaudibly or raucously. They deserve pity clothed in all the respect you can muster, but that's light years from love.

The soul does proud obeisance before an alien grace searching the while for a just, sober language of adoration, not the subjective generalities of "How do I love thee? Let me count the ways," but precision, precision.

A melting pizzicato, a swooning plucking of the strings sounds like a contradiction in terms. But it describes great moments.

In dangerous, dark times, love of a community, a person, a child, hangs like a descant above the cacophony; it is their image that makes danger appalling while energizing resistance.

Sad to say there are besotted moments when senti-mental kitsch has an appeal, because it bears witness to the universality of one's own condition.

"What is your substance, whereof are you made / That millions of strange shadows on you tend?" Here is raised a fundamental question in love's study: Why does an or-dinary human being, if he chances to be in the sun's way, have one firmly attached shadow, while a being that is loved casts a thousand times a thousand simulacra of himself over all and everything? How does a loved sub-stance come so to exfoliate itself without diminishing its thereness? Well, if the world's chief researcher into love's intricacies couldn't answer in fourteen lines . . .

"Reason not the need"—it is love's pride to want its needs divined and generously met. If you have to ask or ask for more, what you get will never give satisfaction.

Love is confirmed when you're admired for your sor-rows rather than pitied.

Nothing so confirms our self-confidence as the convic-tion that our love was well placed.

Luck in love: to have found strength of character and grace of soul.

In early love there are salient moments with circum-ambient life dragging around them; in settled love the now continual occasions of delight have merged with the continuous stream of ordinary life.

Time supersedes itself (it produces bygones) and space is physically exclusive (it allows only one body at a time in one space), and that's what makes love affairs unsound: What kind of love is it that is not conceived as timeless (that cheerfully contemplates its own terminus) and that all but abrogates the law of bodies (that puts different bodies in the same bed in perilously close succession)? Pfui.

When the feeling for a person is imbued with gratitude not just for his being but for his conduct, it has fragrance that won't fade.

The ache of suddenly seeing that other human being as indescribably lovable, inexpressibly beautiful, beyond possible possession, comes from the quandaries inherent in these passionately worshipful apotheoses: You are putting out of reach the very being with which you most want intimacy.

If you want to get off from the shoals of love do it as sailors do: kedge off. Get in a dinghy, set the anchor way off, and start hauling up on it. Soon your sloop's afloat and off you sail. The trick is to set the anchor *way off*.

When speech bears too great a burden of grief, clarifications become simplifications, hurts shape up as complaints, and ramifications come out as repetitions. When you're near tears language regresses. But once launched, the mission can't be scrubbed.

The rich can't retrench and neither can lovers.

In unreciprocated love there's an object and a subject. The object (which may, in its turn, be subject to some other object) is objective—untouched and indifferent. The subject is so denominated because it is both a consciousness and a vassal. Some terminology works.

Of course, leaving each other room to breathe is only the courtesy of Eros, but the panicky fixation on freedom is a contemporary trick and erotically paradoxical. Frequent assertions of freedom in love are graceless. Anyhow, roving love is not satisfactory for women.

When we are past the hormonal age, loving is a gift from the gods—not a willingness which is a disposition we can manage, but the desire which requires a highly specific object. Aristotle speaks truth when he says that it is not desire that comes first but the object that rouses the desire (*On the Soul* 433). And that's the god's doing: the object, *this* human being.

Delight starts in the eye, the panoramic sense, and desire closes the distance until touch, the local sense, takes over and the person disappears and becomes a body. Yet the pleasure even of blind physical intimacy depends on knowing who it is you're with, to wit, Joseph's confounding discovery: "And it came to pass, that in the morning, behold, it was Leah" (Genesis 29: 25 and its exegesis in "Jacob's Marriage," Mann's *Joseph and his Brothers*).

That old ballad about not taking up with the new before being done with the old really speaks to the economy of time. Worthwhile love ought to be time-consuming, absorbing. So aside from the morality of erotic double-dipping, there is the practical fact that it's going to be done undevotedly.

In civil life obligations are reciprocal, not so in love: We can't bind others by the fact that we feel bound. That's because everyone knows that even the unilateral obligations of love are desirable, in fact painful to relinquish.

Love makes us both proud and poor-spirited—proud to take a part in the universal drama and humbled for the same reason.

One asks, "Do you want me?" And the other hears, correctly, "Commit yourself!" And so starts the downhill slide: with the question mark that straightens out into an exclamation point.

Whoever thinks the world is well lost for love will have nowhere to go.

Living in tandem is a life of prepositions: living with, in, for, by, through each other. But of course there's another set as well. They come later: around, despite, against, etc.

People "have relationships," as if the relation was conceivable independent of its terms. And then they "work on" this relationship as if love were fungible, a union contract. Can Eros survive these negotiations, even if the venue is not table but bed?

There is a palpable threshold crossed from playful potentiality to committed actuality. Do we make the choice to cross or is it "always already" too late?

One belated effect of a love is that we become interesting to ourselves (and to others who have their conjectures). And why not? We have the story of a miracle to tell (though if we're wise we don't).

An insouciantly cheerful greeting can plunge an anxious lover into despair.

Stendhal's very French theory of crystallization: I suppose that, regarded as a national obligation, love creates its object, but experienced as a spontaneous event, the object induces the love.

Love can burst in as that proverbial *coup de foudre,* or it can slither in like those sidewinders of our deserts. The devil's in it either way.

Love strikes where there's a readiness to focus light into fire.

It's pretty hopeless when one feels forever deprived and the other perpetually put upon.

The marvel of marvels: that it should be in the light of day as it was in the dark of night—that love has survived a sunrise.

Love is not so much doing good to an other as seeing them well.

The devil's mixed into love insofar as blemishes and misdeeds appear as one more charm. But there are limits: Love can thrive on misguided panache but it can't survive lowness.

The phases of decline and fall are ever parallel and ever out of sync: indifference, irritation, liberation vs. anxiety, recriminations, heartbreak.

The phases of forgetting are oddly counterintuitive: At first the lost figure requires laborious summoning to return as a fugitive form in imaginative space, and only much later does it appear spontaneously, with the presentness of ectoplastic matter. Memory has the power to make time reverse itself, as experiments have indeed shown; it's passage that brings back the past.

The scary singularity of love: It saps the savor from our noblest realm, the universal.

The "at first sight" phenomenon, love's sudden entry through the eyes, is a miracle, but so is its slow insidious growth in the heart.

Who people are and what they do is identical only to a doctrinaire behaviorist; love knows otherwise. For what we love is a being in its mere presence, and its deeds can go pretty far off before they draw us from our beloved fact. We love aspects, not works.

We're logy with love and sodden with desire; our judgment goes soggy, and the outrageousness of it all would come clear only if we told the tale to a third—which what little honor's left forbids we do. We should hang ourselves out to dry. Heraclitus is so right: The dry soul is best.

No appeal more self-defeating than that for pity in love, since elicited pity damps passion.

You can get enough of someone in a good sense too: fully satisfactory companionship.

The ubiquitous one-and-many problem: Love is one unitary fact, and it also has a thousand facets.

The soul on vacation, at once unstrung and invigorated: time divided between waiting and attending, *ennui* and ardor, languor and excitement. And no viable way back to even-tenored work.

We surrender our habits and usages, not to say our very selves, before the first onset of love: We'll be anything we're asked to be. But we snap back, of course, and that's the moment of truth.

Relief that appears as desolation: when we realize that we ourselves engineered the breakup and that it wasn't the loss but the love itself that was unbearable.

The moment love is declared, the incubus of hope and dread takes himself off; then, for a while, love is blithely weightless.

The music of love: the sudden modulation from affection to passion.

Enchantment is befuddling but disenchantment is no relief.

What a lesson in love's mystery: to come face-to-face with the person who has broken another's heart and to find it simply and utterly incomprehensible!

One of love's labors is a strenuous lookout for luck, the attempt to arrange chances.

You can mitigate the ignominious need for incessant proof of love by generously anticipating it; like the ravenous baby's bottle, it won't be wanted before long.

"Sensitivity" means both heightened receptivity to pleasure and overwrought expectancy of offense. The latter has a refrain: "Love doth not so."

Cupid-love may be blind, but Eros-love is rather a hyper-acute state of attention.

There's one test of love: wanting to be together. The rest is diversionary twaddle.

The cognitive arc of love: normal opacity, scintillating mystery, indifferent transparency.

"Familiarity breeds contempt": The mysteries of otherness become trite without having been breached. It's a mean thought and a false way: If the work of love, which is the penetration of an others' soul, is properly performed, familiarity breeds devotion.

Tender by night, brusque by day—the boor-lover.

The impatient assertion that love has been sufficiently declared is a declaration of lovelessness.

Love can be dormant: You know it but don't feel it.

Love's tyranny: It exacts incessant tributes and respects no rights.

Never be flippant with the lovelorn: it's like taking a swipe at a wound.

Rebuffs resonate down the ages; find a weasly way.

The high-wrought music of love: exultant, Elysian— the joyous tension of a Bach concerto.

In love all activities are refracted through one prism.

Admiration can be actively compelled; love is passively contingent.

The life of love begins in the interstices of the working world, and before long it's flipped: Work happens in the interstices of love.

"I love you" can mean: "I have to say it" or "I want to hear it" or "You need to hear it."

The service of unreason is a relentless discipline.

The person you love is the chief actor of a thousand imagined dramas: epic, tragic, melodramatic, domestic.

Time spent together is well understood to have two purposes: pleasure and bonding, and it's so with many activities of leisure, like travelling. We go for the pleasure of being there, and we make memories for the future: we two in that place.

There's a keen but half-guilty pleasure in hearing the person we love talked about, in seeing him in a new perspective, of being in his ambience even in his absence, even of having our protective ire raised.

Is "lovable" a *quality* of a man, woman, child, music? The answer can't be no, because they *are* lovable, and it can't be yes, because it's *them* we love, not their lovableness. It's like that old philosophical puzzle, whether existence is a predicate.

The wish to receive love can be converted into the readiness to give it, with a stiff fee in sorrow.

No need to be a neophyte in love: A childhood rich in affection and an imagination full of figures is preparation enough for sliding into this condition smoothly and naturally.

The love which is in service to a worthy object, poem, or music, has a lovely reciprocity: We give effort, it gives itself. It's fatally different with human beings.

Love's a hermaphrodite; its assaults sometime stab and sometime suffuse.

Once in love, always in love. It can be eclipsed but it can't be obliterated. One night, twixt dream and wake, it's back.

Two barriers to be breached: falling in love and being fallen in love with. People will say we have a propensity for these events, but they are so idiosyncratic, propensity doesn't do it.

You don't expect to learn the three proofs of God's existence from your lover. In fact you're not out to learn *from him* but to learn *him,* to commit him into your soul, so to speak. This works a kind of sympathetic re-formation, new postures and patterns, a new psychic topography. Absorption *in* another implies absorption *of* another, an enormous psychic enlargement; you acquire a second nature. How do you explain the strange fact that you're in effect learning to be a man?

Here's perfect lovableness: fineness without fussiness, patency without loss of inwardness, naturalness without naiveté, firmness without censoriousness, observant keenness without intrusiveness, intelligence without smartness, wit without cynicism; daring and circumspection, generosity and gracious receptivity, pride and modesty. Well, we can dream, can't we?

Love is, among other things, the highest potentiation of agreeableness. Even the best of friends irritate each other by impending too much or by being too distant, by incompatible tempos or by just being themselves—even the fondest of friends find each other finitely bearable. But during the enchantment of love, the lovers are always welcome, in any quantity, posture, or degree of self-sameness.

There *is* a love willing to protect the loved one even from the intrusions of love: parents.

Would that we lost this phrase, "sexual orientation," because it betokens 1. that it's proper to make public proclamation of private affairs, 2. that sex is prior to love, and 3. that the direction of love is predetermined. These are all dubious and restrictive propositions.

"Love is to want another's good." Well, maybe. But it certainly is to want another's presence.

There's a time of inchoateness, of incubation when we're like a cat on a hot tin roof—dreams and intimations: the expectant heart.

Here's valid reasoning with no standing at all: You got me into this, you get me out, i.e., you made me love you, you relieve my longing—the heart's disallowed plea.

There's no way the heart will learn that it cannot demand a return of love.

Affectionless intimacy, inattentive intimacy; the heart fills with liquid lava.

There are hearts that are anechoic chambers: Rosamond in *Middlemarch* and sundry real-life characters.

The long uncultivated heart reverts to wildness with even the briefest break in attention, and over and over you start from zero.

The protectiveness of love: cherishing a superior vulnerability, as of a fine piece of porcelain. When to the cold eye it's just human pottery.

What seemed such an engaging enigma, such an absorbing problem—gone, pouf, when feeling runs out. Yet this attentive involvement with the subtleties of imaginative investment leaves a residue of understanding—the long-term gain.

Mere presence, simple thereness, best assuages grief and gives peace. Or the opposite.

How we take pride in the resilient, flexible felicity of successful love and feel shamed by the fixated vulnerabilities of rejection! And yet the latter demands more bravery: The jocund amiability of the happy vs. the effortful courtesy of the sad.

In early youth, when love is worship, the being we love looks so august, so invulnerable. And then it turns human, woundable, desirous. That's the break point of the infatuation for the young—who are right to scuttle from the sight of their adamantine god's soft interior.

Love is delighted attention; delight is object-induced joy; attention is the soul's stretching toward an object. Ergo: Love is the soul's attention to an object that gives joy. Did that get anywhere?

Etymologies: "Caress" means "endearment" and "care" means "grief," and that about sums it up.

At first love we treat each other with gratuitous care, as if we were the walking wounded. Slowly a little healthy bluffness enters, and then it gets brisk.

Bitterness supervenes when the other's being no longer transcends his actions for us.

Proud lovers are reluctant to taint the beautiful gratuitousness of it all by asking for help. But of course, that is also an admission of its fragility.

The haunts of love are filled with a faint music; does it sound in our absence?

"All happy families are like; each unhappy family is unhappy in its own way"—I think what Tolstoy says is true of love as well. In its upward arch, love's ontogeny recapitulates phylogeny—falling in love follows the received pattern, a grand archetype. But on its descending leg, it's pain is peculiar to ourselves, all ideal-debris.

Some beings concentrate your ardor. Then who or what hardly matters, but how is everything. Love discreetly, decently, and don't make a federal case of it.

21 BODY: FLESH AND DESIRE

Do you want a taste of alienation? Look at yourself in the mirror. Is *that* supposed to be me? Is that my vehicle, my front? Did I shape that face, and if not, what right does it have to represent me? Does it bear any assignable relation to me? I'm put off not by it as a face—it's no worse than most others—but as a supposedly telling mask.

Women, at least, often think they can remake their faces by making them up. What they may gain in attractiveness they lose in expressive verisimilitude.

But then, would we be better off as soul-nudists, going about showing our naked souls to each other? It would not be worse so much as unimaginable. For our inner being does not have a body's compactness. They're diffuse as a mist and expansive as a landscape, my inward prospects. Probably this vehicular container, inadequate as it is to myself, is not the worst way to carry me about outer space and to represent me as a visible person:

But O alas, so long, so farre
Our bodies why doe wee forbeare?
They are ours, though they are not wee. Wee are
The intelligences, they the sphaere.

> We owe them thankes, because they thus
> Did us, to us, at first convay . . .
> (Donne, "The Extasie")

And that's true too; it was as a body that love seized me first and ever after, and as a body that I myself drew love. So let this earthly sphere orbit through its world and it'll be my job to be its governing intelligence. On those terms I'll come back to myself.

The vibrant ties of desire are outlasted by the leathery bonds of need (not always to happy effect); so also loyalty outlives zest and gratitude delight.

The force of possessive desire is inversely proportional to the energy of the contemplative imagination.

There seems to be a kind of human being that spends the day between insipid apathy and acrid recalcitrance and achieves a certain fragrance only in physical intimacy. What a strange lifetime: gray-and-black days with chartreuse nights—a whore's temperament?

It does seem to be a principal property of desire that it wants to outlive itself: At first it appears infinite, wildly or gently insatiable, and at the last it wants to want, desperate to generate itself. Whatever we may well know, our desire never learns: that its fulfillment must spell its termination. So we must wisely intervene: Let's do some work.

Socrates speaks of pleasure as a leaky vessel (*Gorgias*)—there's no true filling up, no definitive fulfillment—not that you can't get enough but that having enough is no longer among the pleasures, that satiation is the death of pleasure, that surfeit is not a satisfaction.

Well, that's the dim view, from the bare soul's point of view. But the complementary truth is: The embodied soul sleeps it off.

What is funny (not very) about pratfalls and other bodily mishaps? In daily life we hardly take each other in as bodies; we make quick, oblique assessments of each other's facade, sometimes appreciative, sometimes devastating (as women's brief, expert glances at each other's outfits). But let the body crash, and we're suddenly *inorganic masses,* helplessly subject to gravity, like a leather bag of bones and blubber. And that has an involuntary, crude first-moment funniness, until we get back our humanity.

Cripples face being mere bodies to the stare all the time.

We long continuously for what is necessarily intermittent.

The eyes can take all they want, but the hands may take only what is conceded.

Promiscuousness is a disturbing sort of enigma: What kind of human being has a heart elastic enough, a soul expandable enough, a mind fluid enough to attend even to two other human beings at a time? Who can maintain multiple loves when the achievement of just one is a kind of special and arduous dispensation? But then, attention and love don't seem to be in it, and that's what's disturbing. I've never been friends with a natural-born prostitute (they evidently exist), but I can imagine discovering a new sort of soul, one gifted for multi-tasking.

The vibrant peace of physical proximity: relaxed comfort with a humming undercurrent of excitement.

Some of us have aging bodies enclosing young souls and that's natural: The soul being partly atemporal, we experience what Piaget calls *décalage,* "unwedging," the desynchronization of stage and age. And so we are "but a paltry thing, / A tattered coat upon a stick, unless / Soul clap its hands and sing . . ." What is unnatural and sorry is a sad elderly soul holed up in a supple young body. Those who caused that hyper-maturation have much to answer for.

The double trouble of abject need is that it repels its own fulfillment.

Insouciance: the panache of invulnerability; adolescent coolness: the pathos of fake invulnerability. The first induces skepticism, the second affection.

The passions are viscous like pitch—it takes a really well-placed blow for them to fracture cleanly.

Far worse than not getting your desire is not relishing it when you do while not ceasing to want, and the same goes for pleasure in general. We are the animal that wants to want past its getting.

It seems like the defining difference between men and women—whether love can endure without erotic possession. But that's nonsense too; think of all the pining poets, the troubadours, think of Dobbin in *Vanity Fair,* think of the heart-loyal boys, our students.

Borne upon the billows of bodily ease and the royal calm of a homeostatic soul anything seems possible—for thirty seconds.

Here is something rousingly irritating, almost beyond bearing: the body left by the self to its own devices and allowed to indulge itself. Abandoned by its psychic regulator it grows compulsive, fanatical: picking, gnawing, scratching, stroking, twiddling, spitting. We are witnessing the autism of the body left to self-cherishing, the rut of self-stimulation. It is infuriating to have to be its witness, unwillingly privy to the body's self-gratification, and it is a hopeless wait for the habit to break; who's going to tell an adult?

There is a brief moment of real bereavement in a close embrace when the visible person is gone and has not yet reappeared in the imagination.

The infidelity of the imagination: at the crucial moment, suddenly, the face we figure is not the one we're with. It's evidently not an infrequent phenomenon and seems to betoken nothing but the wickedly antic side of our curious figurative power.

Cohabitation: when the precious interludes become the mainstream; that's the test. "Marriage," says Kant (I think in his *Anthropology*) "is the moment of truth." This Copernican of cognition, who put all of nature into the single subject, preferred to avoid it.

However immediate the elements of physical embrace may be—surrender, pleasure, fulfillment—when it's over they remain as emblems of love.

In the novels I love to read marriages are consummated, that is, first the marriage, than the consummation. (Actually my favorite authors never get that far, *exempli gratia* Miss Austen.) Since now the sum and substance often precedes the ceremony, we're back, in a curious way, to even older days: marriages of convenience. Here is illustrated one of the few laws of history: Everything comes back again and nothing is ever the same.

The fastidious find that hardest which comes most easily to the rest.

Hope—shafts of joy in clouds of doubting unease: Doesn't what I so ardently desire have an obligation to occur? And when it does, don't call it luck: It was the heart that compelled it by its cunning contrivances.

The sense that sex is a favor bestowed rather than an urgency relieved—is it gratifying or saddening to a man?

Your looks are mine, not yours; *pace* Shakespeare, you are not the lord and owner of your face (Sonnet 94). To be sure, our bodies have, beside their natural build, also configurations and moves that are controllable, by breeding in childhood, by self-discipline later. But those do become second nature, and self-presentation has its limits in everyday life; even affectedly manneristic bearing ends as an automatism, a third nature, so to speak. So your appearance is less yours to present than mine to take up. But there's justice: It works the same in reverse.

Eros keeps his epiphanies sparse; he's an episodic god. If he came to us continually, would that be paradise or limbo?

Is physical intimacy a casual or a difficult achievement—not in the performance but in the psychic preliminaries? Do the generations differ in this? Good heavens, yes. Should we envy the post-revolutionaries? Good grief, no. Love should be a strenuous discipline of the soul which leaves it in shape for more life; pity the life-long callowness of kids allowed to skip the grade with grammar in it.

What body is more remote than that of a former lover? There's a strange psychic taboo that says: not again, no repeats.

How weird it is that we may be fortresses against each other, all the ports closed and the drawbridge up, except that there's a ladder into the sleeping cubicle.

The country of love has an infinite topography all under the same jurisdiction.

Sometimes the bed's a desert, sometimes a slough, sometimes a workplace, sometimes an Eden—the intricacies of intimacy. Cubicular ambitions: to be the classical lover, perfect in spontaneity, exact in synchronicity, replete with satisfaction, and consummate at benevolent pretense. Comical!

What evil demon desynchronized the clocks of love?

Supererogatory responsiveness, such as there never was or will be: wishes divined, aversions honored, confidences kept, silences respected, touchings well-calibrated. Dream on.

Terrestrially, the soul's in the body; cosmically, the body is in the soul, which wraps it round: Plato's most beautiful figure (*Timaeus*).

Who gets to talk of the body with the impunity of expertise? 1. The manual writers who specialize in the mechanical operation of the spirit and 2. the poets, especially if they're divines who clothe candor in beauty: "O my America! my new-found land . . ." (Donne, *Elegie* XIX).

It's strange to me that people would want to proclaim their sexual orientation. Nature has announced pretty clearly what our sex is, but she's said almost nothing about the sex we're to have pleasure with. Why not take her lead of discretion and let private matters be private? If there are wrongs to be righted, my support, at least, would go most enthusiastically to a blind claim for universal rights. But let that be.

Why would we wish to set ourselves in a direction at all? There are in this world all manner of things to be loved: men, women, children, animals, artifacts from cathedrals to vases, music—all to be loved according to their and our nature: as complementary bodies (men and women), as like affective temperaments (women and women), with non-sexual physicality (children), with aroused sensibility (artifacts), with the embodied soul (music, though I had a student once who was simply, erotically, in love with that dark Mozart piano concerto, the one in D minor; he couldn't live without it). And there might even be that love of the disencumbered soul for pure beings, known as philosophy, or for the highest Person, known as faith. Why then would people wish to identify themselves by so restricted a part of their humanity as their sexual taste, and why would they predetermine that taste itself? You love what's lovable, and let its attraction fix your orientation, let the occasion rule. Or so I think.

How lovely is late sex, sex that comes as the natural consequence of forged bonds. Should sex be what stores call a loss leader, an item sold below cost to induce frequenting?

Touch! That so local a sense should have such wide varieties! There are the indiscriminate plebeian intimacies, the bear hugs of jovial people, the crush of masses, the probings of professionals, the puppyish pawings of warm people. There is the heatless sweetness of fondling children, the arm lent the infirm, the ceremonious elbow for stately entrances, the hand-in-hand of young lovers (or old ones feeling young), the light tangencies of friends, and, of course, the gently arousing to fiercely inflaming sensation of erotic touch in a dozen more varieties. Just to name it all makes you go all-overish, and you could write an essay on each of them.

Seeing: Diffused—we glance at everything and nothing, look over, by, through faces to get a general impression, since it is impolite to inspect your vis-à-vis. Focused—we cast manners aside and observe studiously or insatiably suck in the sight. Repelled—we irresistibly avert our eyes and seek the right, the left, the distance.

Why are some hands (figuratively) moist, others pleasantly dry; why do some offers of sympathy make us squirm while others are like cool balm; why do some approaches make us squeamish and others responsive? It's because some souls are moist and clammy while others are dry and light, and it's the latter who have the human reserves. Heraclitus yet once more: "A dry soul is wisest and best" (Fragment 118).

(Excessive) fastidiousness, "being particular," is a nervous condition with a metaphysical root: a sensibility too focused on particulars to rise to wholes or universals, lacking the latitude to let the pimple vanish and the person appear.

Our bodies do betray us, though as revealing not more but less than we mean to: neat dispatch appears as indecent haste, deft turns as gallumphing angularities, etc. And that's because eager intentions rigidify the limbs.

There are fellow humans with bodily ways so impingingly repulsive that their proximity makes us grow wild with aversion—good people. What a disaster!

We communicate both as gesturing bodies and as speaking souls, and it makes us absorbingly complicated. As bodies we are mostly givens. Breeding and self-discipline can modify what we have from birth; we learn to finesse what clumsiness our parents haven't coaxed out of us, though in the end our expressive frame is beyond our control. But *what* we say and, partly, *how* is ours to shape. And so the soul, which configures the body only very partially, has a second chance: We can teach our tongue to *say* what we mean.

Noticed without comment: the poignant corporeality of a body made self-aware by deformity.

When you get to look straight into others' eyes you see that little image, that doll, yourself (pupil, from Latin *pupilla,* little doll). You can only hope you loom larger to your vis-à-vis than that.

When you start dreaming of the person sleeping beside you, distancing is in progress.

Sex is a coming to conclusions, so to speak, since you're closing the very distance through which the attraction first worked.

Romance and sex aren't wired in parallel but in series, I think.

The notion of joyfully unattached sex is surely a myth: Maybe for one partner, but that ends in flight, and then misery for the pair. Maybe there is a sex of pure warm-hearted animal spirits, but the partners would have to be puppies in human form, an eerie pairing before long.

Body: Since it reappears every morning it must be mine, and it's nothing to complain of. Those who got something more elegant don't seem to be more content. That's not it, it's the ever-recurrent surprise that I should have this for my persona, my mask (Latin *persona* means "mask"); or that I should wear a mask at all, that I should live behind a façade, indeed that to be a person is to represent myself in the world, to be my own representative. There's no getting over the curiousness of it.

A conundrum of sex: Is it the separate enjoyment of common pleasure or the common enjoyment of separate pleasures?

Sex has much less to do with sex, so to speak, than with the heart, at least for some women.

Disparity in lovemaking: when the one is engaged in producing pleasure and the other in confirming intimacy.

Lust masked as playfulness is a deadly danger to the innocent.

Promiscuity argues: Why miss a pleasure where it is to be had; it's contrary to nature. Resistance says: And so is it unnatural for me, being one, to distribute myself over many. The distributive law for natural numbers, (a (b + c) = ab + ac), wasn't meant to rule human love.

Bawdiness, comicality in sex: I have a limited taste for it, but there is a warm hilarity in hearing, during an intimately private activity, things called by their common names, the ones that are not usable in public.

The mutuality of pleasure-giving, when you muse on it afterwards, is confounding. Nothing is as egocentric as physical pleasure, and nothing depends more on being a pair. How did nature come to devise that one?

Lovers surely don't quite own their own bodies. It's not only that they've given themselves to the other, but also that they now hold their own body in trust for the other—to keep in shape, I mean.

In the end, these two types will drive each other crazy: those who eventually want to get something done, and those who'd rather do anything than something.

There are adults who have the sweetness of children: inarticulate adroitness, spontaneous affectionateness, uncomprehending tact, physical delicacy. Only they aren't children, and so you could kick them.

Unfaithfulness seems to be tolerable when the partners live psychically askew of one another. But then, what's left?

Being admired induces sedate responsibility, being desired, glorious élan.

In the end the body can only assuage the body's desires; the soul is still left to its own devices.

Great novelists really know the heart's antics, for instance that love declared is love collapsed, at least for a moment: Prince Andrey, having secured Natasha, "looked into her eyes and could find no trace of his former love for her in his heart" (*War and Peace*).

How strange that the person we actually love looks in no particular like the lover of our dreams and yet realizes all our hopes!

Touching, tangent, non-touching: love, friendship, colleagues—limits once set never breached.

Crude but not inaccurate: ocular desire—love; tactile desire—lovemaking.

The plangent pizzicato of high moments.

Justice postponed is, they say, justice denied, but pleasure postponed is pleasure prolonged.

Does the flesh, in particular, the head, express the spirit? We suppose it of others, having no alternative, but we are appalled to think it of ourselves since we consider our soul to be too large and mobile to appear by way of an ovoid with seven openings. If anything, our physical selves are inadequate impersonators.

Amor vincit omnia, most remarkably, squeamishness.

In young men eros is ever-ready and love is fungible. For older women (well, one woman) the particularity that says this one or none is non-negotiable.

Hydraulics of feeling: The pressure of desire is inversely proportional to the availability of fulfillment. Well, of course.

The mission of ulcers is to alert those who are constitutionally content with the world that the guts have independent judgment.

There are opportunistic needs that arise simply from the occasion. Something is on offer, and there we are, eager takers. The hydraulic theory of emotions says that the irruption of desire results from repression. But it's also true that the soul is an inveterate adventurer and opportunist.

Poetry is "an imaginary garden with real toads" (Marianne Moore, "Poetry"); certain desires are imaginary beasts drawn to real watering holes. At a time this seemed to be God's truth.

The Greeks called Eros a tyrant. He's also a totalitarian, a modern type who lets nothing escape his dominion. This god takes over.

The great genera of sexual ontology, courtesy of Plato's *Sophist:* Same, Other, Self, None. Seen in this august light they're all one. But they aren't, as love's dialectic discovers.

There are moments of taut thrumming in the nether regions and swift soaring of the soul when all the boundaries between reality and imagination are down and we are ready for epiphanies. That's the moment to begin a work.

If we are to point to the locus of love it's here (head) or here (chest) or here (groin). Among them they yield love's great modes: purity, permanence, passion.

The wish is fulfilled, and we're on the loose. This is a residue of the reason for our Fall, which was our inability to be happy for cause.

Vexation of the spirit: The senses are charmed and the mind is bored.

Why do we laugh when the phone rings at crucial moments? Because in our demythified world it's a comfort to know that at least the little devils are still at work.

There is a nightmare in which the world is so untuned that nothing resonates to my pleasure or my projects, and being a body is a mere vulnerability and having desires a stark impertinence. It could happen for real; my world could collapse.

America produces handsome normalcy in abundance because our kids drink milk and go to the dentist. But it would be plain snobbish to imagine that because they're well grown in body but underbred in bearing they don't harbor those anomalies which, like a discord in tonal harmony, makes them poignantly interesting.

Any daily companion will be glanced at more often than seen. What a blessing for viable togetherness, that looks can glance off their object!

Everyone, it's said, wants someone. But that's dangerously inaccurate: never *some*one but just *that* one. Which one? Certainly not anyone.

Know thyself! For Socrates the Delphic injunction meant: Think your way soberly through your Typhon-nature, the fiery, fevered, hundred-headed beast within, to a more lucidly gentle humanity (*Phaedrus*). But I'm a modern, for all that, and find the limits of myself in half-dreams: a racking night, thickly enveloped in the specific aura of one human being who poses a relentless answer to which I labor to find the question—something urgent about insufficiencies of the heart, reluctances of the flesh, repulsions of the sensibility, dischargings of debts of love in the false tender of cramped pity. I found myself wanting in both senses that night. And yet I wasn't tossing and turning but lying there very snugly.

22 LANGUAGE: TELLING WORDS

Language shows a gracious civility to thought. Over and above conveying the intention, it adds wit: figures, puns, alliterations, deft turns. And so a stodgily solid notion may attain elegant address.

In cordially casual conversation we sometimes tell things, eventful fortuities, resonant memories, that are fraught with significance for us but become mere apt anecdotes in the telling. They're wonderful touchstones both for the invulnerability of your psychic valuables and for a potential friend of the heart—the one who gets it.

There are many stops for the tongue, but a chief one is the choking detritus of figurings and considerings that repressed ardor produces.

What magic: that diffuse fragrances and expansive visions could be compacted into odorless, sightless words and conveyed to be reconstituted by the irrigating imagination of an empathetic reader!

There's nothing like refusing sympathy for reducing people to skewed, repetitive, and simplistic talk. And conversely, the world's most unlikely orator can be eloquent when sure of his reception.

Are others too lions in conception and mice in utterance?

The more copious the internal flow, the harder the valves are to open. *Controlled* passion is the condition of eloquence.

The word has an almost infinite power of compression: a month's musings—one sentence. Or is it rather a force of deflation?

The loss of the object in our speech: "being relevant," but to what?; "mounting a demonstration," but of what? It's not a mere grammatical solecism, but willful displacement of the final cause.

Reading my own words: What isn't obvious is doubtful, and what's doubtful is often dubious as well.

The easy vulgarity of our kids has only a limited charm. To them it isn't lusty fishwifery but imageless tags. Those of us who didn't hear these words used in public till middle life still can't escape the attendant imagery. What a waste of good—or rather bad—words; especially of the two ubiquitous ones that start with those suggestive sibilants and fricatives.

The danger of word-serendipity is that the elegant prose re-forms the intended thought.

Some great stylists clearly let the words flow and the thought play catch as catch can; I prefer those who form the thought and let the words adhere.

Aperçu: a hemi-semi-demi wisdom.

The mutually exhilarating effect of good talk: The reciprocal trust in being appreciatively heard and readily understood makes the words on both sides flow with controlled copiousness; we delightedly outdo each other in linguistic adroitness.

When "one," when "we," when "I"?: "One" in an anonymously sententious strain; "we" in a companionably confidential mood; "I" in the sparing vein of not meaning to saddle you with my idiosyncrasies.

Does anyone think or muse in full sentences? The apophantic, i.e., declarative, sentence is for public consumption. Within, it's sentence fragments, unasserted, undeclared. The universal "I think" is hardly necessary within, and as for the statement itself, I just announce the topic and I know what I mean. That topic is what comes before the mental colon: Now start spinning.

Since prose is expected to be expansive it usually has to follow a pointed sentence with an explanation, while poetry can articulate the compacted nature of things and leave it there.

How words can simultaneously capture and distance! Tell the moments of your life, and they're at once encapsulated and removed: *Forsan et haec olim meminisse iuvabit*, "Perhaps one day there will be delight in remembering even these things" (*Aeneid* I). Disasters are turned into good stories, shame is converted into a comic episode, defeats are transformed into humanizing lessons: the verbal curing of experience, in both senses.

Sometimes we must force a formulation so as to resolve a debilitating dilemma. The words that tell truth aren't the ones that solve problems—in the short run.

"Aphorism" means, literally, delimitation. It is the curtailment of truth for the sake of wit. It's OK to do it, provided you have a bad conscience the while.

There are writers who sedulously palpate the bruises and peek at the wounds humans sustain from life, but they don't seem to care much for people—yech.

What's the satisfaction in an apt quotation? Well, we are reminded that we are fellow citizens of the Republic of Letters. And we feel confirmed by hearing our thought so exactly expressed. And we feel for the author, known or unknown, a quick, terse friendship.

Writing is a relief both of grief and happiness (for happiness is also oppressive). We articulate them, and as they have now been belabored by us, we are the less possessed by them. Moreover, once captured in words, both grief and happiness yield up their lessons.

There's a whole slew of lovable vulgarities in the language of love. We don't speak Anglo-Saxon for nothing.

When the heart's full, communication gets congested.

Quips, idioms, figures—all the Americanisms express casual freedom. For much of the world that is a contradiction in terms.

Banter is the delicious froth, the frolic of language, where it rises above the sobrieties of workaday communication. To be serious: It's actually a feature of that public sociability that makes republics work; not all nations are good at it; I was born in one that wasn't: the gutturally polysyllabic quips of High Dutch are absurd rather than comical.

Some people's chatter, God bless them, is actually self-expression, but for others it's self-sacrifice on the altar of sociability to join in, and betokens not so much interest in what is being said as interest in the mere expression of interest, that is, the desire to show civility—and to look each other over. Sometimes it gets screamingly boring, and then you catch a glimpse of one of these others feeling likewise—and start a real conversation.

This kind of writing is like the bronze caster's *cire perdu,* the lost wax method. You mush the wax on a clay core: that's the rough-shaping of the soft substance of the matter in thought; you chisel and smooth the surface: that's the first inner formulation, living and true; you cover the finished surface with clay, warm up and run out the wax and pour in the metal: that's casting the shaped thought onto paper; you knock off the clay and start filing: that's the reworking, the eraser's and pencil's last work. What's come about is permanent, a little stiff, maybe a little shiny, even brilliant, but the malleable soft life of the thought has been mostly drained off.

In hermeneutics there's the principle of charity that says: Read the text so as to make it make maximum sense. At least the same should go for listening: Suppose that behind the formulaic babble there's a meaning wanting to be heard, something beyond just "Listen to me," a content. Especially in our more intimate polemics, what's the point of winning eristic battles and driving the other into extremities? On the other hand, you can't be the understanding one all the time—that's diminishing for the other too.

The trick: not to speak either formulaically or rhapsodically but with the crisp accuracy of well-founded conviction.

An anecdote is a verbal snapshot: It catches a lively moment and freezes it.

Telling does lay ghosts, but then, a ghost done in by a bit of daylight ain't a ghost that's a keeper anyhow.

Confidences, even when elegantly achieved, do leave a squeamish sense of gratuitousness, a faint sense of boredom with one's own affairs, and the self-contradictory feeling of having talked both too much and insufficiently, since no finite communication can ever delineate one's life.

"'Tis a gift to be simple"—well, yes, *and* an art, oddly enough, especially for us, now. That's because our normal speech is casual in a phrase-ridden sort of way and doesn't have the dignity of older low speech, the local dialects. But dignity is the *sine qua non* of simplicity.

Language is the body of thought, and we embody our thought first of all for ourselves. We talk to ourselves and write things down so that we may hear and see our thought incarnate; in utterance the soul presents itself to the senses. Very curious.

To speak or not to speak, that's always the question—whether it's better to bemoan an indiscretion or to regret a lost opportunity.

Pleading speech is in a double bind: If it's blocked up with emotion it's embarrassing, and if it's rhetorically fluent it's unconvincing.

To me emotion (from *ex-movere,* "to move out") signifies an easy motion of the soul, easily exhibited, while passion means the deeper affection suffered by the soul. Thus emotion has an exhibitionist element, while passion is passive and preserves its privacy—emotion is talkative, passion taciturn.

Some thoughts press to be almost obsessively repeated over the years—the exorcism of articulation doing its *very* slow work. That shows up in this collection.

Don't we feel sovereignly indifferent to what's said about us, provided it's said behind our backs?

Telephone conversation is comical: gesturing exaggeratedly into thin air. We forget we're just a "far-off voice" (*tele-phone*). I bet when videophones become common we'll all be as stiff as boards.

The pleasures of affectionate teasing: an apt ditty neatly quoted, a foible lovingly exposed, adroit playfulness on one side, the pleasure of being the center of fond attention on the other.

Words have fierce grappling hooks. Nothing can be unsaid. We're like the princess who can't sleep for the pea under twenty well-sprung mattresses: A bad word twenty years ago still pinches. Here too applies the pagan rule: To forgive is charitable, to forget is effective.

All our ways of holding on to ourselves, photographs, videos, recordings, writings, really don't do the trick. Three minutes of the real thing outweighs a stack of stuff. That's at once scary and consoling.

"Louche" isn't in my Webster's (nor are a lot of other useful if outré words), but all the Louises are. Is a boring French king worth more than a wicked French word?

Apothegms and aphorisms are alightings of thought; unless it immediately takes off again, they will have been its lime twigs, its traps.

Utter your thinking and it becomes a thought, a past participle—a posture rather than a progress.

It is an unsettling feeling to have one's waffling, wob-bling, backing-and forthing, turn-tail-and-run-away hy-potheses taken up by eager students, ballasted with influ-ences and provenances, located within an X-ist system, and leveraged into something as august as a position. What Roman emperor said as he lay dying: "I'm turning into a god"?

As long as a day has 60 x 60 x 24 seconds there will not be a pure motive or complete candor. For mentation goes on for at least two-thirds of these moments, and there is probably no selfish motive and no unspeakable thought that hasn't crossed my mind in that time. But crossing and entertaining are worlds apart, and that's my plea of innocence.

It is unwitting perjury to promise to tell the truth, the whole truth, and nothing but the truth. The oath con-fuses honesty with truth-telling. I can promise to be sub-jectively honest, but how can I promise to be objectively truthful unless I'm 1. all-wise, and 2. given limitless time? For every truth has many roots, without which it is, in fact, very nearly an untruth. But of course, they don't mean truth, they mean such factual fragments as can be speared on the "Did you or didn't you . . . ?" fork.

Thought is always young: spontaneous for each thinker, radical in trying to go to the roots of what is given, and subversive in being willing to overthrow cur-rent opinion. Language is old and conventional: con-formist in its usages, conservative in preserving old wealth, and cautious in absorbing current idiom. Good writing is the marriage of spontaneous thought and canonical speech.

Isn't it strange that students who don't write like themselves don't write like anyone else either?

They say that truth is *adaequatio intellectus rei,* "the fitting of thought to thing." Writing is the *adaequatio linguae rei,* "the fitting of speech to thing." So pick a good thing and your writing will be good.

If you choose to write a short book on a big theme you'd better specialize in epigrams and examples or you will be very boring, like a brief history book I recently read that prosed on about agencies, forces, tendencies, and developments (all ghost-agencies), on the false hypothesis that abstractions can serve as epitomes.

We should assume that all of us have soaring poetry in our souls—somewhere. Sometimes it's well hidden behind reams of sodden prose.

In youth we feel bereft, dried out, when we tell others our secrets, but later we learn that the soul, like a well, will fill back up, that our arcana are inexhaustible.

Good writing: intending some nuclear truth and chopping away at its shell until words can extract it, or alternatively having in mind some large notion and compressing it until words can comprehend it. But here's the risk: We retro-shape the object in articulating it.

There is speech with dignity and without: truthful-ness/sincerity, worth/value, trust/credibility, decency/compassion, soul/psyche, dignity/self-esteem, etc.—the second of the pair I wouldn't want to hear at my funeral service.

There are those who sit down and those who seat themselves, those of the band of Gideon (Judges 7:5) and those of the entourage of De Gaulle.

One reason for writing a book: because once you've got the hang of it producing is more soothing than think-ing.

In American sociable speech there are myriads of ways to disguise a condemnation. Since we all know what's meant, why does it work? Because these polite circumlo-cutions have a triple intention: to convey the criticism, to do it without insult, to warn the victim that making a fuss is undesirable. Actually it doesn't always work: There are blow-ups.

If you have nothing determinate to say, there's no rea-son to stop.

Conversation : thinking :: lecture : thought.

"Brevity is the soul of wit" is good: Wit is a mode whose merit is that there isn't much of it. To be witty in oneself or to be the cause of wit in others—neither is re-ally so very respectable.

If you want to get people to tell you what's really on their mind, first relieve them of their urgencies.

It takes ten seconds to inscribe your book, and then the inscribee is left having to write a book report.

Futzing and perfecting: the two stages of writing.

Phrase book of "meeting-speak": "I hate to bring this up"—I'll bust if I don't get it off my chest; "I'll be brief"—This will take twice as long as necessary, so settle in; "I have nothing much to report"—I'll tell you at length why the committee didn't meet; "I'm no expert"—I have strong opinions on this matter; "I'm not understanding . . ."—I totally disagree. Blank pages for everyone's favorite.

Lives interesting to tell must be very distracting to live; lives satisfying to live are boring as hell to read about. Recall the Chinese curse: "May you live in interesting times."

There is an inelegant style in which all the adjectives are wadded together; you could say for it that it suffers from rampant accuracy.

Mencken thought that cellar-door was the most beautiful English word. I've got another, from Latin: *venus volgivaga* ("public prostitute," from Kant, of all people, *Metaphysics of Morals,* 49). And celadon.

Pulling a thought onto a page (a lined yellow pad), screwing a sentiment through a pencil (a mechanical pencil): surely a minimal labor—could it be respectable work?

Caginess and candor: Candor and reserve are easily compatible because no one would want to listen long enough to hear it all. Caginess, on the other hand, is incompatible with reserve, because reserves are just what furtive people, who are spontaneous in nothing, don't have: They have a strongbox of little locked-away secrets, but they have no free-flowing inner wellspring.

There is a delightful tension in being attentively involved with the world while full of just one thing, a love or a work.

Just as we need our identity cards to prove that we are we, so an event needs its story to confirm that it occurred. (Incidentally, here's an irresistible modern Greek word: *tavtoteta,* "self-same-hood," meaning an ID.)

Could these words possibly have been processed rather than scribbled? Consider process cheese.

The sweetly shoddy vernacular of American working life—who can hear it, get it, and not love it?

Later on it might look like "one's own style." But it surely never began by "finding oneself" but by imitating the finest models—which proved, thank God, to be inimitable.

Writing is, to no small degree, felicitous falsification of original impulses and the addition of supplementary serendipities.

23 INTIMACY: INS AND OUTS

If our talk, in internal intimacy with ourselves, was broadcast, would we be very interesting? Surely our obsessive repetitions, our reiterated daydreams, our magniloquent tirades are boring as hell—more. Would we be lovable? Intermittently. Evidently even the most trusting candor should employ a fairly discriminating filter.

In adolescents, just when the desire for self-revelation is most tempestuous, it is also most banal because feelings are a little undifferentiated and language is unpracticed. But that's fine, because their intimacies are mostly with each other. As we feel more subtly, we speak more selectively.

There is a special delight in the light touch and the scarcely audible word.

Sometimes it's good to cut the Gordian knot (located in the stomach) and just to say it.

For intimacy it takes two, and don't I know who's the more recalcitrant?

Who would have thought that domesticity could be not only cozy but exhilarating—if the house is the shelter for intimate glories and vast images.

Intimacy is a middle term held in lovely tension between public distance and the ultimate proximity.

Some people possess a salubriousness of character, a jocundity of temperament, and a comeliness of person that simply overcomes the natural adult wish to keep oneself to oneself.

Some people want to hear, some to tell. It's lucky they're an overlapping set.

Easy intimacy is not quite so sweet as that gained in equal struggle, with partners tripping as much over their own as the other's obstacles. But friends-to-be advance slowly and peacefully, and when the time has come to yield, they do it very smoothly.

Courtesy is the lubricant of social life, but it is the very form of intimacy.

Tremble at touching another's intimate nature but quickly control that; such touch should be delicate but firm.

As long as I tell myself the truth it might be unnecessary to tell you.

A vigorous sense of the complexity of all intimacy plus a decisive "What the hell" equals cool confiding candor.

Nothing opens the world to us like the experience of intimacy.

.

Are there things too squishily personal to tell? You bet. And then there are two telling types, the ancients and the moderns. The most modern of moderns is the Bishop of Hippo. He tells. No one ever told as much as Augustine. He tells his God by way of confession and us for the sake of conversion. This ancestor of all True Confessions outdoes them all because a sense of sin casts the frisson of scandal (a Greek word, actually) over everything, even stealing a couple of pears. The true ancients, on the other hand, tell next to nothing. Homer, Thucydides, Plato didn't choose to appear more than a couple of times in their works. Why didn't they? Were they simply, naively, innocently grand? Or shy? Nonsense. They didn't tell their misdeeds (there's no sin among the pagans) or their passions because they were subtle themselves and expected their readers (or listeners) to be so and to infer a lot. They lived by intimations, and thus they avoided intimate revelations without being completely opaque—open secrets.

The mortal sin in intimacy: inattention.

An incidental lesson of intimacies: You're your own best last resort in human matters.

Misfired intimacy: One thinks it has been said over and over, and the other thinks nothing has been said at all.

There is no intimacy with people whose own inner space is *terra incognita* to them.

Why do reserved people elicit confidences? Because they are inferred to be able to keep a confidence. The inference is right but the imagined cause isn't always: Reserved people don't always actually have reserves; they're often just inertly inarticulate.

They speak of people "you can't get near to" because of their indefeasible privacy or constitutional touch-me-not-ism, but I can't quite believe it. First, even these folks must know that nothing attracts attention like evidence of non-candor. And then, soundly reserved souls come sweetly open when the moment is right. I think some people are inaccessible to others because they're opaque to themselves. Just as I suspect that the great public Mysteries of antiquity were only mystifications, so the personal secretiveness of some contemporaries hides no great secrets but is just a small obfuscation: "There's no there there," as in Gertrude Stein's Oakland.

24 SINGLENESS:
COMPANIONABLE SOLITUDE

There's a type that "wants to be alone"—why? I want to work, think, dream, and we do that in solitude, but it's not aloneness I want—rather its occupation. "I want to be alone" sounds like the need of a brittle soul, a soul in flight.

Two things make the body deft: superiority and solitude—being looked up to and not being looked at.

How can people live, that is, come to, come aware, who don't have some leisured solitude, day by day, for the housecleaning of the soul, for sorting and clarifying the wild stuff that comes in? How can people learn who are too preoccupied to extract the truth from their depressions, to taste nothingness, to participate in the periodic collapse of their world, to take an occasional reckoning down to its roots? Do they float above their lives or are they stuck in them?

Sound solitude goes smoothly into sociability, is ready for interruptions and ready for resumed retreat. Not so with loneliness, which resists contingent relief. Some people are lonely out of loneliness, a sad trap.

In solitude we vanish as "personalities," mask-wearers. We might forget to have an expression, a bearing, certainly a toilette. And yet that's also when we're most within our bodies, make them comfortable, see them unclothed, watch our hands scribble over the lines. Only when alone can we be self-conscious without shame.

Why is privacy a privative word?

Since inner substance is assimilated in solitude, busy people are drawing down capital. Socrates makes a distinction between remembering and recollecting, skimming the stock of memories and digging deep into the soul. In my busiest years I lived off that supply of opinions and reasons laid in before when I had time to go into my books and into myself, and if I'd gone on much longer I would have run out. I think many people who run things have run out, gone bankrupt: tyrants and bureaucrats.

It is easier for that camel (some say *kamelos* is a misreading of *kalos*, rope) to go through the eye of the needle (Luke 18:25) than for a very sociable person to find the entrance to themselves.

Does copious soliloquy encourage self-containment or loquacity? Both, because the proportion of inner to outer talk is so enormous.

Everybody needs somebody, they say, and most of us don't want to be on our own. Thus the loner is thought of as somehow untethered, lightweight, willfully exposed, and unaccommodated—and there's truth in that. On the other hand, being yoked for the sake of togetherness doesn't seem very blissful either. The brisk winds of solitude, a certain stark exile from nesting comforts tenses the soul, and that's acknowledged too in this country: the lone ranger.

Is it possible to live in companionable domesticity and not to seal the windows against the winds of glory?

25 MOODS: SHAPES OF
GRIEF AND GLADNESS

Even a recreational disruption can break the fine-spun cocoon of routine and expose the lurking insipidness of daily life. What a fragile thing the contentment of business is then shown to be!

Wan, morose, and mopish: The world is cracked and Nothing creeps in.

Loose connections where we wish for tight ones, large tolerances where we have very small ones—these are sad irritants in the life of love.

That dark and drafty vacancy of mood when a caving world needs incessant shoring up with wearying ratiocinations and strenuous self-expostulations—is that malaise of the soul *just* a mood or is something deep manifesting itself? Have the courage of your depressions: Choose the more abysmal hypothesis.

There is a high-strung taut twanging as if there really were heartstrings, a desperate high-pitched music of the soul, resounding through its infinite, suddenly uncontained spaces. That is in the all-too silent hours of the night. Morning comes, a call, and the vibrations fade out, comfort flows in—but there remains a faint background strain, a psycho-cosmic background noise, a reminiscence of hell.

I'd rather be afflicted with *acedia* than depression. For the latter there are mood elevators or tranquilizers or whatever, but for the former, spiritual *ennui,* there's nothing but facing it. It's as much a willed sin as an opportunistic sickness. It requires serious introspection. I have to figure out whether I am tainting the world or it is tainting me. To have the courage of one's depression is to consider in all seriousness that oneself might be feeble or that the world might be empty—or both.

Acedia, apathy of the soul, is said to have six daughters: *malitia, rancor, pusillanimitas, desperatio, torpor circa praecepta, evagatio mentis ad illicita.* Don't I know it!—especially those fifth and sixth ones, laziness about learning and wandering of the mind to forbidden things.

To love someone is to want them present, and a present without this presence is an abyssal time, time lost to life, deprived time unconvertible into profitable time. And if the absence was preventable? Then all those twanging little time devils come up to sit on each dragging moment emitting a nerve-wracking stridor.

What has so much weight and so little gravity as the burden of unappropriated and therefore inappropriate tenderness?

During first absence the mood is a kind of swooning pall with rents displaying a remote glory.

When an apprehended excellence finds us in a mood of expectancy—that's glory.

Secret ardor in public places: Pure glory is walking about and no one sees a thing.

There is a doubting mood when facts seem concrete and immediate and contemplation seems abstracted and remote. It's a perverse mood.

"Sensitivity training" is an anger-generating technique combining canned sentimentality with lightly veiled threat, an ideological mailed fist in the velvet glove of compassion.

Clarity lightens a dark mood: my private version of enlightenment.

Two lovely moods: the pearl-gray sobriety of loving laboriousness, the ardor of being altogether at work; the purling pleasure, the light pressure in the bowels that presages bliss in love.

When the vital spirits die down, need becomes acute and demands concrete satisfaction, but when energy returns, the mind is alight and the imagination afire with expectations more fulfilling than any mere fact.

There's at least this satisfaction in the down-heartedness of disillusionment: We join the human race.

Les enfants s'ennuient le dimanche, goes the children's song, and so do adults feel low on Sundays. There is a

Sunday of the soul when warm life seems remote, like an evanescent dream, and the world recedes as if in anticipation of that permanent leave-taking.

Surely moods have a metaphysics. What is behind this rising and falling of the psychic tide, the storms, zephyrs, dead calm of the soul? Whence comes the invulnerable jocundity of mood and whence the cowering anxiety? What is expressing itself and what is it signifying? (There's a philosopher who is supposed to know, but I don't trust him—Heidegger, if you must know.) Are these questions for a next book?

As a grand migraine is succeeded by a delicate, fragile tranquility, so after an emotional seizure there's a delicious levitation, a veritable lesson in the literal meaning of the word "relief," a re-raising.

The "dumping on" phenomenon: First I was miserable and you were carefree, now you're burdened and I feel fine.

Always those psychic hydraulics: the rising tide of expectancy, the draining of impulse, the buoyancy of hope, the billows of bliss, the constriction of the heart.

There are days when the sensibility is appalled by everything that has a body, days such as Gulliver must have had among those Brobdingnagian monsters, when we, myself included, seem gross of matter and uncouth in manners. (Here's the blessed exception: Little children, even with full diapers, never induce that somatic alienation.) Its lesson: Our sensory comfort depends on a lusty sensibility—let that fail, and the organic world becomes inexpressibly repulsive. Squint at things. Pity Swift, who couldn't avert his eyes.

The mind in desuetude: It *fell* into it, but it has to *climb* out of it. Why should down be easier than up? It is the question Lucretius answers when he makes the falling rain of atoms the aboriginal motion, so that rack and ruin are the underlying direction of the universe: It is the down-mood writ large, the poet's entropy. But Lucretius's physics is ludicrous, and the question was put in the wrong mood: Why do we soar though not borne on the wings of eagles?

Sure-fire relief from dejection: from impasse—hot bath; from boredom—sleep; from lowness—candy bars; from lovesickness—love. Three of these four are actually obtainable as needed.

We wake gratefully from bad dreams. But what if we wake into a worse place than we left? It has happened to all of us, but we—I and my friends—live in so peaceful and prosperous a world, given us by this country of ours, that our anxieties usually outrun reality. What a blessed life where fears are worse than facts!

When we are absorbed in work or service we are immune to the megrims. The soul is best fortified when all its forces are thoughtfully engaged without.

There is a congestion of feeling that works an untimely apathy at high moments, as if too much antecedent hoping prevented present fulfillment.

Isn't taking a dim view of things a kind of clearsightedness?

Aristotle minds terribly that we get tired of everything, even the highest pleasure. It is the sign that we are unable to be fully absorbed in our purpose ("to be in the state of fulfillment"—*entelecheia*), because we are immattered, distracted by our incomplete being. For to be in the material way is to be in part unrealized and altogether distractible. So *ennui* is an intimation of mortality and as such to be respectfully savored—and superseded.

You would think the angels in heaven could not be bored or irritated by their attendance on God.—Not so; Lucifer the Light-bringer, the most intelligent and enlightened of them, couldn't bear it—not the shadowless light, not the continually consonant music, and not the perfect, static order. But the last straw was its arbitrary breach—that a Son, lately born, not (as he himself was) made, should be closer to the Throne than any of them. So *ennui* and envy came together—and the world became suddenly much too interesting. I think this unholy story is very much the story of our moody condition.

"'Tis not so sweet now as it was before": For us all bliss is self-blunting.

Why can't you break through to happiness in full knowledge of great good fortune? It is partly because the soul, in its bodylike fashion, is flattened by the emotional overload, partly because luck is such an unreliable giver.

Isn't it odd that the same thrumming, throbbing taut-ness in chest or belly that signals joy also accompanies de-spair? The body lumps together what the soul differentiates. So much for the James-Lange theory that makes emotions the epiphenomena of specific physiological effects.

There is nothing as "mere" as reality uninvested by our mood; the facts stare back blindly and balefully, like those people who won't give you the time of day.

We are borne through life on the artless afflatus of a good digestion. Soul-searching requires a deflation of the animal spirits, a dis-ease, a rub, a puncturing of the naive hybris of mere well-being.

How does a mood differ from feeling? A mood is *of* the soul, a feeling is *in* the soul; a mood is a whole disposition, a feeling a focal affection; distance and alienation are moods, loss and enmity are feelings. Feelings have specific causes, while moods mostly rise up unbidden, and thence comes their significance: They arise under direction from the hinder parts of the soul (which, strangely enough, know more about the world than does the frontage). Then the soul disposes itself to be affected by the world under a particular aspect, and the world responds by being that way. Maybe that's the sense of it: Mood is the affective soul in its aspectual mode. Or: Mood is the affective perspec-tivity of the soul. Well, at least *I* know what I mean.

Not all moods convey news about being; some are just testimony to a lack of sleep.

Some moods bring news from Nowhere, and those are worth interpreting.

Music and work are the reliable non-human tonics for moodiness.

Loneliness and desolation are different; one comes from having no one; the other from losing someone. The latter is more acute but it carries its own consolation: "'Tis better to have loved and lost . . ."

"Why am I miserable?" is an optimist's question; it implies that it's not supposed to be that way.

It's strange how in the long run place wins over persons. Not only is active place memory vivid longer than face memory (I think), but its own atmosphere can wash out the human contretemps it played host to.

The atmosphere of a place answers to the mood of a person: It is the look with which it responds to our disposition, our inward prospect.

People proud of their spontaneity tend to be moody when off-duty.

To keep a snail from withdrawing into its shell keep your hands off; even a slight flip on the tentacles, and in it goes. Likewise, a hint of flippancy with a shy boy, and he's back in his shell.

If you're borne high on the billows of bliss, expect next to be beached high and dry, and if you're wandering about in a haze of happiness, a gust of reality will soon clear the view. It's inevitable, but also a side issue. There's no real reason, none, why the aftermath should vitiate the main event.

Sometimes there's a diaphanous membrane between me and mine that I can no more break through than a brazen wall. It bursts when it will.

The kids have their cool, the adults their nonchalance. Why does Anglo-Saxon pride require imperturbability? (The Mediterraneans demand public pathos.) People think there's a confusion here of affectlessness with masterfulness. But no, feelings held in are *both* intensified and mastered.

There is a mournful mood, a desolate minor music of the soul, singing *quomodo sedet sola civitas:* How did my inner citadel come to be thus abandoned, and I expelled to the outskirts of delight and the margins of my possessions?

Heart narrowed, world lost, life confounded, recourse gone: one word and the heart expands, the world's regained, life is perspicuous, and I don't need a thing. Speak of mood-swing!

What is most fugitive is most poignantly overwhelming: the flash flood of beauty.

I know people who have a lot of animal warmth, but they don't keep their inner barn clean and tend to live in a moping mess.

There's a knife's edge of difference between the tensed energy of self-control and the cramped strain of self-repression. Know when to let up without letting go.

In general only boring people get bored, but there's one exception: enforced entertainment.

There's a mortally trivializing mood in which all mattering is untuned, everything goes slack and indifferent and unpegged. Like all moods, it mirrors a possibility of the world: "The dead shall live, the living die / And Music shall untune the sky."

Pascal worries about the fact that people divert themselves from their mortality by amusements. He wants them to rest quietly at home and have Thoughts. Aside from the fact that most of them would then really go melancholy-mad, does he really think *that* isn't a diversionary activity?

The shutting down of the imagination, except for the flashing views of infinite nostalgia; the need for passive gratification, sleeping and eating; the retreat of the forces of action, not to be rallied; the holding of all things objective as anathema, nauseous; alienation from the day's regime, as if once too often performed; defaulting of the relish for tasks since nothing matters—that's (normal) depression, and it should be counted a memorable experience. For it reveals an aspect of the Nature of Things, the Lucretian side, the rain of atoms into the abyss.

Honor the hours of dispersal, the occasional diaspora of the spirit. It is a miracle that in all this infinity we stay mostly collected.

Kant, of all people: ". . . even depression (not dejected sadness) may be counted among the *sturdy* affections if it has its ground in moral ideas. But if it is grounded on sympathy and, as such, is amiable, it belongs merely to the *languid* affections" (*Critique of Judgment* ¶ 29). He is distinguishing a "sublime" from an "insipid" state of mind. I shall take this to heart and have the courage of my morally based depressions. I can add another not so respectable type, not insipid but acrid: the self-congratulatory existential depression, a French disease.

We are like novas that expand and contract in brightness. In our expansive mood the world is all before us, easy to embrace, lovable in the reflected light of our own warm glow, our inward prospects. Then comes contraction, the world is all dark and alien and only the narrowest, most exclusive objects are acceptable; we need things tailored to our most particular specifications—only this face, this upbringing, this history, is palatable. And as with love, so with energy: Sometimes the world is ours; we walk with the ease and exhilaration of experienced mastery, and sometimes it's all just too much; even the least little effort is a drag.

Emotion : emoting :: passion : ?—which shows that passion is the less manipulable affect. I have a recording of Bach's Sonata for Violin and Basso Continuo in E minor (BWV 1023); there's passion. I have an arrangement of it by Respighi—strings under the solo played with ardent sforzandos; that's emotion.

26 FELICITY:
THE HAPPENING OF HAPPINESS

Billows of anticipation rolling into harbors of bliss.

Sum: the simple happiness of having not someone but *that* one.

Some pleasures are made precious by their fugitiveness: culminations, blooms, comings-together. Others are tainted by their precariousness: peakings, past-it protractions, tenuities.

Carpe diem, "Seize the day," says Horace the Roman. I don't know about "seize," say rather, "embrace." (Way back in Brooklyn College, in Classics 101, a classmate was caught unprepared for a session on the Roman poets: "Well, he said Seize the Day, so I did." Even the professor broke up.)

"This is the day the Lord has made"—and then, kerplunk!

A lovely day: the house in shape, all chores, repairs, arrangements completed. Sun floods the room, the flute all but plays itself, and there is good work just waiting to be done. I'm experiencing that contradiction in terms, domestic bliss, that is, mundane ecstasy.

Wind in the Willows is above all about cosmic domesticity, about a snug world and the *dulce domum,* the snug house, within it, and seizures of contentment are its world-feeling.

The perfection of happiness asks to be defended tooth and nail—and that's just what rends it.

Why is the time out of sight golden? Because in the anticipation of a presence promised the imagination blossoms.

A caesura in engaged activity leaves the soul vulnerable to intimations of paradises bygone and not to be restored.

Why are the bitter reflections of the unhappy regarded as wisdom, while the blithe thoughts of the happy are disregarded as frivolity? Because people think that wisdom has to be hard come by and heavy to bear. But perhaps a certain lightheartedness does the world more justice—or if not more justice, more good?

Middling America: When the absence of a public scene that has some grandeur seems melancholy, recall that mere middling life in its safe sobriety is the better breeding ground for deep reflection.

Re-creation is really a fine word. The best recreations are those in which the intellect goes into its musing mode while the senses are trained on beauty. Good food helps too.

Pleasure can be, as we all know, a compulsion and its pursuit a strenuous chase. Think of sitting in the sloop's cockpit in a hot, dead calm for two hours, to get a half-hour's good run before the wind. Oops, wrong example—it was worth it.

Is it spoiled moodiness or wise forfending of hybris when in the midst of apparently solid happiness there happens a sudden palling of relish rooted in nothing but the sense of the utter contingency of the human condition? We fear the fragility of happiness, and so we break its sway.

What greater mystery than the complementary natures of world and soul: that, be it for happiness or suffering, they are mutually habitable.

The anticipation of happiness is a featureless golden haze shot through with bright apparitions.

A most complete pleasure: facing beauty side by side, looking ahead together: beauty before and love alongside, one seen, one sensed.

The three elements of happiness are love, work, community, in different orders as the years pass. Each elicits its own ardor and ennui, each affects its own security and distress: My country and my college, my reading and my studies, my friends and lovers, live and dead.

Combinatorial happiness: love as the tonic of work, work as the bond of community, community as the source of love, and so on in six glorious permutations.

The prospect of pleasure warms work since then its completion does not issue in the desert of disengagement.

We may think that certain occasions for pleasure are quite spontaneous, but they are really grounded in anticipations that we don't recognize until the event fails to eventuate.

In all the languages I know of, happiness is etymologically luck, what happens happily to happen. But that's only one, perhaps even a lesser, external cause of that internal condition Aristotle rightly describes as the universal end. Were those words, *eudaemonia, fortuna, Glück,* happiness, coined before someone discovered—what a day it must have been!—that one could talk about an invisible, inner self that was nearer and dearer even than that outer personage on whom good or ill luck descends?

Happy love is the continuous availability of delight.

Two-ply happiness: *hilaritas,* meaning both cheerfulness and glimpses of glory.

Possibilities can paralyze; too many options stymie choice. What people want is to get what they want—and before that, to know what they want; the choosing itself is just a stutter of the will, the hesitating effect of our aboriginally irresolute nature—unless you're a kid in a candystore.

There is mere life and the good life. They have the same foundation, the satisfaction of necessities, but they are as far apart as limbo is from paradise—the width of a universe.

Misery of the spirit is quite compatible with comfort, convenience, and commodious living. There is a comfortable desolation, and it's hard to tell which is the better cure: real deprivation or a love affair, the experience of worse or of better.

Happy children: their world is their oyster, or rather it's a succession of Chinese boxes: room, house, street, town, state, country, earth, planetary system, galaxy, universe: a series of homey containers. They sometimes address letters to themselves that way.

Honeybees that "teach / The act of order to a peopled kingdom": "the singing masons building roofs of gold" (*Henry V* I ii): Living in a beehive would surely be unbearable for us who value freedom over substance. But to be a craftsman making music while building a golden dome—that must be happiness, especially the singing.

Activity in and for a community like mine, activity in the light of excellence, is a sober, secure, and high satisfaction—it's what Aristotle calls happiness: an activity of the soul in accordance with excellence. But it's precarious: sometimes the college seems like a vigorous growth rooted in the rich soil of a receptive country, but sometimes it looks like a diminutive, endangered sprout.

We deserve happiness by being happy at the slightest instigation.

There is a worm lurking in a contented life that is supplied with reliable pleasures: In a moment of low vitality this invertebrate turns on the insouciant dominance of mammalian happiness and makes of it squishy spineless rot. But then the warmth of life returns and dries the mess up.

Not all people whose assured safety and sustenance make them candidates for happiness know the simple checklist of its sources: the drowsy invocation of a loved image before the oblivion of sleep, return to a morning of well-going work, the panache of mutually appreciated wit, the sudden glimpse of beauty close to home, the throes of serious reflection in a young face, the completion of a tedious but acknowledged task, fresh orange juice.

Pleasure is the cushion of work.

Happiness too has its misery—its confusions and labors.

The good life is a delicate, complex construct hard to erect and easily damaged by evil design sometimes, yet far more often by blind accident. But recall that in logic "accident" just means "property," and that often these unwelcome interventions can be appropriated to become the properties of a good life. Best example I know: You have to go to the hospital and there, made painless by pills, you get to read *War and Peace* for the third time, in deep long drafts. (The third time is the turning point, from labor to purest love, because you can by now pronounce all the names and needn't worry what comes next—it's a trivia-disencumbered suspense-free reading, the best.)

Happiness just happens. Well, the way any spontaneous event occurs: There's a lot of hidden ingenuity behind it. And its advent has to be ardently hoped for. Ardent hope = openness that's ready to specify itself.

Why do epochs of happiness or misery so often happen as wholes? It starts badly and goes on getting worse until it has played itself out, or it begins promisingly and fulfills itself in glory. I think it all prepares *sub limine,* below the threshold, and, conditions being right, it bursts out and starts happening; thereafter it's self-confirming until it's done. What's the "it"? That is the "it" of "and the rain it raineth every day." As the great philologist Jacob Grimm put it: "It" expresses something "spiritlike, ghostly, invisible, uncanny."

Felicity: that vibrating imaginative mood that lends a glow to locales, a zest to work, elegance to gestures, deftness to motions, exhilaration to encounters.

Does one more day felicitously brought off make us more or less resistant to inevitable calamity? Can we claim a happy day as our dessert, count it as virtue-credit, coverage against outrageous fortune?

My most wholehearted sympathy goes to people who face objective obstacles to happiness: physical defects and evil politics, above all. I feel more grudging a pity for those who don't acknowledge our serious obligation to scramble ourselves into some happiness. Sound-mindedness consists (in part) of a focused intention to find happiness and a steady disposition to prefer it over unhappiness. It is a strange fact that ever since Satan leapt into Eden, having uttered the chilling words "Evil, be thou my good," there have been human beings who're really not quite sure which they want, thus making quite sure which they'll get.

Long ago a sociologist discovered that community differs from society (*Gemeinschaft* vs. *Gesellschaft*, Toennies). So also communal life differs from social life. The former consists of exhilarating conversation about serious subjects with friends you'll know all your life while you're casually dressed and eating food you like. The latter involves you in trivial chat with people you may never see again while you're dressed up and wolfing strangely flavored caloric nothings. It's a matter of pleasure vs. duty.

Who would want to catalogue the forms of felicity?: the exhilaration of a project brought off, the jocundity of domestic puttering, the glory of seeing someone you love in their glory, the pure joy of seeing into a truth, etc. Well, actually I'm tempted to the job.

Happiness is elusive when pursued and tame when possessed.

Can happiness regularly practiced become a second nature? Yes, only it starts going a little gray, as does its possessor.

Do we seek pleasure or *this* pleasure? Both, I think. There are the pleasure-seeking moods when we want to to relax and enjoy ourselves any which way, and there are the keen object-focused desires when all the senses from taste to touch want this one thing; I've seen people in foreign lands long for a hamburger so bad even *kephtedes* wouldn't do.

Is the indifference of contentment a sign that caring has ceased? Not at all; it is simply the proof that you really wanted what you got. Not to worry—it won't last, this satiation. Recall that Socrates says: As desirous beings we are leaky jars.

Happiness is in part the willingness to live in semi-oblivion above the baselessness of human life, in the *de facto* present if it's tolerable, in the *de jure* future as if it owed us redress.

For a long time it was a daily delight just to have escaped the babbitry of Brooklyn, babbitry gone pessimistic to boot, its philistine strangulation, dominating vulgarity, raucous shapelessness, as I thought at twenty. Five decades pass and it gets remembered as a vibrant ethnic paradise.

No one is, I think, native to the land of happiness, because when you're arriving it is with the dawning sense of hardly believing your luck at having found it. But then again it also feels like your country of origin.

What a boon to live a life whose miseries are of one's own origination. There again is that canny Chinese curse: "May you live in interesting times." Here's a wise American blessing: "May you live a life of your own making."

The terrific motions of the soul that are mounted by the heroes—and even more the heroines—of Greek tragedy fit a world in which the gods in their multiplicity combine with Fate in her inscrutability to sponsor humanity's irresoluble messes. But for us such large psychic gestures are inappropriate—flabby word—since our miseries are usually either caused by ourselves, our own godforsaken false choices, or by random and intentionless acts of nature.

The Christians speak of *the* Rapture, the seizing of the chosen into heaven, but all of us are subject to sudden small seizures when the heavens open up. And no one knows why me, why now.

Why are the relaxing pleasures of food, love, entertainment, sleep, our refuge in unhappiness? Because soothing pleasures are simulacra of contentment, present distractions aping better-founded felicities.

"To bethink oneself" is an excellent phrase. Sometimes suddenly I bethink myself with gratitude of this enormous contrivance for human happiness called civilization. We might be living—as some fellow humans still do—in a continual dull struggle for survival, obtusely safe for the moment and obtusely afraid of everything, our lives nasty, brutish, and short.

We have free choice in this at least: We can refuse an irruption of pleasure that tears the fabric of happiness. When Blake claims that "He who binds to himself a joy / Doth the winged life destroy," he must be thinking of something more evanescent than I'd enjoy.

Deep contentment, the homeostasis of the soul, is almost a-pathic: just a runnel of gold down the momentarily still dunes of the soul.

It is a part of virtue to be happy when all is, for once, well—the virtue of gratitude, allied to mindfulness. To think and to thank are, in etymological fact, cognate.

There are irrigatedly expansive and desiccatedly narrow times of life: In the first anything and everything seems interesting and lovable, in the second I see how narrowly tailored to my tastes I require the world to be.

"Ay, in the very temple of Delight / Veil'd Melancholy has her sovran shrine." Be it Keats's ode or the proverbial worm in the apple, it's the same message; does the metaphor matter? Well, the lady in the temple is probably less amenable to unseating than the worm is to extraction.

Socrates' claim that happiness and pleasure are very different is simply right. It is possible to be joyously happy while having a head-splitting migraine, and to make love in despair.

Pleasure is passive, local, ephemeral, and subject to surfeit; happiness is active, pervasive, stable, and you can never have too much. And if there is a somnambulism of happiness, it's nothing like the zombieism of misery.

The expansive golden fluidity of life, the Golden Age, is represented with an accuracy that shows a melancholy knowledge of a paradise lost even by such self-mortifiers as the heavy-hearted Aztecs. Their Tulans, their Greeks, wore blue sandals and were wafted through the air in a fragrant breeze. And the Toltec ears of corn were huge and multicolored.

27 THINKING: PHILOSOPHICAL BITS

Some, looking into themselves, come to the limit and say "I am the ground." Others see no end and say "It hath no bottom." But perhaps you shouldn't search *in* the soul but *through* the soul.

Judgments outlast sensations: That something was sweet is remembered long after the sweetness is gone.

However fervently philosophers may abjure wholeness, I haven't read one who isn't struggling to keep the infinite-headed hydra of Nonbeing from rearing its ugly invisible heads, some by loppings, some by obeisances.

We haven't really assumed possession of even our deepest feelings until they've irritated our intellect into attentive reflection.

Marx: "The philosophers have *interpreted* the world in various ways; the point however is to change it." Revised: The philosophers have indeed changed the world in various ways; the point however was to *reflect* on it.

Skeptics are credited with sincerity. And so they should be, since their lugubrious resignation is a part of their innate temperament. But because *you* are in irons, must *I* stop sailing? To be sure, inquiry makes only an occasional landfall on this or that small island. But doesn't an archipelago betoken an underwater landmass, a common ground?

Philosophy, which was once the queen of the liberal arts, below only theology, is now, the firm having gone bankrupt, a temp of no standing, called in to do special jobs, underemployed, without benefits—although unionized.

"Questioning" this or that is an act of covert aggression. Question-asking is an act of persistent love.

Ancients: *theoria,* receptive contemplation open to intimations of Being; it enters into action through the mediation of practical wisdom. Moderns: theory, a conceptual construct; it is meant to be applied to nature through its implied technique.

I wonder if there is a book about the transformation of philosophical into technical words and the intellectual consequences: Information, the forming of the intellect → information, external data; form, the essence → formula, a symbolic expression; *eidos* (Latin *species*), the being of a kind → species, a taxonomically low grade; *energeia,* being-at-work → energy, the ability to displace objects; etc. Surely the intellectual history of our West can be read off these transformations.

Duals in experience (in geometry points and lines are called duals, because two points determine a line and two lines in turn determine a point): Their imaginative universes bring friends together, and friends together make such a universe. Individuals form communities, and communities shape individuals. The intellect takes in the world, and the world hosts the intellect.

When you're thinking things out it is sometimes in the small far-out ramification that the need for great reversals lurks. That's what gives meaning to "thinking things *out*."

I have little faith in "intuitive" people. They tend to have one intuition per object, and that's it.

The boy with the finger in the dike—that's the feel of the defense against nothingness. There's such a swelling wave of it pressing on the mounded sandbags surrounding our little spots of existence.

"Silence is not denial" says Robert Bolt's Thomas More in *A Man for All Seasons,* and further on cites to the court the maxim "Silence gives consent." So quiescence is not the best way to withhold acquiescence; moreover, it tends toward "learning to live with it." But neither is knee-jerk dissent, reactive oppositionality, the resistance that counts. Somewhere inbetween there must be a way to face the wrong cannily but not evasively, to resist from reflection rather than from reflex.

Many of us feel ourselves to be living on the cusp of time: Great questions are about to be settled: Is nature infinitely transformable, or does she collapse if her own laws are used too intrusively against her? Is human nature indefinitely malleable or does it turn monstrous when pushed too far? How much virtuality can the human imagination absorb before it loses its own actuality?, etc. I don't think anything will be concluded in the short run: Both nature and humans will accommodate to more impositions than anyone imagined and rebel at less provocation than one would have thought, and that way things will maunder on for a long, long time. When the last judgment is ready to be made we'll be long gone.

The sphere of possibility is vibrant only for a while; soon a choice has to be made and the will determined. "All things are possible" and "All things are permitted" are gusto-killers and, worse, incitements to excess.

Searching and researching are as different as a question and a questionnaire. Similarly inquiry and problem-solving: Once you've solved the problem its gist is gone; when you've pursued an inquiry its object is the more there. People who think there are philosophical problems must want philosophy to go away. (That's in fact exactly what Aristotle intimates, Hegel says, and Wittgenstein does.)

Human adaptability is a blessing and a curse—a blessing for making mankind "disposed to suffer, while evils are sufferable," and a curse for making indignities that ought not to be suffered tolerable. Americans have a certain saving rebelliousness; they'll put up with a lot in a pinch, but they don't like being pushed around. Some peoples evidently do. But let them step on this continent, and they drink in revolution with their soda pop; they know their rights. The disposition not to suffer for long is the *sine qua non* of civil freedom.

The acuteness of delight in a thing of beauty comes from its contingent existence—that it is here and now though it might so easily not have been. But the depth of delight comes from its necessary essence, that it needed to be just as it is.

Arguments with people who declare that we have no soul (the contemporary version is that mind = brain) are just tedious to me, while they, in turn, find me "warm and fuzzy" (a pleasant new view of myself). The best thing is to let them have their way, and since they often also believe in the relativity of truth, say: "OK, then, I'll have a soul and you won't."

There are a number of oddities in the mind/brain argument. One is the logic: That a physical system subserves a mental function doesn't seem to imply an identity. That all expressions of consciousness cease when the brain is dead doesn't seem to imply that consciousness has ceased. Another is the science: That certain brain activities accompany and even precede cognitive activity doesn't seem to imply that they're the cause. If brain activity were mentation, shouldn't there be a strict isomorphism between the activity and the thought content, that is, shouldn't it be possible to read the thought off the neural activity? And what theory of observation explains how one material phenomenon (the scientist's brain) applies itself cognitively to another material phenomenon (the subject's brain)?

If I have no soul (or, if you like, if there is no soul and no consciousness) whom have I been talking to all these years? What could have the requisite capabilities for carrying on that dialogue: *intentionality,* an ability to wrap itself around the intelligible being of an object, that is, to think *about* something, and *responsiveness,* the receptivity to the object apprehended and the readiness to respond articulately to its address?

I wonder if philosophy is possible among peoples who keep their temples purposely unswept and foul, like the Aztecs. Just as the marble of Greek temples is flawlessly finished, cusps of the column flutes finely honed, and the interior purified and swept, so the soul has to be clean-swept, purified of mundane preoccupations, for the intellect to go to work. I don't mean made arid or barren; on the contrary, a fullness of heart, an image-rich soul are prerequisites for reflection. I mean that the intrusive detritus of life has to be swept aside and the anxieties that preoccupy the mind have to be washed away for the intellect to become active. The Aztecs were exceedingly clean folk, but that their holiest of holies were kept gore-bespattered shows that they did not think of the highest things as cleanly clear. Yet philosophy, "the love of wisdom," depends on this faith, the faith that clear thinking will be met by a clarity of Being.

We dance on the hot coals of Existence—and long to float in the cool waters of Being.

.

Are all these inquiries of mine arcanely idiosyncratic or centrally human? Or does it come to the same thing?

Concentrated thought is the prayer of the intellect: homage to Being and hope of proximity.

Is the preoccupation with getting the phenomena rightly articulated the road toward or away from philosophy?

Some philosophers give you the sense (I'm thinking of Nietzsche) of writing from deep personal non-experience—especially of normal women, freshborn babies, and decent men.

Thinking is not the emotions' corrections officer but rather its teacher; it makes them shape up and come clean by its discipline, and it makes them firm and complex by its appreciation.

When people get hot under the collar, it's politics. When they are deeply interested, it's political philosophy.

Ordinary questions are jigs; they guide and constrain the answer: What time is it? requires that the answer be a clock time and be given right away. The jig is broken, though, when a great sage intervenes: When asked, "Do you know what time it is?" Yogi Berra said, "You mean right now?" (I once wrote a book about the Yogi's counter-question). But philosophical questions are invitations for the mind to focus; the viewfinder is usually a word and what is spied through it is to be articulated. "What is time?" means: Focus your mind on the forms behind the word "time," though they may be very remote and indistinct. And nothing in the question has jigged the answer. A philosophical question focuses the mind *and* leaves it free to "see" what shows itself.

Why can we ask deeper questions than we can answer? Because the focused mind has an orientation but not necessarily its object in view.

I doubt we want the truth, the *adaequatio intellectus et rei,* the parity of intellect and thing, most of all. Most of all we want the thing we have in mind to be genuine and to be ours, anywhich way.

If I thought philosophical inquiry would take me to despair, would I pursue it? Would I follow truth to hell or nothingness or chaos or cold chance? Some do it wantonly, exulting in terror, some do it cagily, gambling that a special grace is reserved for the uncompromised. So would I? No. The love of truth derives from its lovableness; did truth prove dreadful, I'd go look for mere beauty.

Soundmindedness depends on one conviction, an open secret: that good is really better than bad. The devil's party is continually tempted to think otherwise: "Evil, be thou my good," unforgettably says their leader, about to irrupt into Eden. Among its temporary members are the young who want to experiment. "Experiment" is what Eve did in Paradise, and to think that the interesting world-historical consequences justified the transgression is to belong to Lucifer's side. We all do with some part of us.

Experimenting is a real Lucifer-trick: to seek excitation on the pretense of illumination. But then, soundmindedness, *sophrosyne,* is a pagan virtue.

Here is what seems to me a good life: to animate the world a little by reticent teaching, to pursue clarification without scholarly paraphernalia, controversy, or regulated accountability (except to myself and discerning friends), to have a working world that is scaffold to my ardor, to be sometimes illuminated by the life of the intellect, to complete some small, neat work, and to be part of a large one.

The light of the intellect and the warmth of the imagination: when these are in play Dürer's Melencolia herself might cheer up.

Even the intellect flourishes on habit, and to resume one's wonted ways leads to bursts of mental energy: the reopening of the workplace of thought after a siesta.

The Law of Contradiction, the stay of soundness in reasonable people, can be a bludgeon in the hands of importunate rationalists: "Either A or non-A, make up your mind" is a precipitous demand. It might be neither A or non-A because they were false or inapplicable terms, or it might be both A and non-A insofar as I want to keep things indeterminate or want to set aside the law's restriction "at the same time." Or I might have intimations of Heraclitean and Hegelian reasons too deep to specify at the moment.

Thinking is affected by paradox from its very nature: It is *about* something, so it is not what it's about, yet that is what it strives to become. But that's, as the Russians say, "discovering America"—or Athens.

How could philosophy be a help in a pinch? It's a noble leisure activity and doesn't tolerate pinchings. What does help is stored dogma, literally: codified opinion. What you need in an emergency is not to think but to remember the Rome (well, perhaps not the best city for the purpose) to which all roads lead, or, to shift metaphors, what you need to be able to resort to is the residue of all the sifting done over the years. Alternately put: In a pinch it's not the *love* of wisdom you want but a little sediment from that love.

Truth-telling is always hung about with ifs and buts, which translates into lots of technicalities. But they're not boring: What's boring is dramatic wrong-headedness. *Thus Spake Zarathustra* is a boring read.

Do we proceed from or to prototypes? Do we grow out of or into ourselves? Do we discover who we were meant to be or do we invent that as we go? Probably different people develop in opposite paths. As for me, I think a discerning adult would have known roughly what was to become of me, excepting perhaps the fortuitous colorations of circumstance. Probably the chief of these is the dye of the English language, the imbuing luck of my life.

Here's a seductive falsehood: the truth, being forever, can wait while I do other things.

Against anti-reason: Of course not everything is in principle explicable, and some things are better off unexplained. But for the rest, why declare a mystery when something may yet be clarified? Truth may be unreachable, but in the manner of an asymptotic approach: The curve may approach the axis as close as you've got time and focus for.

If you let the mainstays go untuned, the mast will start rocking in heavy weather. You should keep your opinions taut against the moment they're needed so you don't sway about when challenged.

For the contemplative life the conversation of friends is what's wanted, but for action you need the co-operation of colleagues. Friends and comrades—it's great to have both. And one can turn into the other in a wonderful moment.

Dead seriousness, incessant self-denigration, terminal moralism—these are all, to my taste, forms of self-importance. Irritating.

Socratic inquiry is a search into the interior of the appearing world, a search that leads to heights when it might conceivably lead to abysses. So is it driven by a longing for the true or for the sublime?

Some thinkers care much more for honesty (subjective) than for verity (objective). They seem to get a sort of raw joy in discovering complex kinds of nothingness which attest to the severity of their probity.

Deadly serious persons put you under twenty-four-hour surveillance for levity. Don't they know that playfulness is an expression of trust in the sturdiness of the enterprise? No, because they suppose that not trust but suspicion is the mark of probity. But I like the honesty that is sweet candor rather than desperate recalcitrance.

What do intellectuals think of when they're making a cheesecake?

The desire to profit from one's agonies is not the most trustworthy beginning for philosophy.

When everyone says the same thing, it's likely to be a truth in caricature. Commonplaces need to be morphed back into verisimilitude.

The jocund, dry, comic ordinariness of mere people is a much better way to truth than the strained exorbitancies of the intellectuals.

Resignation does open the senses. Give up hope of doing something, let the thing go, and out in the street you find yourself absorbed in the unobligating looks of things.

There are—brief—moments when the absorption in crystalline objects of learning makes the somatic world almost repulsive.

Of course the intellect can govern our passions, certainly over time. It can file down and shape them, it can penetrate and expose them, and at moments of psychic harmony, it can illumine and confirm them.

People who are mentally mostly out to lunch resent those "who are always thinking." To them this unaccustomed activity consists of rationalizing, critiquing, judging, calculating—something ruinous to peaceful existence. When in fact thinking just makes you be there twice: implicitly and explicitly, a lovely double life.

Thinking—not rigorously, which constrains the mind past reason and deforms its object, but clearly—is evidently not as common as one might expect, man being a rational animal. There's a whole slew of people who think that independence of mind is expressible as elaborate eccentricity; they get together in little therapeutic-spiritual cults with a complex gobbledygook philosophy.

Esotericism and philosophy seem to me to be incompatible. For one thing, secrecy is redundant when, as Heraclitus rightly says, "nature loves to hide." For another, Being is *the* common human business, so its pursuit is restricted, if at all, to the club of the self-elected.

Thinking deliberately and acting accordingly are not linked necessarily. Often people think hard and act jaggedly, and others who act on impulse do it deftly. Going from thorough deliberation to smoothly decisive action is a gift.

Are we ultimately separate or connected, alone or together? Bodies play out parodies of penetration but they're ultimately impenetrable, they can't be in the same space—that's what it means to be a body. Souls rejoice in being one, but how can that be one with another which is, on the one hand, not always at one with itself yet, on the other, an unconjoinably independent "I"? "A friend is another self": an *other,* a doubling, of the self, not a merger.

I think I've got this word usage right, and here's an illustration: The desire for conversation is mutual, but the talking should be reciprocal.

Philosophical discoveries may be *recollections* of the mind's prenatal knowledge, but moral decisions involve the *remembrance* of models later laid up in the imagination.

Don't underrate the intelligence of good people.

Axioms: very respectable prejudices.

The heart can seduce the head and the head can outtalk the heart, but eventually it's a good marriage.

Agonizing isn't thinking; in fact, when the latter kicks in, the former gives up.

There's a pusillanimous fear, encouraged by people of feeble feelings and rigidified reason, that thinking undermines one's capacity for passion. Not to worry. Right reason subjects the soul only to appreciative and preservative scrutiny; it acknowledges, shapes, records what we feel, and leaves it twice-lived.

Thinking: We find ourselves attached to a belief and want to uncover the why of it—not to undermine it but, on the contrary, to ground it, and sometimes not even that but just to know ourselves. So also the notion that we ask our students to reflect on their opinions to upset their faith is ludicrous. The deepest questions aren't driven by suspicion of error but by longing for light. We don't "question beliefs"; we ask questions about them, precisely not to eradicate but to root them.

Philosophical scavengers: Vultures feed on dead bodies, and some professional philosophers (apologies to the soaring kingly condor) play vulture on living doctrine; they pick it apart and seize on bits. Example: Take a little bit of Plato, tear it out of its context, discard the pedagogic playfulness and dissembling, flap away the silently engaged participants within the drama and also those without (meaning the critical readers)—and behold!—a logically vulnerable bit of vulture-do.

How could there be professional philosophers: a credentialed guild of lovers of wisdom!

Stereotype: We overlay a ready-made template *on* an individual. Type: We see an archetype *in* the person.

Being original: the gift of putting one's own spin on a subject or even of being oneself the origin of the matter. Philosophical originality is a contradiction in terms, since philosophy requires letting things be what they are (no small trick). Seeking origins, looking for the principles of causes of things, not with brilliance but with insight—that *is* philosophy. Some famous philosophers are very original, and their works should be read accordingly—with suspicion.

Thought and passion play leapfrog. One overleaps the other until they face about and fall into each other's arms.

There is a fact-truth distinction: between what is merely so and what is meaningfully so. There is a value-worth distinction: between what has an assessable price and what is esteemed priceless. These are nice discriminations, useful in fixing one's ideas. But that famous fact-value distinction, in combining the less noble first member of each pair, seems to me to construct a universe of discourse I don't want to impose on my world.

My experience: Believers in relativism are in theory tolerant and in temper irascible. Adherents of principle are severe in their judgments and in life quite easy. (At least this is often true.) So I like the second group better on both counts: sturdiness and sweetness.

I learned one useful thing in graduate school (from my numismatics professor, imagine!), worth a whole library of "Mirrors of Princes": Pure principle, corrupt administration. Anyone who's been in the position knows what he meant: Know what ought to be, and do what you can.

The wonder with which philosophy begins is astonishment at the normalcy of the normal, not at the marvelousness of marvels. If the world appears monstrous or uncanny or even ravishingly beautiful, sleep it off before you think.

The mental indolence of some of the faithful derives from the sense that someone somewhere knows it all: live well and you too will know, and without laborious cogitation. They could be right, but it is too big a chance—the risk in taking up Pascal's wager (that God exists) is greater than he lets on, not because we might lose the bet but because we might lose just because we bet—when we should have pondered.

When the breezes of living thought blow—some people slip into windbreakers.

Department of opinion-having (which we all belong to): The trick is to keep one's mind at once determinate and open, to train it to be springy, and to turn its firm perches into elastic springboards.

Any truth has a problematic aspect which our opponents have focused on more acutely than we have.

Though I believe (in the absence of contrary evidence) that all human beings have a pretty similar range of intellectual capability, there does seem to be an abyss between those peoples to whom a grand idea has come and those who haven't yet got the word. For example, the Aztecs seem to have truly lacked the idea of a lawful nature moving independently of the gods.

The marvelous fact seems to be that ideas are absorbed (which does not mean that habits are changed) overnight. I read somewhere of an American Plains Indian receiving with delighted recognition the idea of the relativity of motion; I think he was asked whether the Earth moved under the horse or the horse over the Earth. The keyword is "recognition": Human beings are all the intellect's natives.

Universal, kind, species vs. particular, instance, individual—the latter would not be discernible except in the light of the former, but conversely, we are brought to the former by thinking about the latter.

A thinker engaged in a close-up, Jacob-like battle with the angel of doctrine is an awesome sight, but when he limps away victorious, can he still entertain questions?

Feelings can be bent to the will but not thinking. A controlled feeling is a feeling still; a willed thought is not thought thought at all but the ventriloquism of the mind.

Advice to myself concerning nescience:
1. Simply admit ignorance of what others do know (facts, theories). 2. Don't be boastfully modest about not knowing what no one else knows either (first and last things). 3. Either resign yourself to never knowing what you ought to know or make a project of learning it, but don't fuss. 4. Don't claim that something important is unknowable; it's pure presumption. 5. Try to exult in newly discovered perplexities. 6. Don't display dithering nescience; it's just annoying. 7. Remember that unknowableness is the least persuasive antidote to dogmatism. 8. Make no boastful protestations of your large ignorance of expert's expertise. 9. Don't say "I don't understand" when you mean "I don't approve."

Let's hear it for reality. All that constructivist fantasizing can make one into a hard-edged positivist.

I can't escape the sense that the phenomena, everything that's around me and offering itself to the senses, are an emergence, configured below and inside and pushed into appearance, risen like an iceberg—"This iceberg cuts its facets from within" (Elizabeth Bishop)—and like an iceberg more out of sight than in. That underworld is surely very cold and possibly crystal clear.

Is it possible to have metaphysical propensities without something of a mechanical intelligence that can discover linkages, discern the seating of parts, detect problems, and devise solutions? Not because the mechanical model is applicable to first philosophy but because it isn't. Quite a few high metaphysical notions depend on a deliberate imaginative subversion of such a model, for example, the Unmoved Mover and Hegelian dialectic.

The fact that most of us feel confusion as burdensome indicates that clarity has primacy.

To turn a lax ambiguity into a taut paradox—there's an accomplishment.

A human being at work thinking, especially a young one, is interesting even if what issues is not exactly news.

The cosmopolitan individual: different from all, alien to none.

No one has the answer ≠ There is no answer. The latter implies the former but emphatically not the other way around. In embarking on an inquiry it is in any case irrelevant to the business who claims to know what and a statistic to be considered last of all, if ever.

Philosophies that dance on a tightrope over an abyss seem to me frivolous daredeviltry. Human life is lived on an open plane and wants ex-planations, not antics.

To conclude that nothing is knowable and to understand that one knows nearly nothing are experiences worlds apart. The first is a devastating crisis of faith, and the second is that famous Socratic wisdom.

Three sorts of philosophizing: craftsmanlike working out of problems set by the tradition; eccentric spinning out of idiosyncratic preoccupations; inspired composing of original systems. In the *orbis intellectualis,* the first fills the middle regions, the second goes on at the margins, the third takes the very center. But I think that dawdling at the marginal extremes brings you closer to the center than being busy at the broad middle.

To my mind what is absolutely intractable is also perfectly pointless: radical untranslatability, impenetrable privacy, existential absurdity, complete contingency. Glance at it, to be sure, but why focus on it?

The further you've climbed up the approaches the larger the mountain of knowing must loom.

Be reasonable just to prove that reason can command loyalty.

The Greeks say *chalepon to kalon,* "the beautiful is hard"—hard to come by, hard to do. Experience makes that seem so obvious: There are fewer excellent than ordinary people. The perfect zephyr for an afternoon sail is rarely up. There are many mediocre and few good paintings. A good man is hard to find. And so on. But why? Why on earth are not the many, *hoi polloi,* the noble and the few the low?—even Jefferson, that reckless republican, speaks of a "natural aristocracy." Is it a flaw or a perfection of the world that in it our presumedly self-evident human equality with its unalienable rights is countermanded by apparently indefeasible inequalities with their irresistible arrogations?

Why is it so hard for professional philosophers to say "In my opinion . . ."? They develop strategies, take positions, declare problems disposed of. You wouldn't guess that three decades later the strategies will be superseded, the positions vacated, and the problems as live as the hydra's heads. They seem to think that they owe it to their profession to know definitively, when they really owe it to their calling to be knowledgeably ignorant.

Metaphysics, which is now and ever was and always will be about Being, is a valiant activity requiring a cleared soul and an unoccupied heart. But there is another activity, allied yet antithetical, nothing like comprehensive contemplation, more like probing penetration, less an ardor than an obsession, less discovery than therapy. It obeys the pressure to catch life *in words:* preserve nuances of passion and accesses of nothingness, catch moments of delight, and capture the pangs of pain. As—Aristotle teaches—nothing can come before the intellect that was not first figured in the imagination (*On the Soul* 431 a), so nothing can come to reflection that was not first expressed by language, because thinking needs to fix itself in sensible form before it can reflect (literally: "bend back") on itself. Thus a mania for articulating the world in words might, after all, be phase one of getting beyond it.

28 TRANSCENDENCE: ABOVE AND BEYOND

The pursuits that go down, back, and beyond, should sometimes have priority over those that go up, out, and on: the rectification of the soul over the accumulation of knowledge.

Life without archetypes is unreferenced, baseless. Prototypes are built in the world to test a design; archetypes arise in the soul to give depth to events.

The price we pay for living without reverence, for a kind of petulant egalitarianism in the face of the high and the august, is nerves, anxiety, and panic. Roots and reverence give us gravity and dignity. That holds especially for children.

Hierarchy sacralizes even mediocrity. To be a very middling member of a sacred order is still to be involved with heights. We are high even in being low on a holy ladder.

Here is a way to look at our tradition, the works of intellect and sensibility that choice and chance have handed down to us: It is a secular hierarchy, a rank order, so to speak, in the horizontal dimension, that is, distributed through time, and as in any hierarchy, even a minor member may serve and reflect its greatness.

Can human passion run high without running rampant if there is no regard to something sacred?

Can we be wholly ourselves unless we feel contained by something larger than ourselves, something beyond?

Devoutness is a disposition not to be bored by what is old, grand, obvious, and given. Its opposite is "innovative creativity," avidity for clever commotion; we need some people to be like that, but not everybody, for God's sake.

Some of us denizens of modernity (for let's not forget that most of America is very religious) know the sacred only by involuntary accesses of holy terror, by inexplicable correspondences and coincidences, by sudden manifestations of sublimity. We seem to have to be caught by surprise to experience a moment of belief. Which tells me that we ourselves are in our way: We are caught in the cross hairs of recalcitrance and probity.

There sits a realm of grace athwart our working world with its honest pedantry and industrious production. Sometimes the world and the realm are suddenly aligned.

Just as music is central to my life although I'm practically unmusical, so faith is central although I'm effectively unreligious. I keep having the sense that these matters can wait; it is certainly feckless, perhaps blithe. Now is that belief or unbelief?

When the psalmist sang that "a thousand years in thy sight are but as yesterday when it is past, and as a watch in the night," did he model the divine experience on our own, on the indiscernibility of our days? Years of daily living collapse into a day, a day of days, the Day of Routine, which we experience as the one just gone by: "yesterday when it is past." Isn't that an intimation to mortals of that infinite condensation of time through which a divinity would have to apprehend human history?

The memorable punctuations of our routines, on the other hand, act as pegs upon which time strings its lines and by which these same mortals experience time as having extension, stretches articulated by moments.

Here is a suggestion to Satan for a new mode of hell, or rather limbo: a demonic mood in which you are not present at the present and look at it from afar with an acrid nostalgia. But of course, he's already familiar with this mood. It's one of the varieties of his sins called *tristitia*.

People believe in God because they feel comforted when they ought to be, by all rights, in despair; also because things come together when they ought to (if entropic nature had its way) fall apart.

We have all the causes for anxiety Pascal thought of and then some: Inserted between two infinities, the vast void beyond us, with only a few sinkholes of energy and concretions of matter to interrupt it, and the sub-sensory world of ever-divisible, raving elements below us, ourselves a precarious composite of a vulnerable external body, with the Lord knows what catastrophic diseases already latent within it and a mysterious interior territory kept in a fragile state of peace by who knows what—how do we manage to live our lives in relative comfort? It's by practicing a sort of sensible recklessness, a sound obtuseness.

We're duplicitous beings, one way or the other: now a roiled surface over a reservoir of serenity and again a cheerful veneer over a dark abyss.

I feel myself to be a true pagan: enchanted by visible gods and trusting invisible Being.

How comforting is ex-plaining thought that brings things to the surface and makes them plain to the human intellect, as compared to these close-up struggles with a God who is, apparently, opaque even to himself!

If there were no sort of divinity at all, why wouldn't I be utterly alone when I'm by myself? Superegos and sub- and un-consciousnesses are inadequate explanations of that sense of the third, attentive auditor in these internal conversations between me and myself. Sometimes, to be sure, the third is a real friend I've taken within, sometimes an imaginary listener I've made the silent interlocutor. But all that is as child's play carried on under the unobtrusively attentive eye of a Monitor. It's absurd to presume that I do—and am—it all.

How did Heaven change when Hell was founded? It's a paradigm question on earth for anyone who loves a place. When Lucifer fell through the void, Heaven must have been forever altered by a taint of anxiety, knowing well that the Creation now had that Adversary on the loose. Just so every terrestrial demi-paradise must fear its excluded evil. Lucifer leaped half-way back up to operate in Heaven's favored colony, earthly Eden. How will our adversary enter? Can we be infected? Isolated? Swept under? Compromised? Or worst of all, die on our posts of defensive rigidification? "It is . . . a small college, yet there are those who love it," Daniel Webster said, himself in tears and before a teary Chief Justice Marshall (Dartmouth College case). Can we keep ours up?

The poets, Blake says, are of the devil's party, and I can see why. Unrelieved bliss bores the bad, and poets are talentedly bad. Where would I have been in that great civil war? On the side of a proud and beautiful and bad adventurer or the all-surviving wise old establishment? I hope with goodness, when all is said and done, which was not too soppily boring after all, viz., the glorious march-by of Heaven's victory parade Bach recorded in Cantata 50 for Michael, Heaven's general.

To know why "bad" means "magnificent" in ghetto language read *Paradise Lost,* Book I.

Hell is a recognizable place, familiar in its cozy horror, its bleak grandeur, its melodious, thrumming despair. It is built as the imagination builds: "Anon out of the earth a fabric huge / Rose like an exhalation, with sound / Of dulcet symphonies and voices sweet, / Built like a temple, where pilasters round / Were set, and Doric pillars overlaid / With golden architrave . . ." (*Paradise Lost* I 710. Why Doric, I wonder? I would have said the more florid Corinthian). And the music there, "though partial," takes "with ravishment the thronging audience" (II 552). It's partial, self-favoring (my edition glosses: prejudiced *and* polyphonic), here on earth too; we only listen to what suits us and prefer polyphony over plainsong.

What is that devilish attraction exercised by beings that are doomed, damned, demonic? It's the frisson of moral dissonance. Such creatures are not amoral or immoral but dis-moral, to coin a word, perversely moral. Amorality has the odor of nothingness, immorality has an offensive smell, but dis-morality has the appetizingly disgusting fragrance of certain soft cheeses.

I would respect agnostics more if they were suspended rather than settled. How can one take a *position* of ignorance? What is the difference in the end between determined noncommittalism and careless indifferentism?

Two questions that leave me monumentally nonplussed: "Why is there something and not nothing?" (Leibniz) and "Where wast thou when I laid the foundations of the earth?" (Job 38:4). Did it make itself? Was I involved? Both possible answers are sayable but not intelligible. What am I being driven into?

This week a friend looked shocked because I reckoned with a possible God. Last week another was grieved because I didn't. Truth to tell, I'd rather shock than grieve my friends.

Some things that aren't so great have an unbeatable point in their favor: They *exist*.—Better a live dog than a dead lion. But for really bad stuff it's the opposite.

The paganism of the old philosophers seems to me to consist in an exaltation of the sensible; they want to find the underpinnings for our ordinary virtues as well as the sources for our extraordinary intimations, to confirm the gravity of the former and the legitimacy of the latter.

Honest people say they just can't believe; not so honest people say they believe because they need to. When in *real* life was needing something a cause for its existence? But then again, when did real life have the last word?

Phidias (or his architect) expressed his faith in the holographic vision of the gods by finely finishing the back of the statues in the pediment of the Parthenon. I'm about something similar when I correct misprints in the books on my shelves—following a feeling that the world's backsides and insides are visible and monitored by something or someone, that an all-seeing perfectionist divinity is watching.

Tobe, Welt, und springe; / Ich steh' hier und singe / In gar sich'rer Ruh', "Rage, oh world, and caper; / Here I stand and carol / In secure repose" (Bach, Motet S. 227). The world's approval means a lot, but it means more that, when the moment comes, I *could* and *would* brave its encroachments, and sing serenely in the storm.

However loath I would be to make declarations of faith, I also would not wish to adopt principles that would debar me from recognizing divinity, should it ever deign to manifest itself.

1. The way it is, is a curable corruption of the way it ought to be. 2. Whatever is, has first-comer's rights. Both true. Figure that out.

Does everyone wake up from the day's sleepwalking now and then into a moment's dark illumination: the sense of the absurdity of marching through the world in this particular body, carrying about my peculiar atmosphere, demanding welcome, respect, even appreciation? The best cure is to get back to busy oblivion, but I've seen what I've seen: a tiny pursing of the universe's mouth.

Faith or works? It's not really my business, but I trust the church of deeds. For one thing, the one-upmanship of deeds is less than that of faith; the soul is best served by the knowledge that a decent deed redeems an evil thought, and above all, the credo of deeds makes for a certain hilarity, a humorously indulgent view of human capacities. If faith matters desperately, everything becomes dead earnest. Am I a closet Catholic? Perhaps, if it weren't for that Son, whose godhead is to me a mystery with a small "m" and whose humanity seems all too familiar from my youth in Brooklyn.

29 IMAGES:
WORK OF THE IMAGINATION

Every night—no, many nights—we wake up into another world. It has, as Descartes observes, some basics in common with this one we are pleased to call real: place, configuration, number, time, motion. Is it coherent as well? Is reality so coherent? Are all the dream realms in one system? Are all the waking human worlds in one universe? These are questions not for thinking but for musing, not for solving but for dwelling: They're half-serious and all-important.

On certain nights, bad ones, the world unravels, and is respun into its protective cocoon only in the warmth of the day's routine.

Desire is like an agitator (the kind in a washing machine), shaking apart imagination and existence; its urgencies insist on reality.

A recurrent dream: I crash land on the seam of a reedy lake, a few columns are standing, some drums lie in the sand. Pan, I know, is hiding in the rushes. There's a shed, an archeological *apotheke,* a storehouse, where shattered antiquities are put away. Major nostalgia!

What is so moving as vivid reminiscences of scenes never seen and souls never known and the haunting strain of unheard music—and not just those off that marble urn in the Louvre either, the one Keats talked to.

The imagination invests the world but only if the world has earned that dignity. Some of its spaces are unimaginable, definite and dull, stark as a dirty-gray Roman marble.

In dreams our companions appear in the aura of their essential being, their fragrance-essence.

Three forms of imagining: Precise figures and topographies effortfully summoned or composed from the memory—imaging more than imagining; the essences of things, their fragrances, auras, penumbras—the misty mode, deeply accurate yet without acuity; iterative daydreams—lax envisioning, taut pleasure.

Sometimes the imagination develops an object clearly seen by interpolating its own references and resonances to enhance its objective beauty. Sometimes it envelops an object scarcely discerned in a pathos that invests it with subjective beauty.

Surely flagellating the imagination with hallucinogenics is a huge admission of its failure.

Under the shock of loss, the imagination cuts out. It won't be co-opted as a comforter, won't make shades appear on demand or lend departed figures vitality. It collapses before the annihilation of existences, because it is itself the realm of non-beings. But in its own time, when no longer oppressed by demands to produce existence, it returns the lost figures to us and sends up the shades, unbidden, round and ruddy, like the souls in Homer's Hades who've drunk blood.

Behind the appearances of the imagination there are just more appearances. Down to its immemorial depths we wander in a spacious Augustinian topography. But there, in its hindmost recesses, we make the *metábasis eis állo génos,* a "transition into a different kind" of capacity, into the intellect.

The world comes to us as appearance, and we return it to itself as meaning.

We take in and we put out: Imagination is fed by the world and in turn nourishes it, or alternately, it is given the wool and it returns the web.

Nothing matters more (and this is not hyperbole) than the stocking of children's souls with sound and shapely images—emphatically not to be found in the rambunctious cuteness of the toy store but in the grave beauties of real children's books. For these accumulated visions and events will someday be the true (if unacknowledged) ground of real action; for example, *Wind in the Willows* is a *civic education.*

How many metaphors for the work of the imagination there are, and all accurate: the distilling alembic, the testing titration, the purifying sieve, the transforming workshop, the secure treasure house—and the last best refuge?

Imagination is expansive, desire constrictive. Love puts them in their tensest tandem.

Biography of the spirit: In youth we're so close to our imaginative archetypes that we expect them any minute to emerge into being. In young adulthood the theoretical intellect, vigorously preoccupied with its intuitions and constructs, drives the imagination into eclipse. (Who reads novels in their twenties?) In maturity the practical intellect is at work building and maintaining the world in the image of long suppressed images. Then, one year, the imagination wells up, even gushes out, after its long compression, and lo and behold, imagination and intellect turn out to be each other's complements.

Imagination is interiority made internally external, the soul's non-extended spatialization of itself, the non-appearing made manifest to nonsensory sight, *the inward prospect.* You could write an eight-hundred-page book about its sum and substance and yet not understand this discarnate incarnation of the spirit and still have no clue to the mystery.

Utopias are a. precise projections of the imagination, but b. sometimes regimented by ideology; a. can be lovely, b. is perforce horrible. It's the difference between utopian and dystopian vision.

"Imagination" is cognate with "imitation"—we share that capacity with mirrors and puddles. But human imagination also has a power of place, of siting its figures in an atmosphere.

Do heroes step out of their mythical setting, coagulated, so to speak, from its aura, or do they first bring their enveloping archetypal world into being? I suspect the former, encouraged by this story of ours, that makes man wait five days to be created while his world is made ready for him.

Suddenly, when the mood opens up, myths invest the scene and intimations take on shape and the essences of lost times fill the air. It's soon gone, but it's magical while it lasts.

Aristotle, who can't be faulted for romanticism, nonetheless defines "place" in a way hospitable to the imagination: the envelope of a being. And a being's place is where it belongs. So as in *space* there are Cartesian coordinates, numbered loci marking extended configurations, in place there are intensive beings, at home and snuggly embraced. The imagination I cherish is our place-making capacity.

When music sounds in a place (real music in a real place) its people suddenly become inexpressibly charming: our normally impish kids singing angelically at the Christmas Collegium Musicum.

The music of a place summons its bygone inhabitants back into a ghostly life.

Some places have little to adorn them except that they are the depository of dreams.

Suddenly a room will go misty with pity, passion, grandeur, as if the dream was about to embody itself or a fiction about to materialize.

There are many places in Augustine's "spacious fields and palaces" of the memory, and they light up seriatim as friends converse.

Human attachments are the indirect lighting of worldly venues, and places go dark and cold when this illumination fails.

The imagination has no more effective tonic than stretches of ardent intellectuality, and conversely, thinking is vivified by dreaming.

Strenuous thinking is activated by opposite causes: either the sighting of a crack in Being or a glimpse of its exemplified perfection.

Anticipation of fulfillment can overwhelm, flood out, the image of the object longed for: the blind futurity of desire.

It's wise to respect others even in the imagination, to deal with their image only as they would wish to be dealt with in reality, though we may take this liberty: to hold them closer than we do in fact. That's on the hypothesis that if they knew us from the inside, they'd wish it. So that noble reticence comes to naught.

Second visits are wonderful because you see anew while summoning memory.

Between the imagination and its realization practical arrangements intervene and so its materialized shapes bear the marks of work done. Nothing imaginative wanders unmodified into life.

Suddenly you come in real life on a scene you'd sometimes remembered in dreams. It's like a loud psychic click, a corroboration that the dream was no dream. Does the dream then withdraw for good? Happily not.

"It's me," we say ungrammatically but sensibly, meaning that we are the object in view. So also in dreaming or daydreaming we don't turn up in the first person nominative but as objects viewed by ourselves. But is that figure in the imagination, which is identifiably me, more a first person than any others that turn up in that odd place? Surely the imagined Me is no more the host of the entire entertainment than any other figure, while I am certainly its impresario. Anyone willing to consider that question earnestly will be my friend.

Sometimes the world suddenly shifts, and you can't tell whether it's gone askew or come aright.

In youth: "In dreams begin responsibilities" (Delmore Schwartz). In age: "In obligations are dreams maintained."

There are what dreaming aborigines call the "big dreams," which will have shifted the world when once we wake, which dominate the day and come back by night. They are a *déja vu* even on their first dreaming in their utter familiarity, and each recurrence is, in the words of that sage, Yogi Berra, "*déja vu* all over again." But in their redolent aboriginality they're no laughing matter.

If music be the food of love, so are the fragrant decoctions of dreams.

Those daydreams are truly sound that could step into reality with only minor modifications.

In dreams there is often a back room, doorless, where some reunion is waiting to take place. What if that unknown friend broke into the dream? And then into reality? Well, if step one occurs, then we'll worry about step two.

Are dreams real? Nothing so low as that.

There is a time of psychic vigor, when the barrier between possible and actual is vanishingly thin: not only are images on the brink of materializing, what's more, it makes no difference.

Revisiting scenes of graduate study: the place looks as if it had awoken from a half-century of refreshing sleep and knew not me—or I, it. Suddenly a building springs into memorial action: pangs of bygone times, more for youth passed than pleasures recalled. In fact Yale had no imaginative resonance for me, and I learned mostly what to forget.

No hallucinogens—lest my imagination lose its innocence. No tranquilizers—lest I miss the lessons of pandemonium.

There are musing moods when I see my loved venues and their figures as if from beyond; I am a revenant but they too are ghosts in a bygone world—an eerie fantasy with a residual message: Return to the present gratefully.

Reality claims the distinction of being one world. Is the imaginative world a territorial union? Oh yes, for us cosmopolitans.

A standing atmosphere becomes opaque; familiarity blinds.

Those floating hours when the tough diaphanous membrane between the world we wish for and the world that exists billows, like the humongous soap bubbles children blow through plastic wands, a long way into existence . . .

As a bulb flares up brightly before it burns out, so the image of an impossible love flares up just before the final abnegation.

One dreams and the other plots—misery in the making.

The imaginative content seems to be inversely proportional to the real resolution of the image. What's the attraction in watching that never-improving low-grade stuff in ever-improving high-grade imaging? TV is okay, I like it, but its technical advances are like putting a high-gloss paint on a rough-cut board.

There are dreams that are a visible asking. You spend a laborious night trying to articulate the question.

Here's a self-correcting daydream: The devil grants my wish to have as many dollars as there are leaves on my willow oak. But there's one condition, he says: *You* count them, and if you're off by one you get nothing. And your life is gone.

Demythifications probably give satisfaction to the enlightened minds that perform them. But why isn't the world less deluded when they've done?

Anyone who has a nice, innovative scheme for shaking up a working community should be required to submit a plan in closely imagined detail of a day under the new dispensation. Who, for instance, gets a key to what?

The defect of reality is that it's imperfectly realized— that takes imagination.

The imagination's chief mode is discarnate visibility and yet it can rouse the flesh.

Empathy, feeling your way into another's feeling, is blind without the imaginative reconstruction of the other's imaginative life.

Revisiting the places of our childhood: the strange experience of seeing the archetypes of our life reappear as instances of themselves.

Our memories are recursive: They embed the remem-berings of memories, memories of memories, way back to a first memory which was, in its time, itself the memory of a timeless archetype—or felt that way. (I experienced this as a child, a half century before I read it in Husserl's great work on time.)

Sleeping dreams are rarely wish fulfillments—much more likely to be revelations of the wish itself. It's the waking dreams that are unabashed gratifications.

Escalating dreams I really dreamed: First week—a huge glowingly beautiful balloon rising with a fine-spun ominousness over a green-and-gold horizon. Next week—a huge, potent doomsday chopper doing the same. What's my imagination telling me?

Plans for innovations that have no content but their own novelty are the hallmark of people with more drive than imagination. And it's perfectly well known that all these improvements are only redistributions of trouble. Yet let no one think that just because over time enough it's all a wash, nothing is lost. The peace and quiet that breed substance are lost.

How could anything that goes on over hundreds of channels 24/7 (as they now say) possibly be of uniformly great quality? It's no use complaining about TV. Turn it off if you're not amused. I think what we must ponder is the format itself, the "medium," that is, the means by which images are conveyed. Among many items: First, since by an ancient convention, we divide the day into twenty-four parts, every imaginative event is now one twenty-fourth part of a day long; if you look at your watch you know exactly how far you are from the de-nouement. Second, all the figures are pygmies not by reason of distance, but right in front of me. Third, if I don't like what's going on, I can switch to a different channel plumb in the middle of someone's sentence. In other words, the medium discombobulates my natural rhythms, my sense of scale, my human consideration.

Imagine according to the rules of possibility; don't fantasize. That will neutralize reality's revenge.

30 PASSAGE: TIME AND LIFETIME

The heroism of maintenance is severely underrated. It is the resistance to human and natural entropy—that cosmic downward trend (which Lucretius symbolized in the fundamental fall of his atoms), that tendency toward deterioration and featureless homogeneity that will obtain if the world is left alone. (In Washington State I used to see a dentists' billboard saying "If you ignore your teeth they'll go away.") But it isn't only nature and humanity in its natural course that needs to be kept going against time's grain; we also need a counterinsurgency against mindless novelty. Between entropy and innovation— that's where my heroes are at work.

"Vacation" is a sad word, the vacancy of time after the press of business. "Leisure" is a lovely word, the freedom of time for long-breathed projects.

Who doesn't, in middle age, feel a gnawing anxiety for a life now half-gone that might go to its end half-unlived? Some of us then look for last-chance raptures, some of us for new-life projects. The projects are more apt to work out than the raptures.

You emerge from a period of solitary eventfulness into public time and find that you've got nothing to tell. It makes you empathize with the children's refrain "Where did you go?" "Nowhere." "What did you do?" "Nothing," when the unspoken answer is: "Arcane places; clandestine deeds."

From childhood to old age this desire persists: To see realized in the outer world the inner landscape and its native figures, our inner prospects—either to find or to help found it. And then to protect it.

Those who experience their times as responsible insiders are in for a noble misery, while the determined outsiders, who practice *sauve qui peut,* live in somewhat ignominious serenity—no, it's more likely to be suppressed anxiety. But being an insider doesn't mean being a full-time participant; that would be a little nutty.

After our hurdle-ridden daily passage, filled up with scheduled duties, appointments, even time-bound amusements (movie starts at 9:20 P.M.), leisure is like a long draft of cool, fresh water, delicious in the drinking and restorative in the result—restorative not as rest but as activity in Aristotle's sense: being fully immersed in fulfilling work.

Nighttime is the leisure time of the busy—free not only of interruptions but even of the expectation of interruption, silent not only with an absence of distraction but with the enveloping, focusing silence of the night. Nothing wrong, incidentally, with being responsive to the world's calls—by the ubiquitous gray of day; it's the dark-girt island of the midnight lamp that should be inviolable.

When we consume food, we degrade organized, tasty, textured portions, having extracted nutriment into you-know-what. Isn't that what some of us do to culture?—or to time, an even more expensive commodity to be used up in precise parcels when we're in a business mode and when we've got nothing left to do, a worse than worthless, insipid mass for us to eliminate as best we can.

Aristotle, ever loyal to the immediately apprehensible, thinks that acceleration, change of change, is impossible (*Physics* 225 b). But that's just *our* contemporary temporality. So for us the meaning of motion is no longer the prolonged fulfillment of a capability but a mere instant to which is attached a differentiable quantity, the mere rate of its change, which can be differentiated in turn to obtain acceleration, the merest mathematical abstraction, a rate of a rate of change. No wonder the human meaning of "accelerating innovation" is somewhat dim to us.

There's futurology vs. Prophecy, rational conjecture vs. Divine Revelation, prudence vs. Providence—I'm not sure that I'd want to rely on either the new methods or the old ways for knowing or facing the future. My notion is that it's best to back into it: hang onto the past-rooted present and mind that prickly feeling at the back of your neck.

Those managerial souls who regard social life as a set of soluble problems see the present not as their moment to *be* but as a hurdle to be leaped over into a future of resolutions! When's life to happen?

Modernity, the just-now time (from *modo,* just now), rushes past itself, from inchoateness to obsolescence and the reverse, so fast now that they're all but simultaneous. That's for high-tech stuff. But try to change a school system!

Stuttering temporality: instant replay, the artificial *déja vu* of events before they've even passed from iconic (photographic) to stored memory. We take this duplication of the specious present in our stride, but doesn't it devalue the original moment?

You can think of the future as the unformed not-yet or as the shape of things to come, sliding inexorably over the knife's edge of the now. If the motions that matter to us were cyclical or obeyed fixed laws of change the latter view would make sense. But seeing that there is genuine newness—not the unforeseen but the unforeseeable—the future has to be unformed for us. Newness seems to me a no lesser mystery than creation; in fact it is intratemporal creation—or is there someone who still adheres to total determinism?

Maundering restlessness: when my time is vacant and your company unavailable.

The Titan Cronos (interpreted as Chronos-Time) ate his children. That's antiquity; in modern times the children also gobble up their progenitors: The present can be seen as being devoured by the past or as gorging on it: reckless obsolescence or heedless inheritance.

How uncannily recognizable is the aura about one's birth! It's neither my infant experience nor my adult taste that makes me resonate immediately (albeit with a shudder) to the Europe of 1929: the radically experimental, the perversely abandoned, the romantically demonic, the rebelliously idealistic and doom-laden atmosphere before the catastrophe. I'm as sensitive to it as litmus paper to acid—a whole slew of visions, for all their ruddy luridness somehow homey, flutter about any reminiscent artifact, say a movie like *The Cabinet of Dr. Caligari,* or a song from the Youth Movement and the Spanish Civil War. I was a protected child—how did I absorb that world, lost by the time I came to, as an adolescent? It's enough to make one believe in a *Zeitgeist*—a notion otherwise barely plausible even in its Hegelian context.

From youth to middle age we—well, some of us— grow both less aggressive and less malleable, more accommodating but also more determinate in shape.

Some outlying parts of our interior territory are bound to become deserted in the course of a concentrated life. But it's just from these that renewal comes. As the desert blooms in delicate profusion with even a light watering, so with a little cultivating these deserted parts come gratifyingly to life: I read hardly any lyric poetry for the first half-century of my literate life.

Why should the millenarian dead be any more dead than last year's deceased? How dead you are depends on who's attending to you.

Let there be a sudden hiatus in the round of thinking and rethinking, doing and redoing, and a lovely passivity takes over, a mood oppressed and delighted by glimpses of returning dreams, twinges of renewed desire—all but lost lands, long hidden prospects looming up through the mists of memory. Just a small break in the clangor of action—and you can hear the continuo of the inner life.

Middle age: a faintly incredulous recognition that roots have established themselves in the soil of daily life, the plant has assumed fixed contours, and its reliable fruit tastes like blessed tedium. Then stirrings of longing for a glorious uprooting: grandeur and battle. Do other people get over their youth?

Archeology, my first calling, was a way to delve into time by digging into dirt, to go backward by going downward. Space had been time's safe-deposit box. So we dug through the undisturbed strata (the archeologists' virgin soil) and got out the testimony and put it into a museum. Now what happens when that museum's holdings return, as all things must, to dusty earth, to a pocket in earth's strata? We'll have discombobulated time—and perhaps some fellow archeologists millennia hence. Not my worry, actually.

The wakeful disillusionment of those who have seen through our time's hopes is much more comforting than the blind expectations of our time optimists. But so also is a cheerful trust in humanity's good sense more sensible than the panicky self-spooking of the apocalypticists.

In life, artifacts get junked and are survived by their users; in death, the users return to dust and ashes, while their pots live on in museums.

Getting older = being closer to home free.

We humans are temporally rooted in the world, atemporally in the soul. Good communities mediate these two realms of the secular and the transcendent: Their members live their daily life mindful of something beyond.

Great Gatsby is right. He's offered the bromide "You can't repeat the past." "Why of course you can!" he says incredulously. You can, you should. It's the same as being loyal to a dream. You don't have dreams *of* the future; you have dreams *for* the future, and if you have them in earnest they come from way back. All practical dreaming is of renascence, and the dream of dreams is Paradise Regained.

In youth all study is really self-making, self-production. At some point it should turn into production, namely when the self is made.

In youth the cold clear air that tastes sweet to the intellect and the warm misty aura that the passions thrive on oppose each other like two weather fronts. Later on the heart and head are better balanced and the temperature of the soul mellows out.

At the end of youth you've pretty much discovered how the world limits your ambition; at the end of middle age you find out that the limitations could have been much tighter, for all you care.

"Killing time" is a dead metaphor that deserves new life. For anxious waiting, joyless diversion, paralyzing fear, moping inertia—these are all ways of putting life on hold. But since our biological clock keeps running, that doesn't work; when we "kill" time, especially when it's already running short, we're literally contracting life and introducing premature spasms of death.

The sweet rhythms of leisure: bedding down to a sleep untrammeled by obligations and undisturbed by alarums, pottering about and caught up in a long-postponed home improvement, pigging-out on TV and returning to the exhilarating night-concentration of work with expectations of sleeping in—these usages of temporal freedom are a ritual that never becomes a routine.

Some people think being overworked is a badge of martyrdom; it's actually the sign of a vice you might call "task greed" (always excepting single mothers).

The course of time expenditure: Hurrah, free time—profligacy; time marches on—procrastination; time's coming close—pressure; time's up—flailing into action.

In youth I wanted grandeur and clarity, in middle age roots and clarity, in old age readiness and clarity. "The readiness is all" means something to me: to ponder presentiments of your own death while it's still a fairly insouciant topic.

It's because all things do pass that we should value everything that deflects that passage into a loop: regular observances, ritual returns.

If a day went missing from our lives, would we be different? Are we borne to our present along a continuum whose every now-point was needed for us to pass to this present? Was that continuity a mere abstraction or was each past-present a substantial bridge into our present being—are we at this moment concentrated continua all of whose moments are successively embedded in each other? Are we recursive accumulations or rather somewhat accidental accretions, parts of whose timeline could fall into oblivion without affecting our present?

"Punctuated equilibrium" in evolution says that speciation is not continuously incremental but geologically sudden with intervening periods of stability. The human psyche seems to me to work on this model: Without supposing that there can be truly abrupt discontinuity in our lives (barring utter catastrophe), we do seem to undergo moments of reconfiguration which we then settle into for a life-epoch.

Human nature really does not seem to change—the Lascaux painters' awesome visions look awesome to me (I've seen them, the real ones, Lascaux I), and Homer's Ithaca is home to me. But our artifacts change dramatically. I couldn't wear what warmed the wielder of that fur brush in the cave nor (more's the pity) Penelope's *peplos*. Which means that historical, non-cyclical, time shows itself in what the Germans used to call *realia,* or rather, the quantified change of artifacts *is* (in the absence of texts) historical time. And that is what is so strange: that history is people feeling and thinking and doing the same thing dressed up and outfitted differently.

The course of being in love neatly exemplifies the phases of time: anticipatory dreaming (hopeful futurity), urgencies relieved (poignant moment), melancholy fade-out (bemused passing).

We grow older but we don't grow up. Of course we age in body (some people actually manage to grow an attractive bark of age, more corrugated, like the free-form sheathing of a plane tree, but also more figured, warmer). But inside? Well, most things have happened many times; there's some indifference, some serenity (limited); there's an accumulation of coping tricks and of knowing what's what. But the child's childishness, our perennial brat, is still alive, and so is the child's childlikeness, the readiness to be made purely happy by wishes fulfilled.

Life, under the day's dun sun, is current, contextual, continuous, but some people have the gift of making it abrupt, of casting it into discrete episodes, each with its own dramatic lighting. Their account of things is usually a bizarre fantasy on a theme taken from reality. They're fun to live around (but not with), these anecdotalists of life.

Dailiness and mundaneness are better repellents of nothingness and chaos than higher order beings. For these terrors turn tail before subdued routine and secular ordinariness.

How oblivion-prone our life is—most of it has simply flowed into the sinkhole of forgetfulness. (I don't know the current standing of Penfield's old claim that our time-contents are never lost, just inaccessible.) There's that

Borges story, "Funes, the Memorious," about a country person who remembers in minutest detail everything he sees, including the cloud configurations of a certain day. It seems to me that such a person is caught in a devilishly impossible dilemma: In just remembering everything up to the present, he needs to borrow time from the future; also things have changed and these changes too are remembered; but noticing change requires remembering an earlier memory, so he gets farther and farther behind in his remembering, while he becomes increasingly recursive, embedding a primitive memory in a memory of a memory of a . . . , etc.

So oblivion is a blessing. It is also an economy: Most of our days pass in relative sameness, and to them a practical version of Leibnitz's "principle of the identity of indiscernibles" applies: the near identity of all-but indiscernibles. What would we gain in remembering three thousand versions of a nearly identical non-event? So we're twice blessed: Not only aren't we caught in uncannily excessive time expenditure, but we actually economize on lived time by being immemorious.

Does the round of routine and diversion reveal or obscure the human condition? People talk of living one day at a time, but maybe it's our lot to live one day at all times, so that in memory, which is not good for large numbers and small differences, we've lived essentially that day, the day that we've been allotted. Or is our daily routine only the thorough bass beneath the melody that's never twice the same and whose variations we are intended to discern and relish? I think we live in both ways: memoriously and forgetfully.

Free time, vacant time, vacation, is a blessed sabbath in a full life and the voidest void for an empty one.

Nearly a half-century's days, say some eighteen thousand, in one place are unsurveyable. The first day stands out and this present one and in between this or that memorable—and dateless—moment is conspicuous; the whole of days is at once uncountably long and fugitively brief.

The heart becomes freer—or should—as the die of our life is cast. The more settled our circumstances, the more established our position, the more liberated we are. It may be nothing grander than no longer taking things personally or not being as choosy: content to take companionship for love, health for looks, safety for perfection.

There's a smug superiority to fate in returning to the stormy places of one's life in calm and mellow indifference. Living well *is* the best revenge.

The dimensions of time and space are all askew: I'm in the right location but the wrong time (in Athens, 2400 years too late), or at the right time in the wrong place (right now, when a living friend is elsewhere)—though the latter has a real-time cure.

To me, who managed to undergo a European adolescence in Brooklyn, N.Y.—protracted, intense, intellectual, passionately reactionary, and flailingly radical—the condition of adulthood is a never quite abating relief: balance, moderation, tolerance, large casualness, in short, American.

How is it that something as precarious as life and as flimsy as happiness manages to subsist through more than 27,000 days, each of which could have ended life itself or its goodness? Retrospectively it induces a—false—sense of sturdily well-meaning fate and a matchingly amiable world. To be sure, there's also some work, some coping, some good choices in play. But take it all-in-all, it's miraculous. (Here's some apotropaic gratitude!)

Waiting: what a strange temporal mode! Time dedicated to mere futurity, energies in abeyance, reposeless dancing on hot coals, preoccupation preempting occupation, the soul in limbo. What's needed is distraction from distraction: spray graphite into all the creaky hinges, dozens of them.

Two kinds of routine: dull, insensate passages of indiscernible daily cycles that don't accumulate but just run off, leaving the time balance low and life empty, or diurnal rituals, the daily reflection of that cyclical time which is "the moving image of eternity" (Plato, *Timaeus*).

It takes a lot of leisure, time's leeway, to sail out of the shoals of pressures and complexities into one truly golden day.

What's the greater fear: that luck should fail or desire?

There is a certain serenity to old age and it seems to come partly from knowing oneself to be a diminishingly rewarding target for fate, partly from having cared long and hard enough to have been stretched a little past the bouncing state, and most of all from knowing—now and then—just what to do.

The miasma of unreadiness: better do the random thing than breathe it too long. But there's also a perfectly sound sense that it's best to stand by and do nothing—which is, as Milton knew, a mode of readiness: "They also serve who only stand and wait."

Why is our time-grain so irregular? Places of crazy-making bunched oscillations and then stretches of deflatingly flat nothing. There's a time demon behind this.

In old age we are no longer so absolutely sure, or so totally confounded. Things are still mysterious, but that's now a precise category.

When I was young, it would not have occurred to me to demean my tragedies with light diversions. Now that's about all that does occur—and behold: The tragedies are mostly quite willing to be ignobly assuaged.

When you're old, would you want (it's ludicrous to consider, but let's do it just for instance) another love affair? No, you certainly don't want it, all the phased rigmarole from dawning hope to tail-turning departure (and the wonders in between), nor the multitudinous labors of love. But you'd take it, for sure.

Everybody knows this—that pleasure is temporally discrete and happiness continuous. But here's one reason, not so well known, why it works that way: You can't be experiencing pleasure and not know it, but you can be unconsciously happy.

Time fatigue: the motor of change is sheer boredom as much as irrepressible innovativeness. And the results are according.

They say war is tedium punctuated by terror; peace is routine interrupted by crisis—similar but vastly preferable.

The heaven of Heaven is its atemporality: never-failing ardor, unceasingly fulfilling activity, music in the endless repeat mode, and no tedium at all—all the content and none of the passage.

It's so strange that life is unforeseeably numerable: When it's done it's a definite sum of days, but up till then it's endless.

Here's the task: to maintain a small margin of advance over the tendency of things to fall apart. Or seen another way: Lucretius's atoms would rain straight downwards into the abyss were it not for that tiny random swerve that causes them to become configured. Impose a smidgen of intention on that swerve. Make it serve a purpose.

What's a grown-up? Someone who's gotten through and over everything without being done with it.

The prudence not of the reason but of the feelings: preventive panic and apotropaic trembling.

Free time, briefly vacant time, flows differently from long-breathed leisure: At first you expend it mindlessly and then you hoard it anxiously.

Once a long-feared danger is avoided its non-eventuation begins to seem like an ordained necessity. And then we fools think that what didn't happen couldn't happen!

This slightly obsessive fear of mess: neglect a small thing and that's cresting the slippery slope to chaos. Let loose ends whip around in the tempest of time and you'll get lashed. You're on call, somehow, by something, and need to be ready, everything snugged down and shipshape. Skippers are perfectionists, obsessively anticipatory, and control freaks because the ship is small, ever-deteriorating, and storm-prone. So is life, and perhaps my skipper's mentality wasn't so crazy.

The almost eventless life is also close to timeless; provided there is internal eventfulness, it might even be the most Edenic.

A danger of being old: mellow and callous are pretty close.

There is a pleasantly scatty kind of procrastination, doing this or that little job, ambling through the morning and racing after the fugitive day in the evening—time once more brought to naught.

I'm averse to moments of truth. Why should life use a sledgehammer when I would have been receptive to a tap?

"The grave's a fine and private place"—but of course it's neither, less than half full of nothing and altogether public, since graves tether solely the living. For it's true that we are bound to the site where—well, what? A loved one lies? But in no sensible sense! You don't want to think that one out, or why it's true that over time the bond makes itself more felt.

A sabbatical is for the recreation of the soul. Behold, it works, and the next decade will rush toward death with renewed vigor.

Procrastination is a tough and recalcitrant unwillingness to face it, and, if pushed, mounts pleas of unreadiness and complaints of tyranny. How do we summon so much will *not* to act?

What is at one time a sheer impossibility—to act—is later sheer incomprehensibility: Why didn't I?

Acedia, time-wasting indisposedness, may be a curative vice: The soul takes to its bed.

Killing time with small, sallow pleasures and unsavory anxieties: Weed the garden instead.

When talking with young students you have to remember all the things that haven't happened to them yet and that therefore the things that have happened weigh so much more heavily.

The supposed wisdom of old age, which comes from the wearing down of the soul's snags, isn't very useful to the young who sprout snags by the week.

Commitments, those occupations of the territory of time, are refused at the peril of living in a temporal locale of vacant lots.

Weeping now for losses to come is the most unprofitable—and unavoidable—providence.

A bourgeois: one who cannot enjoy the moment's blessings until they're secured for the future—that famous Protestant ethic; Jews and other sensible people in fact feel the same.

The old know that joys will come and pass, but the young in trouble don't even know they'll come.

There is a nostalgia for the present, like a telescope held the wrong way round which diminishes the sights that are close.

The timeless soul in time: essence coping with its accidents.

The mail came: Yesterday—everything was painfully, anxiously iffy. Today—of course, what else, next thing.

Days dawned more beautifully when I was young, but by noon I'd had enough. Reliable energy comes with age.

Time limits on liability: by forty you can't any longer call on your childhood for absolution from your nutty defects (except if you had a Jewish mother).

Where do people get these two time-truisms? 1. Change or die, 2. You can't bring back the past. If they're true so are their opposites: 1. Change is dying, 2. If you can't bring back the past, you can't bring anything back. When you have opposing truisms, is it a wash or an enigma?

General observation: Age goes rigid if youth was loose, but if youth was intense, age will be open.

It's easier to leave off doing what you're doing successfully than to down tools in the midst of a mess. You can't properly say adieu to what you're not done with. And life is the same. Its emblem is an arc: Until the second leg is drawn you can't go in peace.

Old is what you get if nothing worse happens. It's the best-case scenario.

Contrary motions: The young at their best are intensely introspective but all their dreams are for the world. The old are in fact rooted in that world but their meditations turn inward.—Like passing ships, they send tenders across and board briefly, bringing news and victuals. Less fancifully, coming and going, we've got things to tell each other.

Why are age of body and soul so out of sync? That's a silly question: The soul's time is not arrow-time, as is nature's. Is it a blessing or a curse? Well, a blessing, of course. Who needs a wrinkled soul?

Self-love doesn't end in maturity, but it becomes too cagey to show itself, though also too involved in useful work to be quite its old insistent self—and, at last, too self-aware not to think itself comical.

Not hope but expectancy gives life its vivifying tautness. Hope looks to things wished for possibly to happen, but expectancy is a sense of great things sure to eventuate.

How strangely the biographical sum contrasts with life lived minute to minute: a grand configuration of settled designs as against tiny movements of inchoate free-forms.

Tears wept for oneself in old age are crocodile tears: Sure, there's still some thrashing about, some free-floating anxiety, some eating-out of hearts, but all without much conviction: lucky so far and the end in sight. Now crying for others, that's different.

Unblushing candor, sedate working habits, pretty reliable serenity, grace in authority—boons of age. We'll leave the debits alone.

The present is time's mirror of Being, and so the moment matters most. Planning is for the future and accounts are from the past, but living happens now.

People (disease apart) tend to get the senility they deserve: sweet for the sweet, crabbed for the crabby, expectant for the faithful.

Isn't the last stage of growing up mostly getting it out of your system? And does passion fade biologically or get worn out psychologically? Silly question: neither.

Who doesn't wish even in old age for a grand passion—not that obsessive narrowing of the world to one being within it, but some large fervor: a discovery, a founding, even a battle?

After forty, they say, people are responsible for their own face. Well, we do engrave our own character on the tablets of our inner nature. ("Character" is an onomatopoetic word meaning something scratched in—grrr.) But does that engraving work its way out onto the face? Can we tell a good or bad person by their visage? Not reliably: I have known a low-browed prognathous type who had a refined sensibility. And wouldn't a deceiver give himself a deceiving face? It seems to be in its expressive mobility that the face does give away something of the soul—in a four- or forty-year-old. Moreover, though facial expression may be supressed (to wit, the poker face), it's not subtly controllable; a fake smile or false sympathy are not beyond detection. (In fact, psychologists have itemized the tell-tale indeces of facial fakery.)

Probably it's temporal passage that marks the flesh, without much regard to accurate disclosure: "And careful hours with Time's deformed hand / Have written strange defeatures in my face" (*Comedy of Errors* II i).

31 RECOLLECTION:
"THE SPACIOUS PALACES OF MEMORY"

Of course memory is the mother of the Muses, in human terms the source of the arts. It has both a frontal and a dorsal intake: the senses out front, which deliver the appearances of the world, and the great intellectual hinterland, which contributes the structures of thought. Between them—and this makes sense and thought the grandparents of the arts—they give birth to the image-memory which is the Musical matrix.

Public places of memory, "the place where" this one was born, that one worked, another died, these spots of space where the stasis of place countermands the motion of time, are invested by memory not only with the shade of the local hero but with the shadows of a thousand pilgrims, with the intangible residue of their respect, a mysterious fragrance palpably different from the miasmic deposit left by gawking tourists.

Most memory is accreted slowly by small discrete deposits, so that the assaults of incessant fast change leaves us all but memoryless. One explosively singular event, however, leaves us with one sudden, searing insuppressible memory: the Twin Towers.

There is a melancholy even to fresh beginnings: In closing out past accounts we briefly readmit past pains, reopen healed wounds, and find ourselves weeping for now-to-be-superseded losses. And that's because we know very well that in consigning the past to deep memory we are also protecting it from oblivion—it's *au revoir,* not good riddance.

Where are the joys of yesteryear? Well, they're in memory, in hiding from the depredations of our fallen nature which can't bear happiness.

It is possible to be held in the bonds of a memory, and for that enthrallment to make one free of the world: Knowing ourselves to be in some part securely moored to our memories, the rest of us is at liberty to cruise the universe.

The stage fright of memory: We want to bring an experience back up onto center stage by writing it out, and straightway it goes into hiding in the wings. It was all so alive a moment ago and now it's gone. We have to drag it back by the shirttails. Practically speaking: if we can recall a key word, we can unlock its closet.

There are evidently loves—my longest and deepest was one—that are strongly unmusical, without much aura or atmosphere—more a comradeship made for common work, an eros aroused by excellence, a passion moved by magnificence than an ardor of the imagination. Such love doesn't leave much memory residue because it passes completely into one's active being. It's not made for remembrance because it's forever in actuality. Yet sometimes a picture comes back . . .

The loss of a loss: when bereavement ends and it's not entirely a relief.

Distance sometimes coagulates simple longing while attenuating the particular object's power: The proportion of mere wanting to wanting *that* miscreant increases.

Afternoon naps: You wake up on the wrong end of the day, and there's a day-mare: obscure sins of omission and commission, alien-familiar memories inducing murky nostalgia. Was afternoon tea instituted as the specific to this dis-ease?

Although it is all eventually dimmed and then occulted, nothing is ever gone. It comes back in sleeping dreams or in those vivid insomniac musings when one's ghosts walk as eidetic images (a class of vivid, external-appearing imagery).

There are two pasts. One is passive: nostalgic, melancholic, atmospheric, essentially bygone. The other is active: sharp-edged, invigorating, archetypal, effectively present.

Since bodies are opaque and ghosts are diaphanous the beauty of a place is more visible when it is invested by crowds of memories than by hordes of fellow tourists.

32 ENDGAME: "TASTE OF DEATH"

Melancholy, relief, and exhilaration come together, now that the term of life is in sight: melancholy that the world which contained me will before long be emptied of me, relief that I may yet make it to the end relatively unscathed, and exhilaration as of a wild surmise.

If we ever have a craven impulse to shun our dying friends it's mostly because we are so hopelessly ignorant of the subject most on their minds.

It's—probably—with death as with life in this respect: As in a problem-tainted relation leaving is a misery and absence a wrack because everything is unresolved, while in a happy relation leaving is a warm sorrow and absence the happy guarding of an unclouded memory, so a happy life might be easier to say farewell to, when the time has come, than a life which was unfulfilled and must now remain so.

What a relief it is to contemplate one's death—at an indefinite distance.

Fear of death not taken seriously is the spice of life: sailing in a squall with the jib ripped, the main not reefed in time, all the aerial demons screaming and the skipper at the tiller battling them. Or, alternately, sailing far too close to the wind, as we young idiots at the tiller sometimes would, with the skipper curled up in his bunk with the ship's supply of Southern Comfort in his arms, accusing us of creating internal shipwreck before relieving us.

If a person has thoughtfully determined that certain worldly goods are irreplaceably necessary to happiness, then, if they're hopelessly lost, suicide *is* a permissible choice, to my mind.

Let's lay this out: 1. We die and pass into nothingness; that's hardly to be contemplated before and profoundly indifferent after. 2. We die and whatever in us was essence returns to the great reservoir; that's cool comfort on this side, since our accidents, which we love, will be lost, but it might be satisfying after transit into the realm of Being. 3. We die and come to in a venue not utterly unlike earth, only much better or much worse, according to our deserts; this is consoling because wherever we are sent, we will be at home in the main: There will be space, figures, time, and motion—and it *could* be superlatively beautiful, blissful. To try to decide among these seems to me ridiculous, not only because we have no evidence from beyond at all, but because nobody is more incompetent to think about being dead than one who is alive. For we cannot think without our imaginations, and the imagination naturally drifts most easily to that third possibility which the intellect least readily admits. The best we can do is so to familiarize ourselves with the options as not to be taken utterly by surprise. And even in that we may be frustrated, if it turns out that there are more of these than are dreamt of in our philosophy.

Death is beyond us but dying is part of our life: May it come painlessly and suddenly, leaving no time for thought. For I know from thought experiments and reports from friends who've been at death's door, that I would embarrass myself with the triviality of my reflections. We don't meditate well during emergencies, and here surely is the ultimate emergency. It would be good if for my friends' sake I could summon some insouciance; perhaps there might even be real serenity. Anyhow, what matters now is not how to die but how to live toward a certain end of uncertain date, an event at once indeterminate and impending. As for emulating Socrates, who was not only serene but *interesting* on his last day . . .

In moments of near-perfect contentment the difference between life and death seems negligible. But that's a great illusion arising from the fact that life is then so smugly dominant.

When life seems insipid, imagine yourself dead and gone and a ghost among the living, unable even to say "boo."

When we hear that an acquaintance is incurably ill, we immediately look for a blameworthy cause: She smoked, he drank, she overate. It's clear why we do it: so that the sheer, random ill luck of it all won't stare us in the face and say: Why not you? And there's no right attitude toward having escaped this time either. To thank the fates is provocatively arrogant, to congratulate oneself is bottomlessly stupid, to sheer off and evade it is just a bad case of being in denial. In the face of brute luck a feeling of intense inadequacy is in order; you might fancily call it "existential embarrassment."

There is a night wind that comes in soft puffs from the center of things and lifts the hangings with which we curtain off hard truths. We look on our own leave-taking; loves and loyalties recede. We see ourselves displaced from our snug, smug seat in life; our ultimate event, our passage out of time comes into view. But there it abruptly ends; there's nothing more to see; the wind dies and the curtain drops.

Sometimes, when the thought of death intrudes, the imagination gets to work and produces extraordinarily round, ruddy, real visions of all I've loved, as of people gathering at the gate to say goodbye. Well, it's premature but probably good practice.

That anything so evanescent, insignificant, and realistically speaking *de trop* as a human life should matter so much! But it's a fact, a brute fact, not susceptible to proof or disproof, that it matters, indefeasibly. When Kirillov tries to demonstrate that we are as gods to whom death can be a lightly exercised prerogative, his ultimate moment proves him dreadfully, bestially wrong (*The Demons*).

Could nothingness be not a trespasser on the world to be ejected with the vital force of Being, but its true proprietor, and we the brief intruders? The soul's landslide into the abyss: Could we, it, the great globe itself, melt into air, thin air, and "leave not a wrack behind"? What thought is there "to still my beating mind" where even deep Prospero despairs? (*Tempest* IV i).

The thought of Nothingness can be intoxicating because, since by us being-bound beings everything is brought under the rubric of Beingness, even Nothing gets its essence and its properties: Nothing has the pearl gray sheen of colorlessness and the acrid energizing odorlessness of ozone.

The most effective way life prepares us for death is that we wear out.

This place was never quite home anyway.

Secular grace: small blessings deeply appreciated. It lightens life, and I imagine it will ease death.

I've read that the "pursuit" of happiness in our Declaration doesn't mean chasing it but practicing it, as we pursue our calling. I can't think of a better passage toward death than day by day to ply happiness under the aegis of our founding document—ply happiness and mind the store.

What seems to me best: a small-scale life largely experienced and death *in medias res*.

Even those of us who have managed to live our way around disaster notice an occasional rent in the fabric of equanimity when the fragility of all we depend on shows through. Our worldly works and successes, our planned pleasure and comforts, our careful contingency plans and reliances—all that may fail, and so may life itself.

Everything always needs fixing, and who can think of death when there's a spreading stain on the ceiling? Is our busyness an anodyne masking reality or perhaps the real answer?

God protect us from the people who want to reform American self-indulgence, consumerism, comfort-seeking, sugar-eating, rights-demanding. I think people who have lived softly face death better than those sitting on the sharp edge.

It is a truism that we are sometimes careless in life of those we mourn in their death. It's partly a supply-and-demand matter: An existing person is readily available, a dead one has made himself scarce.

Best: to be gone suddenly, without pain to myself or fuss for others. Next best: to fade away, soul and body together, in good-natured undemanding old age. No good: all else.

I'd fight like hell were my life threatened with force, and I'd be despondent beyond present imagining were I terminally ill, but being faced with a certain term, to be sure, but also with a blessedly indeterminate one, I think of death with a strange excitement. After all, it will either be nothing to me or will be the most interesting thing that has ever happened to my self. The thing is to get oneself to and over the threshold in reasonably good shape.

What a strange paradox that we are so alone in death by reason of undergoing the one absolutely common fate.

Some variable must satisfy the equation of our life and solve it. Were we to know beforehand that value, as it has been figured in the actuarial tables of heaven, could we carry on? Some people may in fact know their number, but they are marked, while a normal life is precisely one unmarked by a fixed fate. Prometheus gave mortals *blind* hope—even Oedipus thrashes about to preserve a blind normality.

The world without me: Well, they'll get over it, and I won't be there to mind.

Socrates' humanity: saving the women the trouble of washing his corpse by doing it himself, and leaving his best friend—a plain good man, this Crito—with a witty request that gives him a last ceremonial service to perform, presumably while tearfully smiling: to sacrifice that cock to Asclepius, which Socrates owes to the god of healing for having cured him of life. Oh, to do likewise!

"Cowards die many times before their deaths" says Shakespeare's Caesar. And here's how it happens: The terror of death can so darken our day and devalue life that it affects the very thing it fears, death—the death of a nullified life. So be valiant and taste of death but once.

Some Greeks thought that death is not just the end (*telos*) but also the goal (*telos* again) of life, and there was a modern German philosopher who thought the same— that we live toward our death. But how can that be a goal which is unavoidable? You can't have the inevitable for a purpose, can you?

33 LEFTOVERS:
VARIATIONS ON NO THEME

Dolce far niente: For us of the northern climes "sweet doing nothing" is less sweet than anxious. That's because we're used to thinking of our leisure negatively—"free time," "relaxation," "vacation," meaning empty hours, going slack, vacant weeks, to be filled with "a-muse-ments," museless diversion. There is a third way beyond doing nothing sweetly and diversionary time spending. It's that leisure from which business (which the Romans called *neg-otium* "no-leisure") is a diversion. It is time not merely filled by labor but fulfilled by a work.

The live heart has no habits, is ready for anything, can fall with ease into new circumstances and snap back without slack into the wonted ways. It is, in fact, per-fectly elastic.

If you want to praise acceptably, be very precise. Inat-tentive praise is almost an insult.

What the uncultivated affections don't know: the im-portance of observing first and last moments, of making public acknowledgments, of avoiding small slights. But if you teach someone untalented the ways of the heart they will, from sheer docility, ape them. It's probably worse than raw nescience.

It is very profitable to advertise your psychic infirmity. No one will dare to make any demands, and the usual duties of humanity are cancelled.

When all your emotional eggs are in one basket, your whole lot can be cracked by the stroke of one word. And that doesn't even make an omelet.

A drop of existence can water a desert of want, but so too, a splinter of reality can puncture a bubble of bliss.

It is too genial a view of paradoxical people that they are uttering wise inconsistencies out of large minds. They are often simply living a very practical life, levitating above those grounds on which the paradoxes of appearance might be resolved.

I have my misgivings about "rich, full, active" lives. Think of those writing spinsters of New England, our South, and the English shires. Their outward lives were comparatively narrow and restricted, but their inward prospects were incomparably eventful.

When we are divested of our civilized panoply do we look natural? Not at all; we look more or less defiantly embarrassed.

Spontaneity requires complex arrangements to produce and lots of help to clean up after.

Acquaintance-adoration is embarrassing, not only because it's overdoing it, but because I suspect that it is aroused by something not quite solid in me.

In life, we can't be much hurt either by those who want to just because they do want to or by those who don't want to just because they didn't mean to. In love, it's the opposite: We're surely hurt when it was intended and hurt worse if it wasn't, because that betokens indifference.

We run our lives by psychic algorithms, which is all right as long as we don't imagine they're principles. Example: Duties deemed boring by me clock out as overtime, to be credited against the next obligation.

What does Pascal mean, "The heart has its reasons that the reason does not know"? To be sure, our affections have a mind of their own (to coin a phrase), but with patience and thought the heart's logic comes clear enough. There is, when all is said and done, only one me.

Living single has invigorating aspects that are the exact obverses of the obvious downsides: guiltless freedom, unnegotiated leisure, and the sharp, pure air of independence—not for everybody.

A great lesson slowly learned: In arguments every retort is a set-up and every sarcasm an incitement, and being in it at all a self-defeating stupidity.

Contempt for those who think otherwise and disdain for those who do other work is natural as a first motion of the soul. As a second one it's pure stupidity.

Imagine the somatic epiphany of those Greeks of mine: absurdly undersized stature, garlic-breath and bad teeth, crotchety dispositions, tempestuous coldness. Let them stay in their graves with those pots I used to study—and I get to say what their incomparable writings mean with nobody but my live colleagues to gainsay me.

Here's the test of knowing your mind: Can you say no to an "experience"?

Efficiency is not a virtue, at least not in me. It's activated hatred of the world's business: Get it done = Get it over with. The object of efficiency ought to be leisure, that is, the freedom for lovable work.

Life is full of portents. If one had the virtue of prudence one would know which to shrug off and which to meet with preventive hustle.

Marriage is a great idea, but then, it turns out, it has to be to *this* one, and that's not such a great idea.

First rule of life: Consider everything. Second rule: Eventually.

We can discover the oddest desires, most outlandish thoughts, quirkiest tempers within ourselves with a shrug of our psychic shoulder *if* we are confident of our baseline sanity, of our fundamental soundness. Then what's ours is *ipso facto* sane; we're the standard.

You can look with love and see a face as the frontage of the soul. Or you can look with science and see it as the chief location of the five senses. Or you can, in a Swiftean mood of appalled alienation, see it as a most outlandish apparition: a mouth working away in an ejaculatory or masticating mode, the nose poking erratically into space, two eyes, gelatinous globes that draw in the world but give nothing out. Our imagination has these odd topological moods: bizarre deformations that stay just short of tearing up the world altogether.

There is a certain soundness in trivial and shallow people: They sense that depths and abysses are hard to keep apart, and they are, wisely, keeping away from either.

Facts are bearable and unbearable for the same reason: because they're facts.

It's wonderful that many people readily discern quality and wisdom, though they can't specify the excellence or repeat the lesson.

A perceptive and bold intruder into our life can surprise us into confidences. But these episodic revelations have no chance for clarifying addenda and corrective modification. So you let her go with relief, even with the hope that you weren't heard and won't meet again.

There are people who possess a kind of nescient observation which expects anything and suspects nothing: Anything can register and nothing signifies.

People say they like people. But they seem to mean new ones, not the ones at hand.

Limited people tend to offer a kind of vacuous resistance to new ideas on the principle: When in doubt, balk. The best thing is to drop off one's notion and come back later. P.S. Limited doesn't imply stupid—it means slow, as if the mind were a viscous medium.

Can you believe what people say about themselves? Well, they ought to know. So, figuring in linguistic inexactitude, defensive camouflage, insufficient self-knowledge, you'd better accept it.

The unambitious seem sometimes to suffer from inordinate pride. And the unaligned similarly. Goethe: *Wer sich über den Parteien dünkt mit stolzen Mienen / Der steht zumeist beträchtlich unter ihnen,*" "He who, with a proud air, fancies that he stands above the parties, mostly stands considerably beneath them." (No one born in Germany may fail to mention this rococo Olympian at least once in a writing; my editor notes that I've done it thrice.)

What a felicitous coincidence! We are inclined to despise something and happen to judge it despicable.

Why I can't convey my life's experience: Because the chief lesson is—I've forgotten at the moment.

Adult fanaticism as observed in me: tunnel vision and wild generalization; bug-eyed credulity and balking at counterevidence; paranoid cocooning and dreams of domination; manic mentation and mindless proscriptions: a prolonged Walpurgis Night of the soul.

One effervesces blithely through life while the other stands anxiously by—and then picks up the pieces.

If one side, unwisely but unstoppably, breaches the dam of complaint and lets the flood of recriminations roll—no, that's the wrong metaphor: If one side, irresistibly driven to psychic arson, lights the accumulated deadwood of griefs, the other side has no defense against the firestorm but to set a backfire, to conjure up some countercomplaints. That might contain the fire, but the end is scorched earth.

Being idolized is no pleasure. (Sometimes it is fatal: "Mistah Kurtz—he dead.") In fact, it works a sort of petrification—for the satisfaction of the worshipers you become impenetrable—an idol, in fact. And then to scotch it, you have to evince more fallible humanity than you really want to own up to.

Truth can't be derived from facts; real empiricists (actually quite rare) often infer correctly and conclude badly.

Who teaches what's worth knowing? Lovers of sensuous experience given form in language? Lovers of bodies and their motions rationalized in mathematical models? Lovers of wisdom grounded in the nature of things? Poets, scientists, philosophers?

It is a touching but strange notion that to know each other better is to love each other more. Why should a maxim hold for all cultures when it is manifestly untrue for many couples? And yet it's the premise of globalist education.

The closer you come to people the harder it gets to distinguish their deliberate intention from the congenital patterns of their nature.

When there's no echo, shouting becomes a little frantic and then fades away.

Beware the quiet, inarticulate hell-raising of gentle people who've been wronged.

There are certain bonds not made for prolonged use, for the wear and tear of daily time and the irritations of proximity—exquisitely fleeting intimacies of unlikely partners unlike in everything but this taut, one-stranded connection.

We whistle apotropaically in the dark and hope that a pretense of sanguineness will scare off a lurking fate.

When the power is out and communication ceases—it's then that conversation comes back on.

Thinking that a pound of chocolate kisses during the day is redeemed by one salad at night is as workable as the idea that a bad life can be saved by one momentary access of grace. It couldn't possibly work that way. Or could it?

Ockham's razor applied to life: Make a minimum of experience go the maximum distance. The same goes for information: Get just enough to neutralize your opponents' fact sheet.

Two features can make me believe that a supposed truth is really true. One is that it all hangs together, that it is coherent. The other is that all roads did lead to Rome, meaning that I got there along several, radial rather than parallel, approaches.

The litany of the poor in spirit, a fluttery hemi-demi-semi-quaver of wisdom: needing to be alone, conserving one's energy (unavailable when wanted), needing time to think (procrasinating past the moment), resisting pressure (balking at sensible suggestions), etc.

It seems that often people whose appearance is quite bizarre turn out to think very sensibly, while those of inhibitedly sober mien are full of wild notions. You can't tell a soul by its mortal wrap.

Aimless friendly jabber is engaging in life but excruciatingly boring on record.

"Many things are terrific but nothing that walks the earth is more terrific than mankind" (*Antigone*). That is to say, we are both wondrous and terrifying just by being human. I wonder where Sophocles would put those hyperwonders, the geniuses?

Nothing, to my taste, brings out human vulnerability like a uniform and the uptight bearing that goes with it; from middies to admirals our naval neighbors look so indefeasibly young.

The unexpected happens like clockwork.

The art of judgment: take in each detail as evidence of an intention—or lack thereof.

Honors late in life: perhaps a little vexing if omitted, but not particularly gratifying when offered. And if the presentation contains errors, one's irritated, and if the tone is fulsome one could sink through the floor. But it's nicely meant and should appreciatively be accepted. And then I like that little pile of honorific paraphernalia: fake vellum diplomas, canes, baseball caps, T-shirts, multicolored ribbons good for wrapping presents.

Winning has its downsides; for example you're stuck with the fact that your tricks worked and by your agency is human iniquity once more rewarded. Who wants to march around feeling like the incarnation of malefaction triumphant? Not me, except losing is even less desirable.

Righteous anger is a *perpetuum mobile,* self-moved unendingly.

The revenge of the grudge-litigant without a case is making work.

Apotropaic panic: Anticipate the worst at 4 A.M. and by lunch it's dissipated; wake up unsuspecting and by noon it's got you.

Why is the pious injunction to see their side not normally accompanied by the reverse? Why do the blamers get to hold the moral high ground? Here's one (pretty aggressive) defense: Tell them with articulatedly accurate empathy what's to be said for their side, and then say: "Now you do that for me." If they ever did, you'd *have* to hand it to them, from sheer surprise.

Really talented manipulators always take you by surprise. You know their every version will be skewed, but you never guess the latest obliquity, what complexity they'll have you enmeshed in. It's a no-win game: If they trump you, you're ashamed of losing; if you get them, you're ashamed of having known how.

Insecure people are self-centered. Is it cause or effect? A psychic conundrum.

One shouldn't wait for the public debacle to have one's crisis of confidence. Again and again, practice preventive panic!

Human nature requires conventions, and all their exegeses lead back to this: Conventions are according to nature. That famous antithesis, nature vs. convention, ought really to be a subordination: conventions are a sub-class of nature.

The longer you know certain human beings the harder it is to sum them up. That's why you should store as accurately as possible your first impressions, when each of them was still just surface and all one. Sometimes these first takes come back in dreams to assert their inaugural function.

Experience, which gives you a fair idea of what follows on what, should endow you with calm nerves and steady judgment. But sometimes all it does is to replace vagrant anxiety with focused fear. Besides, at moments of crisis the world jumps its tracks and one's coping tools come unjigged. Anyhow, whoever is guided by practical experience and worldly wisdom to the exclusion of dreamy images and unworldly principle is likely to be safe *and* sorry.

Life's like a tippy little sloop I used to own. You're sailing gloriously before the wind and before you know it, you're broached to and watching a slow, dreamy, unstoppable capsize. This sailor's simile is an *exact* figure for life's antic behavior.

The despising spiral: Each climbs to the next higher, tighter turn and despises from there. Why not let the whole coil collapse into itself, so we can all despise each other on the same plane, as neighborly equals?

What is more hilariously comforting than to discover that a supposed paradigm of normalcy is, internally, a tried and true crazy, a kook, a dedicated deviant?

Experience teaches that experience teaches very little. The large lessons come from imagining well, not from experiencing much.

How lovely is a silence where talk is easy—just wordless speech.

Here's a closing thought from Merrill's "The Broken Home."

I have thrown out yesterday's milk
And opened a book of maxims.
The flame quickens. The word stirs.

Might that happen?